WITHDRAWN

Hart Crane's Holy Vision: "White Buildings"

Hart Crane's Holy Vision: "White Buildings"

by

Alfred Hanley

DUQUESNE UNIVERSITY PRESS

Copyright © 1981 by Duquesne Univesity Press
All Rights Reserved
Manufactured in the United States of America

No part of this book may be used or
reproduced, in any manner whatsoever, without
written permission except in the case of
short quotations for use in critical
articles and reviews

Published in the United States of America
by Duquesne Univesity Press
600 Forbes Avenue, Pittsburgh, PA 15219

First Edition

Library of Congress Cataloging in Publication Data

Hanley, Alfred, 1942–
  Hart Crane's holy vision, White buildings.

                          Bibliography: p.
  Includes index.
    1. Crane, Hart, 1899–1932. White buildings.   2. Crane,
Hart, 1899–1932 — Religion and ethics.   I. Title.
PS3505.R272W534   811'.52   81–12656
ISBN 0–8207–0151–3   AACR2

Contents

Chapter

   I.   *Introduction*   *1*

  II.   *Spiritual Gates*   *16*

 III.   *But Echoes*   *33*

 IV.   *New Thresholds*   *56*

   V.   *Beyond Despair*   *112*

 VI.   *The Incarnate Word* *150*

VII.   *Conclusion*   *185*

      Selected Bibliography   *189*

I

Introduction

Frosted eyes there were that lifted altars.

"*At Melville's Tomb*"

In a now famous letter to Harriet Monroe, Hart Crane explained the above line as one that "refers simply to a conviction that a man, not knowing perhaps a definite god, yet being endowed with a reverence for deity—such a man naturally postulates a deity somehow, and the altar of that deity by the very *action* of the eyes *lifted* in searching."[1] This is a very telling statement, for it reveals as much of Crane as it does of his subject.

In one of Crane's earliest surviving poems, "The Moth That God Made Blind," written when the poet was about fifteen, an intriguingly similar image is used to convey a similar visionary attitude. A moth, born blind, has the obscuring "tissues" burned from his eyes while flying too close to the sun—"a black god to him"—who, having allured the moth, grants him a vision not given to the others of his "race" . . . a glimpse of "Great horizons and systems."[2] The vision, though brief, leaves the moth ravaged, evermore hungry for a "spark in the sand," but with "a tongue

---

[1] *The Complete Poems and Selected Letters and Prose of Hart Crane*, ed. Brom Weber (New York: Liveright Publishing Corp., 1966), p. 239. Hereafter, all citations of this source will be shortened to "*Poems*."

[2] *Poems.* All quotations of Crane's poetry will be from this source. No reference to page or line numbers will be made.

that cannot tell." In Crane's last poem, "The Broken Tower," composed only weeks before he died, the poet confesses that he had only "entered the broken world / To trace the visionary company of love"; and after questioning his success in projecting the "crystal Word," as it is bequeathed by the "tribunal monarch of the air," he finds solace in the silent contemplation of love within the "quiet lake" of his inner vision.

Certainly there is no comparing the quality of these two poems which bracket the works of Crane. But the sense of anguished longing for purer vision and the supplicatory attitude toward the "God" of the sky who vouchsafes such vision represent a pervasive attitude in the poetry of Hart Crane: an almost unabated search for the holy—the absolute, the ideal, the true, the beautiful, the saving—the Divine. Crane's poems, however, are not just *about* God or the Ideal; they are not just *about* the search for divinity. They are the "very *action*" of that search. Crane, in fact, cautioned us not to ask poetry to explain "man's relationship to a hypothetical god" because "poetry, without attempting to logically enunciate such a problem or its solution, may well give you the real connective experience, the very 'sign manifest' on which rests the assumption of godhead."[3] It is the purpose of this study to describe and interpret that experience, that sign, which is Hart Crane's poetry.

The focus of this study is Hart Crane's first book of poems, *White Buildings*, published in 1926. My thesis is that in *White Buildings* the major theme of Crane's entire poetic work, and specifically of *The Bridge*, is anticipated in all its aspects and fully developed in some, and that this theme is the sustained pursuit of an Ideal or Absolute clothed often with the attributes of divinity. Integral to this thesis is the idea that the collection, *White Buildings*, has a unity and delineable structure, an artistic integrity and development, comparable to, even analogous in kind to, that of *The Bridge*.

Before proceeding to the more particular task of interpreting the theme and arrangement of *White Buildings*, I will explain

[3]*The Letters of Hart Crane, 1916–1932*, ed. Brom Weber (Berkeley: University of California Press, 1965), p. 237. Hereafter, all citations of this source will be shortened to *"Letters."*

more fully what I mean by Hart Crane's "holy vision" as it applies to the entire body of his poetry, outline the *modus operandi* of my analysis, and respond to the common criticism of Crane as a willful obscurant.

In most of Crane's poetry there is a constant attitude of worshipful reverence or longing before an ideal or idea—a supremacy—which is variously imagined or symbolized, "the pure possession, the inclusive cloud / Whose heart is fire" ("Possessions"). So exalted, beneficent, desirable, and true is this perfection that the poet praises, thanks, supplicates, and propitiates it as its priest and victim, prophet and disciple, dedicated to the procurement of its favor, the proclamation of its goodness:

> And obscure as that heaven of the Jews,
> Thy guerdon . . . Accolade thou dost bestow
> Of anonymity time cannot raise:
> Vibrant reprieve and pardon thou dost show.
>
> O harp and altar, of the fury fused,
> (How could mere toil align thy choiring strings!)
> Terrific threshold of the prophet's pledge,
> Prayer of pariah, and the lover's cry,—
>
> > "To Brooklyn Bridge"

In the face of such beauty, such regenerative power, the poet sings as the Psalmist does chanting ritualistically the scripture of its divine attributes or abjectly lamenting his own unworthiness or promising his fidelity or begging its gracious condescension or simply contemplating its holiness; but always, and sometimes desperately, aspiring to its sacredness:

> Migrations that must needs void memory,
> Inventions that cobblestone the heart,—
> Unspeakable Thou Bridge to Thee, O Love.
> Thy pardon for this history, whitest Flower,
> O Answerer of all,—Anemone,—
> Now while thy petals spend the suns about us, hold—
> (O Thou whose radiance doth inherit me)
> Atlantis,—hold thy floating singer late!
>
> > "Atlantis"

The matter of how Crane the poet comes to apprehend the holy is of particular importance. Crane is not, as some have mistakenly considered him, a transcendentalist of any school or to any degree. His approach to the Absolute is neither Platonic nor Neo-Platonic, but what I shall call "incarnational." Crane seeks not to transcend the material realm, or the "quotidian" as he liked to call it, but to experience the ideal in and through the "real"— *not* by analogy as in Plato's system. Though full development and substantiation of this idea is deferred until my discussion of the individual poems, it is important that it be defined here as pivotal to my thesis.

To commune with the All-Good, a dynamic transformation, comparable to an alchemical transmutation of a base material into something imperishably precious, is necessary. This transfiguration of experience differs from the general sense in which all poetry is transfigurative, for it does more than let us see things in a new way; it is far more radical in its transformation of both knower and known. It might better be understood by comparison to a sacramental "transubstantiation" of mere bread and wine toward communion with the Divine—who is no longer transcendent or the distant object of one's ascent but becomes incarnated within the bread and wine now tasted as the Body and Blood of God. R.W.B. Lewis also sees this same analogy when he refers to sacramental transubstantiation as a "supernatural process akin to Crane's process of poetic transfiguration."[4]

This spiritualization of the sense world into something immortal, supernal—yet experienced sensorially—can be illustrated by reference to a rather early poem, "Carmen de Boheme" (1918), in which the transubstantive vision is as yet, admittedly, only incipient. (I draw from Crane's juvenilia to demonstrate that both the vision and its mode are at the very root and origin of his poetic output.) In a setting anticipatory of the roof-garden party in "For the Marriage of Faustus and Helen," awash in the sights, sounds, and smells of what seems to be a Gypsy celebration, the protagonist begins to experience a transformation of what he senses and how he senses (though the poem makes no such distinction):

[4]*The Poetry of Hart Crane* (Princeton, New Jersey: Princeton University Press, 1967), footnote, p. 291.

There is a sweep,—a shattering,—a choir
Disquieting of barbarous fantasy.
The pulse is in the ears, the heart is higher,
And stretches up through mortal eyes to see.

Carmen! Akimbo arms and smouldering eyes;—
Carmen! Bestirring hope and lipping eyes;—
Carmen whirls, and music swirls and dips.
"Carmen!," comes awed from wine-hot lips.

Having touched some "higher" reality in Carmen—seen with "mortal" eyes something not mortal in Carmen's "smouldering eyes"—the protagonist is left with the lingering dream of "Carmen's mystic face." One hesitates to call Carmen Incarnate God, but whatever apotheosis she becomes is not separable from her sensual "flaunts." She incarnates what the poet now "knows" (if not possesses) through transubstantiation and communion.

Crane, on more than one occasion, acknowledged the "religious" quality of his poetry. In a letter to his benefactor, Otto Kahn, referring specifically to *The Bridge* and its symbol of Cathay as representative of "spiritual unity," he adds, "A rather religious motivation, albeit not Presbyterian."[5] This playful disclaimer of Presbyterianism is Crane's appeal to his readers not to seek to "validate" the religious thrust of his poetry by strict reference to a systematic or orthodox theology. This should not, however, prevent us from responding to the religious content of the poems within whatever religious context we find ourselves. If in this study I sometimes use Christian terminology and concepts to explain or relate to Crane's poems, it will not necessarily be to make a case for the Christianity or even the godliness of the poetry. Crane himself uses much traditional Christian image and language—if not always from a Christian perspective.

Our understanding of all that we seek to know is, to some degree, analogical. Although we certainly do not require the object of our knowledge to be identical—even in part—with what is already familiar to us, we look for similarities that will enable us to comprehend and talk about the new object of our knowledge. Such will be the function of my application of Christian and other

[5]*Letters,* p. 241.

established categories of thought and language to Crane's poems. But neither do I deny a traditional religious consciousness in Crane's poems, for if the poetry sometimes conforms to or complements Christian belief or biblical precept—or Hindu piety or pantheism—it should be acknowledged and responded to as such.

In either case, I would affirm with T. S. Eliot the propriety of "the application of our religions to the criticism of any literature."[6] And with Eliot, I would refute a critical attitude that scrupulously skirts any encounter of faith in literature and criticism:

> And if we, as readers, keep our religious and moral convictions in one compartment, and take our reading merely for entertainment or on a higher plane, for aesthetic pleasure, I would point out that the author, whatever his conscious intentions in writing, in practice recognizes no such distinctions. The author of a work of imagination is trying to affect us wholly, as human beings, whether he knows it or not.[7]

Monroe K. Spears, who smells merely "the odor of spilt religion" in Crane's poems, admits that "one's final judgment in this matter cannot be separated from one's religious and aesthetic beliefs."[8] And so, while certainly not trying to squeeze orthodox belief from the poetry of Crane, this essay is written in large part with reference to the Judeo-Christian experience—its symbols and ideas.

In another letter, conceding to Herbert Weinstock "the essential religious motive throughout my work," Crane comments further, "This last-mentioned feature commits me to self-consciousness on a score that makes me belie myself a little. For I have never consciously approached any subject in a religious mood; it is only afterward that I, or someone else generally, have noticed a prevalent piety. God save me from a Messianic predisposition."[9] Horace Gregory is right in surmising that Crane was

[6]*Selected Essays* (New York: Harcourt, Brace and World, Inc., 1960), p. 344.
[7]Eliot, p. 348.
[8]*Hart Crane* (Minneapolis: University of Minnesota Press, 1965), p. 45.
[9]*Letters*, p. 350.

embarrassed about his religious impulse because "In the late 1920s
and 1930s to confess religious emotion in New York literary
circles was far more damaging to whatever went by the name of
'poetic prestige' than the confession of any number of sexual or
moral irregularities."[10] Yvor Winters confirms the unconscious
motive of much of Crane's poetry with this recollection, "He told
me once that he often did not understand his poems until after
they were written."[11] Here too, acknowledging the "essential" if
unconscious religiousness of his poetry, Crane asks not to be read
as a proselytizer. The spirit of Hart Crane's poetry is not that of
the Book of Proverbs or of the Gospels, which seek in part to
convert by means of maxim or instructional narrative. Crane's
poems are not discursive or didactic and are to be experienced as
one would the Psalms of David or the Song of Solomon or the
Revelations of St. John: as passionate aspiration to, as sensual
apprehension or ecstatic envisioning of, the Divine.

From the beginning, critics have observed the religious and
visionary nature of Crane's poetry. Yvor Winters, regarding *The
Bridge* as a fundamentally religious poem, calls Crane "a saint of
the wrong religion" because "he had not the critical intelligence to
see what was wrong with his doctrine."[12] Prescinding from the
problem of seeking "doctrine" in psalmic-lyric poetry, we can see
that Winters obviously read Crane as a religious poet and found
therein a major obstacle to a positive response to most of his
poems. Samuel Hazo, in one of the earlier book-length studies of
Crane, several times points to the religious tenor of the poems as
in this reference to the "Atlantis" section of *The Bridge:*

> Crane, like Shelley, had a cosmic conception of poetry's function
> and poetry's power. This power, according to Crane, could save
> man from the daemonic tragedy of the tunnel; it could animate all
> nature with its vitality. Possibly for this reason Crane identifies it as
> a gift from God, transfigurative in its potentialities and apocalyptic
> and eternal in its very nature.[13]

---

[10]*A History of American Poetry: 1900–1940* (New York: Harcourt, Brace and
Company, 1946), p. 476.
[11]*In Defense of Reason* (Denver, Colorado: Alan Swallow, 1947), p. 585.
[12]Winters, *In Defense of Reason,* p. 602.
[13]*Hart Crane* (New York: Barnes and Noble, Inc., 1963), p. 116.

Characteristic of a common critical attitude toward Crane's poetry is Vincent Quinn's thesis that "the central theme of his inspiration was the desire for absolute beauty and love."[14] Such an inspiration can only be called religious. Brom Weber, in his intimate analysis of Crane's life and works, does not focus on Crane's religious vision but establishes Crane's "faith" as a clear premise of his book: "In an age distinguished by the rapid decline of belief in a divine being and his agencies, Hart Crane stood apart as one who saw God ('Elohim, still I hear thy sounding heel!') and who dedicated his major work to God's glory."[15]

The above citations are just a representative few of many that could be made. Most critics, whether they are affected positively or negatively by Crane's poems, acknowledge their visionary or religious content. Many shorter analyses are built on the premise that Crane is a spiritual poet in the classic sense. Only one extended study by R.W.B. Lewis, however, approaches Crane as a religious poet comparable to George Herbert or Gerard Manley Hopkins in his persistent preoccupation with a worshipful supremacy and his relationship to it. Lewis is explicit: "If, as eventually I do, I claim for Crane the role of religious poet par excellence in his generation, it is because such a combination of love and vision seems to me to partake indisputably of the religious imagination."[16] And Lewis sees this "religious imagination" as utterly pervading Crane's work: "Using the word more laxly, though not, I think, irresponsibly, one can accurately say that from 1922 onward Crane never approached a subject in anything *but* a religious mood."[17]

It is such an attitude that I bring to this study on Crane's poetry, though the angle of my approach will differ somewhat from Lewis's. As indicated above, I consider Hart Crane more orthodoxly, less romantically religious in his idiom, his medium of praise, petition, and propitiation; and in his sacerdotal posture as priestly mediator and prophetic voice for the "Word."

[14]*Hart Crane* (New York: Twayne Publishers, Inc., 1963), "Preface."
[15]*Hart Crane: A Biographical and Critical Study* (New York: Bodley Press, 1948), p. 6.
[16]Lewis, p. x.
[17]Lewis, p. 11.

The identification of this classically religious impulse in the poems is not an attempt to explain Crane's principles for living, except inasmuch as poetry reflects the beliefs of any poet. The focus is on comprehending a sure strain, a substance that informs the corpus of Hart Crane's poetry.

This examination of *White Buildings* will not be a formal analysis of Crane's poetic method—the imagery, prosody, and rhetoric—for its own sake. Assuming the premise of the organicism of poetry and acknowledging that content and form are not really separable except for discussion, the manner of the poetry will be treated specifically as both expression and outgrowth of its matter. Unless one understands the complex of mind and heart, the soul, which gives body to a poem, one cannot truly experience the poem. This study, then, is an apologetic for an approach to a deeper appreciation of Hart Crane's poetry based on a fuller comprehension of the visionary animus of the poems in *White Buildings*.

Without, then, denying the validity or usefulness of reading Crane's poetry within another frame of reference, such as the romantic tradition, or from another perspective, such as the psychoanalytical, I wish to demonstrate the plausibility, even the necessity, of seeing the religious consciousness described above as fundamental to the meaning of Crane's poetry.

There have been a number of dependable studies of Crane's poems in relation to their actual order of composition—a technique that provides us with indispensable knowledge of Crane's artistic and personal development. Three rather exhaustive studies of this kind are: Philip Horton's biography, Brom Weber's biographico-critical analysis, and R.W.B. Lewis's more purely critical work (see Bibliography). This study will focus on the arrangement the poet gave his work as an equally important consideration.

Because of the artistic/thematic integrity of *White Buildings*, each poem will be examined as it relates to the others in the volume and with reference to its place in the book's sequence. In addition to noting each poem's special participation in the generally religious vision of Crane, I will, where appropriate, refer each poem's thematic and structural role in *White Buildings* to its counterpart in *The Bridge*, as the two books have considerable similarity in motif and construction. Within this framework, the further plan of this study is to: (1) fully explain the Ideal to which the poet gives homage, being particularly detailed in interpreting the different figures that incarnate it; (2) explicate the process by which the poet "wrings" the Ideal out of sense experience—a "transubstantiation" of the quotidian; (3) describe the priest/prophet persona of the poet as it is imaged in the poetry; (4) examine the often ritualistic, prayerful, "scriptural"—the psalmic—style of the poetry that complements, derives from, and is, after all, one with the poet's holy vision; (5) demonstrate how some of Crane's favored writers (Plato, Whitman, Blake, Nietzsche, Ouspensky, Hopkins, Joyce and Rimbaud) relate to and illuminate the principal ideas of this study.

By way of preamble, I would like to generally acknowledge the common critical objections to Crane's achievement as a poet and respond briefly to one of these criticisms. The more detailed interpretations of Crane's individual poems, which will constitute the body of this study, will always implicitly and sometimes explicitly refute them further.

The most influential early appraisals of Crane's poetry were written by Crane's acquaintances and fellow poets, Allen Tate and Yvor Winters. Tate and Winters, both of whom considered Crane capable of writing unexcelled lyrical poetry, faulted the larger body of his work on three grounds: (1) an extreme subjectivity or unnecessary obscurity, an abuse of the objective meanings of words and normal syntax; (2) a lack of structural coherence or thematic unity in *The Bridge;* (3) a tendency to indulge his emotions for the sake of emotion without reference to any definable idea, any consistent, objectifiable, or (when discoverable) acceptable philosophical or theological base for his poetry such as we find in Dante or Milton.[18]

It seems to me that, especially in the past twenty-five to thirty

---

[18]These criticisms can be found in their most comprehensive and developed forms in: Allen Tate, *Reactionary Essays on Poetry and Ideas* (Freeport, New York: Books for Libraries Press, 1968) and Yvor Winters, *In Defense of Reason,* cited above.

years, the objections of the Tate/Winters school (including such other prominent figures as R.P. Blackmur and Edmund Wilson) have been adequately answered. There is one charge, however, I wish to respond to at the outset: that Crane is more often than not incomprehensible, needlessly and impenetrably obscure. I am responding to this critique not, to repeat, because it has not been effectively refuted. The relatively recent scores of sensible interpretations of many of Crane's poems along with the more deliberate rebuttals of this charge of the impenetrability of his poems provide an imposing refutation. Crane himself gave perhaps the best defense of his poetry against the first accusations of obscurantism (as will be discussed below). Nor do I take up this matter only because my study depends upon the decipherability of Crane's poems, which it does. I front this issue because in demonstrating the comprehensibility of Crane's poetry, we must get to the essence of Crane's idiom—of Crane's mode of comprehension and expression; and in penetrating Crane's idiom, we pierce through to the essence of Crane's vision. For, as we have seen, what Crane envisions is inseparable from the "very action" of his envisioning it because, he tells us, poetry "is both perception and thing perceived."[19]

To Allen Tate's first charge of obscurity (1924), Crane protests, "I have always been working hard for a more perfect lucidity, and it never pleases me to be taken as wilfully obscure or esoteric."[20] Certainly a poet's own protestations, however sincere, are no final response to Tate's or later Winters's indictment of Crane for using words too privately, too subjectively, and rendering the denotative meanings of words almost negligible.[21] But Crane did more than protest. In a letter to Harriet Monroe defending himself against the same accusation, he explained for the first time what he termed the "logic of metaphor." After conceding the "illogical impingements of the connotations of words on the consciousness," he points out, "This may sound as though I merely fancied juggling words and images until I found something novel or esoteric; but the process is much more predeter-

---

[19]*Letters*, p. 237.
[20]*Letters*, p. 176.
[21]*In Defense of Reason*, pp. 585–86.

mined and objectified than that. The nuances of feeling and observation in a poem may well call for certain liberties." This "dynamics of metaphor"—inseparable from the language used to communicate it—must be understood by readers, Crane contends, with reference to parallel experiences they have had, not in relation to the fixed categories of thought and language as they are unaffected by experience: "The logic of metaphor is so organically entrenched in pure sensibility" that it "demands completely other faculties of recognition than the pure rationalistic associations permit."[22]

This principle of the logic of metaphor (which, to repeat, bears directly on Crane's use of words) is further developed in the important formulation of his "General Aims and Theories" where he more explicitly relates metaphor to language: "The terms of expression employed are often selected less for their logical (literal) significance than for their associational meanings," for the words must reflect the "organic principle of a 'logic of metaphor' which antedates our so-called pure logic, and which is the genetic basis of all speech, hence consciousness and thought extension."[23] Declaring that "new conditions of life germinate new forms of spiritual articulation," Crane uses a phrase from "For the Marriage of Faustus and Helen" to illustrate and support his axiom: he insists that "nimble blue plateaus," though it has no correspondent in objective reality—it attributes the nimble quality of an aircraft to the sky itself—"*is* completely logical in relation to the truth of the imagination."[24] One either affirms or denies such a "logic" depending on one's own sensibility or the experience to which Crane asks us to refer. There is, however, an objective factor here; it is the common imaginative experience that, because it is universal, should be communicable and recognizable—*within* the "subjective" terms by which it is experienced.

Philip Horton, who wrote the first comprehensive study of Crane's life and work, testifies to the universality and understand-

---

[22]Crane's complete explanation of the "logic of metaphor" can be found in the letter to Harriet Monroe, *Poems,* pp. 234–36.
[23]"General Aims and Theories," *Poems,* p. 221.
[24]"General Aims and Theories," p. 222.

ability of Crane's vision: "Indeed, what is surprising in these poems is not their obscurity, but their constant preoccupation with moral and spiritual evaluations."[25] Hilton Landry, in his penetrating essay, "Of Prayer and Praise: The Poetry of Hart Crane," contends that "a reasonably sympathetic reader who is willing to work seldom encounters confusion or lack of control. . . . The more one carefully studies the poem, the more one becomes convinced that he knew what he was dong."[26] Vincent Quinn finds corroboration for the "logic of metaphor" in the tradition of scholastic philosophy as interpreted in Jacques Maritain's notion of the "nonrational" faculty of the soul, which includes creative intuition as part of the "intellect" by which we apprehend reality. According to Maritain, the expression of what the "preconscious region of his being" experiences will be necessarily obscure—that is, not subject to the laws that govern the logical faculty—if the poet is true to what he sees because the preconscious region is "nonlogical," not illogical.[27] L.S. Dembo clearly connects the medium of Crane's vision with its content: "The 'logic of metaphor' was simply the written form of the 'bright logic' of the imagination, the crucial sign stated, the Word made words."[28]

If, then, we are to understand Crane's vision, we must understand his mode of apprehension. The vision is not abstractly or rationally comprehended because it cannot be—it is not its nature to be logically explained. One might better say it "comprehends" Crane who, imbued with its being, speaks its nature through intimate communion. This immersion in the mystery causes the rational mind, the memory, the senses, the emotions, the very categories of ordinary experience (time, space, causation, etc.) to exceed their normal boundaries and partake of each other. It charges words with meanings that depend almost entirely upon the images, ideas, emotions, and other words with which they

[25]*Hart Crane: The Life of an American Poet* (New York: W.W. Norton and Co., Inc., 1937), p. 179.
[26]*The Twenties: Poetry and Prose,* ed. Richard E. Langford and William E. Taylor (Deland, Florida: Everett/Edwards, Inc., 1966), p. 24.
[27]Vincent Quinn, pp. 124–25.
[28]*Hart Crane's Sanskrit Charge* (Ithaca, New York: Cornell University Press, 1960), p. 34.

interplay. The result is an "organism" knowable and communicable only as the poet experiences it—by the laws of the "logic of metaphor"—knowable through a dynamic orchestration of all the faculties, rational and nonrational. The result is neither emotional chaos nor intellectual confusion nor an anarchy among the faculties of knowledge but an irreducible balance of thought, feeling, and imagination as they contribute to spiritual apprehension.

"The Wine Menagerie" is a testament to (not an explanation of) this process of realization. Although more detailed treatment of this poem is deferred until its proper place in this study, a brief exposition of the poet's discovery of the visionary mode as it is communicated through this poem would both support and clarify the above comments. The first six stanzas of the poem detail barroom observations that in their apparent distortion of ordinary sense and rational experience frankly puzzle the reader, and yet the observer's "sight" is said to have been redeemed by the very wine that deranges it. For instance, "Slow / Applause flows," "Percussive sweat is spreading," "the alcove of her jealousy recedes"; these actions defy literal explanation even in the context of the poem. What is "percussive sweat" in any absolute, denotative sense—or "flowing applause"? There is a fusion, a conflation of the senses that goes beyond the ordinary function of synesthesia in poetry. And a woman's emotion is perceived in terms of, identified surrealistically with, a spatial observation, a receding alcove. Then, without any apologetic, other than the faithful documentation of what he sees as he sees it, the poet declares, "New thresholds, new anatomies!" The word "anatomies" suggests a new analysis of truth, a new kind of understanding. The speaker has experienced a transformation of vision, fathomed, somehow in his "blood," the nature of things "Wherein new purities are snared."

Hart Crane was in constant pursuit of a reality that could not be known by the ordinary way of knowing. And though the express dependence on alcohol and other "anesthetics" diminishes or disappears in his later poetry, the insistence on a new way of seeing does not. And once seen, the object of this radically transformed vision must finally bring the poet through wonder to praise and through praise to prophecy: a calling of others to praise, "to bind us throbbing with one voice" ("Cape Hatteras").

In a 1922 letter to Allen Tate, Crane exhorted his new found friend to "Launch into praise."[29] This direction Crane himself followed through the central thrust of his poetry. Given the profound influence of Walt Whitman on Hart Crane, one might also point to Whitman's "prophecy" as the prime call answered by Crane:

> The Prophet and the Bard,
> Shall yet maintain themselves—in higher circles yet,
> Shall mediate to the Modern, to Democracy—interpret yet
>   to them,
> God and Eidolons.[30]

[29]*Letters,* p. 94.

[30]*Leaves of Grass,* ed. Sculley Bradley and Harold W. Blodgett (New York: W.W. Norton and Co., Inc., 1973), p. 755. All subsequent citations of Whitman's poetry or prose will be from this edition.

II

Spiritual Gates

The question of thematic unity, consistency of purpose, or proper ordering of the sections of *The Bridge* has been much discussed since its publication and still remains an open question even for some of Crane's admirers. That *The Bridge* ought to possess the integrity of a single, sustained poem, however, has been the contention of almost all students of Crane's poetry and was the stated intention of Crane himself. But few have sought or carefully noted a similar unity or meaningful order in *White Buildings*. Surely Crane did not intend his first collection to be read as one poem in the same way as he hoped *The Bridge* would be. The poems of *White Buildings* were almost certainly written without any thought of how they might be ordered or how they might affect or complement each other when collected. Once the prospect of a collection became likely to Crane, though, there is good reason to believe that he took great care to give the book an order that would provide thematic development as well as an aesthetically pleasing balance—more meaningful than a random or merely chronological anthology of his best poetry.

The evidence for this claim is mainly internal, the book of poems itself which has a thematically and aesthetically significant thrust and progression. But there is some external evidence of Crane's unusual deliberateness in ordering his poems in *White Buildings*. In a letter to his mother referring to his plan for a first collection of his poems he says, "You know one makes up one's mind that certain things go well together—make a book, in fact—and you don't feel satisfied until you have brought all the pieces to a uniform standard of excellence."[1] This penchant for grouping poems is even more evident in Crane's interest in seeing to press a collection of Malcolm Cowley's verse (which later came out as *Blue Juniata*). In his zeal for his friend, Crane actually took editorial charge of the collection giving particular care to its arrangement. As Cowley remembers it, there was much discussion about which of the poems "belonged together, and in exactly what order" because "Hart believed that emotions, and the poems that expressed them, should follow one another in the right sequence. He thought naturally in terms of structure and of 'the book,' which, he insisted, should be more than a random selection of poems by one author."[2] After the order of the poems was agreed on, Cowley quotes Crane as saying, " 'Really the book as we now have it has astonishing structural sequence' "—about which Cowley observes, "thus ending the sentence with two of his favorite words."[3]

It is that "structural sequence" that I will examine while, of course, respecting the fundamental independence of each of the poems. Though the separate parts of *The Bridge* were, for the most part, composed with the whole book in mind, what Crane says of the montage unity of *The Bridge* bears as well on the independently composed poems of *White Buildings*: "Each is a separate canvas, as it were, yet none yields its entire significance when seen apart from the others. One might take the Sistine Chapel as an analogy."[4] Vincent Quinn, for one, detects an artistic wholeness and thematic unity in *White Buildings* noting that "the grasp of one poem enhances the reading of another until the entire collection is seen as a mosaic by a single artist."[5] It would be premature to seek to trace in detail the pattern of the mosaic before the content, the shape and color, of each of its "pieces,"

[1]*Letters*, p. 199.
[2]"A Note by Malcolm Cowley," Susan Jenkins Brown, *Robber Rocks: Letters and Memories of Hart Crane, 1923–1932* (Middletown, Connecticut: Wesleyan University Press, 1969), pp. 103–4.
[3]Cowley, "A Note," p. 105.
[4]*Letters*, p. 305.
[5]Vincent Quinn, p. 31.

each poem, has been established. For now, I will just sketch the structure of *White Buildings* and describe each part's particular function in the picture as I discuss each poem in detail.

"Legend," "Black Tambourine," and "Emblems of Conduct" introduce the volume by defining the role of the visionary as well as providing a preliminary glimpse of the vision sought. This done, the eleven poems from "My Grandmother's Love Letters" to "Repose of Rivers" provide a romantic reflection upon the various encounters of the Ideal ("North Labrador") or create artifacts of the Ideal to be contemplated ("Garden Abstract") or speak lamentations over its unattainability, trancience, or loss ("Pastorale"). While in no way attempting to reduce these richly varied poems to stereotypes, I hope to show that together they provide a sustained and nicely modulated meditation upon an as yet remote vision. The unity of these otherwise diverse poems is like the distinctly colored facets of light refracted from one prism. Only "Chaplinesque," which stands exactly at the center of this sequence being the sixth of the eleven poems, does significantly more than the other poems—while contributing to the ambience of reflection. Its sorry harlequin reminds us of the sacrifice ("Legend"), alienation ("Black Tambourine"), and sadness ("Emblems of Conduct") of the devotee to the Ideal.

With "Paraphrase" there is a notable shift in tone, technique, and focus. The poem's central idea—a hallucinatory experience of death—engenders a dire, deliberately morbid feeling that contrasts with the more wistful, elegiac tone of the book's first half. Crane's poetry is almost always difficult to understand because of its extraordinary compression; but, technically, "Paraphrase" seems to me the most concentrated and difficult of the poems up to that point in the collection. It anticipates the extreme density and crypticism that characterize the poems from "Possessions," which follows "Paraphrase," to the end of the volume. "Paraphrase" is placed almost squarely at the center, the halfway point, of *White Buildings*. If you count the parts of "For the Marriage of Faustus and Helen" and "Voyages" as separate pieces, the collection contains thirty poems, of which "Paraphrase" is the fifteenth. If "Paraphrase" were not, however, the physical center of the work, it would still be its thematic pivot, for it shocks and plunges the reader from the gentle revery of "Repose of Rivers" into the "antarctic blaze" of annihilation. "Paraphrase" is the artistic axis, the "dead center," the fulcrum of the collection, lifting it from the contemplative into the psalmic postulations of the second half.

Through this emptying out, this "bottoming out," come the intense discoveries of the "bright logic" to which the poet pledged himself in "Legend": the "bright stones" that are promised him in "Possessions," the "Nazarene and tinder eyes" that redeem him in "Lachrymae Christi," the "improved infancy," the "glittering abyss" entered in "Passage," the "New thresholds" crossed in "The Wine Menagerie," the healing of fragmentation, the "salvage"of time itself made whole ("All hours clapped into a single stride"), in "Recitative." All five of these poems between "Paraphrase" and "For the Marriage of Faustus and Helen" are poems of anguished discovery of a deeper reality by an intense transmutation of knower and known. The tone, to repeat, is no longer the more elegiac one of "In Shadow," nor is the style nearly as transparent as in "North Labrador." The speaker is doing more than reflecting, lamenting, or casting emblems; he is being made new in a crucible forged first in "Paraphrase."

The climax of the process comes in "For the Marriage of Faustus and Helen" where the separate notes of the previous five poems are strung into a sonata, a harmonic song of celebration and praise for the blessed aspiration and for the transportation to the holy, "For golden, or the shadow of gold hair." "At Melville's Tomb," while providing an elegiac interlude, a transition between the major movements of "For the Marriage of Faustus and Helen" and "Voyages," also recalls to us the sacred role of the seer, much as "Chaplinesque" does in the first half of *White Buildings*. Homage is again paid to one who has known "silent answers" and been thereby translated: "This fabulous shadow only the sea keeps."

"For the Marriage of Faustus and Helen" ends on a far less excited, more meditative, note than the "cultivated storm" of the poem's center. "At Melville's Tomb" continues this brooding mood, which is amplified and sustained in "Voyages." The tension of "Lachrymae Christi" and "The Wine Menagerie" has been relaxed, and the tenor of the poetry seems to be once again that of "Emblems of Conduct" or "The Fernery"; but this does not signal a return to the contemplative attitude of the book's first half. Though the tone contrasts with the tautness of "Possessions" or most of "For the Marriage of Faustus and Helen," "Voyages" continues their theme—that of a transubstantiation of experience, a communion wit 1 what is now called "The imaged Word."

Although consistent with and furthering the theme of the section introduced by "Paraphrase," "Voyages," in its quieter voice, aesthetically complements the tone of the first half of *White Buildings*, bringing the collection back to the more wistful idiom of "My Grandmother's Love Letters." The collection has not turned in upon itself—it has spiraled to a peak realization through an incremental metamorphosis of the vision sought and a gradual transformation of the seeker. The "spiritual gates" only remembered in "Emblems of Conduct" are "crashed" in the second half of *White Buildings*.

The unity of the collection, put simply, consists in this: the "perfect cry" of "some constant harmony" aspired to in the book's first poem is answered by the "unbetrayable reply" of the last. *White Buildings* is about the pained pursuit of that holy truth that begins in quiet speculation and passes through the clamor and fire of experience to tranquil illumination.

"Legend" was written later than most of the other poems included in *White Buildings*, yet Hart Crane placed it first in the book as it keynotes perfectly the theme of the collection and, one might say by extension, the theme of Crane's entire poetic work. Like the "Proem" to *The Bridge*, "Legend" provides a brief symphonic overture of *White Buildings'* thrust and meaning with traces and strains of its major movements.

The very title of the poem suggests a key, much as the "legend" of a map is a key to our interpreting and understanding the whole. It is in this sense that Phillip R. Yannella understood the term as "a 'legend' by which one can be aided in reading Crane's visionary poems," adding that "it introduces the reader to the ontology, epistemology, and imagery of Crane's maturity."[6] But this is not to obscure the more obvious meaning of the word that

[6]"Toward Apotheosis: Hart Crane's Visionary Lyrics," *Criticism*, 10 (1968), 313, 315.

denotes a mythical story. Here too, however, the suggestion is the same; we read or hear legends because in them we find significant, archetypal truths—*logoi* to the meaning of things. Considering also that the word "legend" relates etymologically (through the Latin *legere*) to *logos*,—in Greek the "reason" behind reality—we might well take the suggestion that this poem is the "logos" of *White Buildings* and of Crane's larger vision. The additional connotation of the word—"unreality" or "fantasy"—is also likely intended by the poet, but only to be reversed, as we shall see, in the poem's last line. Hyatt Waggoner is right in saying that "Legend" is "at once about poetry and about vision."[7] "Legend" is the poet's manifesto of his consecration to the visionary and a declaration of the course to be taken—the course *White Buildings* itself will take. The first two lines, "As silent as a mirror is believed / Realities plunge in silence by . . . ," suggest, in fact, a state of unreality. What is a mirror but a reflection, yet it is believed as true much as Plato's cave dwellers believed in shadows as true. The unspoken premise in posing this illusion is that the "realities" now merely mirrored must be apprehended in themselves. The protagonist, in the second stanza, refuses "repentance" and "regrets." But to repent of and regret what? The answer to this question is contained in the action of the moth that "Bends no more than the still / Imploring flame." The point, despite the shades of Platonism in the opening lines, is that "reality" is not found by a withdrawal from the fire of experience, a cooling of the passions and transcending of the quotidian, as Plato had called for; but, as with the flame-drawn moth, by an immersion into the very life that consumes one—without repentance or regret. For it is in this consuming, this consummation, that the primal reality is touched; and though the moth, the seeker, be singed to "white falling flakes," he finds therein that "Kisses are,— / The only worth all granting."

This implicit motif of sacrificial immolation to the "light" is intensified in the third stanza in the direct admonition to the visionary that to learn what "This cleaving and this burning" means one "Spends out himself" repeatedly. One must continually, "Twice and twice," enter the flame's radiance "Until the

---

[7]*American Poets* (Boston: Houghton Mifflin, 1968), p. 499.

bright logic is won." This image is reminiscent of, and perhaps inspired by, Whitman's characterization of the visionary, the poet, who "glows a moment on the extremest verge."[8] But there is a cost, for the valued token, the "souvenir," is "smoking"; and the Ideal, the "eidolon," is "bleeding." The realization is not separable from the victimization of the protagonist who finds *within* his own sacrifice to the flame the flame's "bright logic"—which is now, however, not "silent" but "Unwhispering as a mirror / Is believed." When, then, will the mirror's silence be shattered and the reality it feigns be clutched? It is not until the "word" is spoken that the fruit of the sacrifice is manifest, when "drop by caustic drop, a perfect cry / Shall string some constant harmony." Only then will the "legend," the phantoms of "youth," of illusory vision, be passed through to the brilliant truth of "noon."

But this is a "Relentless caper," a constant escapade, a desperately gay leap into the fire of experience, not a Platonic or stoical shunning of the quotidian for an ethereal realm..The "bright logic," the "constant harmony" earned is not transcendent but incarnate, found embodied in the poet's own passions, in the poet's very self—but transfigured, transubstantiated, by an entry into the fiery ordeal, a sacrificial shedding of blood, and a crying of the word. The sacrificial/transfigurative aspect of "Legend" is identified by Samuel Hazo as part of a larger paradox: "Its theme evolves from the tension between death and renewal, giving and receiving, immolation and transfiguration."[9] But the renewal, reception, and transfiguration are as yet potential, pointed to, promised in "Legend."

This concept of the aspirant to the Ideal as the priest who immolates himself as his own victim toward communion with the holy is not picked up again in *White Buildings* until "Possessions," which also escalates the process of an almost violent plunging into experience. But the positing of a "bright logic" to be revered and sought is the prescription to all the poems of *White Buildings*, which at first just seek, meditate, simulate, or mourn the loss of that "bright logic"—then, after "Paraphrase," extract, transmute it from the seemingly base elements of experience. And just as the

[8]Whitman, "Preface 1855," p. 718.
[9]Hazo, p. 18.

"Terrific threshold to the prophet's pledge" ("To Brooklyn Bridge") is crossed in "Atlantis" to the "Answerer of all," the "constant harmony" strained for in "Legend" is heard in the "unbetrayable reply" of "Voyages."

"Black Tambourine" is a very apt sequel to "Legend," for it speaks of the alienation of the artist/victim introduced in "Legend." "Black Tambourine" is not just about the artist; for when Crane is writing about the poet or visionary, what he says should not be applied just to the artist because Crane, like Whitman, considered the poet the representative person: "He must, of course, have a sufficiently universal basis of experience to make his imagination selective and valuable."[10] Crane would have said with Whitman, "And what I assume you shall assume."[11]

The poem is ostensibly about a "black man" brought, at least ancestorally, from his home in Africa but given no home in the New World where he is consigned to a subterranean, subhuman existence:

> The interests of a black man in a cellar
> Mark tardy judgment on the world's closed door.
> Gnats toss in the shadow of a bottle,
> And a roach spans a crevice in the floor.

Crane discourged any moral or social interpretation of the poem, despite what seems a morally charged first stanza. His statement is worth quoting almost in full:

> The word "midkingdom" is perhaps the key to what ideas there are in it. The poem is a description and bundle of insinuations, suggestions bearing on the Negro's place somewhere between man and beast. That is why Aesop is brought in, etc.,—the popular conception of Negro romance, the tambourine on the wall. The value of the poem is only, to me, in what a painter would call its "tactile" quality,—an entirely aesthetic feature. A propagandist for either side of the Negro question could find anything he wanted to in it. My only declaration in it is that I find the Negro (in the popular mind) sentimentally or brutally "placed" in this midkingdom, etc.[12]

[10]"General Aims and Theories," *Poems*, p. 218.
[11]Whitman, "Song of Myself," p. 28.
[12]*Letters*, p. 58.

It is always dangerous and perhaps presumptuous to gainsay a poet's own explanation of his own poem, but it is a generally accepted truism that artists are not always fully aware of, nor do they usually like to explain, the implications of their own images. One could make at least a liberal extension of Crane's own comments and, hopefully, not contradict him. If the critic knew nothing of Crane's attitude toward his poem, that its quality is "entirely aesthetic," and had heard only what the poem says, he might note that the black man is also an artist, a musician, as indicated by his tambourine and by his comparison with a fable maker and fellow slave, Aesop. The black man is suspended "forlorn" in a "midkingdom," "the key [word] to what ideas" the poem contains. One likely idea here is that the artist like the black man (or the black man like the artist) is in a "no-man's-land" between what he was, "a carcass quick with flies" (suggesting a savage but dead past) and what he cannot yet be, "his tambourine, stuck on the wall" (suggesting impeded articulation and thwarted celebration of what he knows). "Driven to pondering," the alien finds "Heaven" in the imagination, in metaphors appropriate to his own condition—in animal lore, with perhaps a very faint promise of eventual recognition in the image of the patient tortoise that will in time prevail over the hare. And upon his death, he bequeathes only puzzling fragments of his vision, "Fox brush and sow ear top his grave," or cryptic formulations of his art, "And mingling incantations on the air."

The poem sustains the interpretation that it is at least in part about the state of the artist and true visionary who is displaced and misunderstood. It is not clear, nor is it necessary to know, whether the artist is alienated because he sees differently or he sees differently because he is alienated. The condition of "Aesop" is the focus, and he "Wanders in some mid-kingdom." This is Crane's subtle, maybe unconscious, message to the pursuer of the "bright logic" defined in "Legend": that the visionary must expect to experience alienation, a message consistent with the theme of *White Buildings* but participating more specifically in the contemplative, preparatory spirit of the first part of the book, in which the "relentless caper" is merely anticipated, delineated, and in which the legend has not yet been stepped into noon.

The style of "Black Tambourine," though characteristic of the tighter, elliptical idiom of Crane, is in the comparatively looser, less intensely wrought style of the first part of *White Buildings*, the syntax and diction less strained—which is also consistent with the ruminative quality of the first half of the book.

Various portraits in the first two sections of *The Bridge* similarly establish the "mid-kingdom" role of the solitary seer: the detached speaker/observer in the "Proem," "Under thy shadow by the piers I waited"; Columbus in "Ave Maria," who has left Genoa, where for "truth" he was an "exile in her streets," and is now poised afloat "between two worlds"; the addressee in "The Harbor Dawn," given revelations "midway in your dream"; Rip Van Winkle who, sprung free of time, "was not here nor there"; the ageless, shiftless "hobo-trekkers that forever search / . . . Holding to childhood like some timeless play." And, as we shall see, this subtheme of the suspended visionary persists throughout both books for it is basic to Crane's poetic outlook.

"Emblems of Conduct" continues the brooding, meditative tone of "Black Tambourine," which is also in keeping with the tenor of the first part of the collection, although its style is more tightly wrought than most of the other poems in the first half of *White Buildings*. Along with "Legend" and "Black Tambourine," "Emblems of Conduct" forms a triptych on the theme of the nature of vision and the role of the visionary. After "Emblems of Conduct," the book explores and finally exposes the vision as a response, so to speak, to the challenges, directions, and questions posed in this opening triad—much as *The Bridge* searches for and finds "Cathay," the "*ultima Thule*" posited in its first part.

"Emblems of Conduct" is in comparison to "Legend" cynical about a devotion to the visionary, which it suggests may be only remembered, not "won"; and it comes considerably closer to despair than "Black Tambourine," which concludes nothing as it leaves the black man/artist suspended, not resigned to merely recalling "memories of spiritual gates." When Crane wrote "Emblems of Conduct," supplied with the images coined by the deceased young poet Samuel Greenberg, he must simply have felt the skepticism the poem communicates—a skepticism he experienced and tended to suppress but expressed again, later, in "Quaker Hill," "Key West," and the first part of "The Broken Tower." But when collecting the poems for *White Buildings*, Crane

26

must have seen a proper place for a melancholy resignation as
part of the proposition, the prelude to the book—as a common,
predictable doubt and counterpoint to the visionary's faith:
"There is only one harmony," the seventeen-year-old Crane once
told his father, "that is the equilibrium maintained by two oppo-
site forces, equally strong. When I perceive one emotion growing
overpowering to a fact, or a statement of reason, then the only
manly, worthy, sensible thing to do, is build up the logical side,
and attain balance, and in art,—formal expression."[13] Such doubt
provides aesthetic balance as well as a question to be answered, a
problem to be solved.

The title of the poem functions similarly to that of "Legend."
"Emblems" like legends are signs embodying values, symbols
containing, here, codes of "conduct." The poem opens with the
artist, again as in "Black Tambourine," a "wanderer," sketching
"graves" against a background of disturbingly frenetic occur-
rences. The implication is clear enough that the visionary is
recalling spiritual values that will never again be viable, "com-
memorating spiritual gates" along with the less aware "Orators"
of stanza two.

The "logic of metaphor," as we have seen, defies prosaic, purely
rational paraphrase; and certainly an "apostle" giving "Alms to
the meek" while a volcano erupts "With sulphur and aureate
rocks . . . / For joy rides in stupendous coverings / Luring the
living into spiritual gates" escapes any final explanation. Yet some
explication, however partial, consistent with the logic of argu-
ment is both possible and in order here. If *true* spiritual value is
dead, then what can the "luring" of the "living" by the "apostle" be
but a counterfeit of the truth disguised by a spectacular and
strident style, and reinforced by the buying, with "alms," of their
followers, "the meek"? And the joy the evangelists proffer is not
real though it comes packaged in "stupendous coverings." Such
"spiritual gates" are a mirage, a delusion.

Though he respected religious expression, Crane had a pro-
fessed dislike for the carnival barker tactics of at least one very
popular evangelist of his day, Aimee McPherson, whom he heard
during his stay in Hollywood. Though he went to California some

[13]*Letters*, p. 5.

five years after the writing of "Emblems of Conduct," the attitude of revulsion for her type must certainly have predated his encountering her. His comments on her may enrich our understanding of the "apostle" and "orators" of this poem:

> My philosophic moments are few, but when they do occur it is almost always possible to turn on the radio and immediately expose my soul to the rasping persuasions of Aimee McPherson, eternally ranting and evangelizing to packed houses at the great palm-flanked arena of Angelus Temple. She broadcasts the news that people are frequently carried out in pieces, arms broken, heads smashed in the stampede for salvation which she almost nightly stages, thereby emphasizing the need of arriving early (so as to save one's body as well) and thereupon lifts her voice into a perfectly convulsing chant, coaxing and cuddlingly coy about "Come, all ye —" (You can catch her in it on the Victor) the chorus of which would make a deacon's bishopric leap crimson and triumphant from the grave. . . . I haven't seen her, but they say she has beautiful long, red, wavy tresses.[14]

The deception of the race by such high-pressure, false prophets in stanza one is matched by the more subtle directives of the "Orators" in stanza two, who with "dull lips" presume to comprehend the "universe" they "follow," and thereby to edify and instruct, to "radio the complete laws to the people"; and who, along with the "apostle" who "conveys thought through discipline," seek to substitute system and law for beatitude and grace.

This sense of the death of religion through its institutionalization is a stock romantic attitude and may be traced back to just about all the authors whom Crane read with more than ordinary interest (Blake, Whitman, Nietzsche, Rimbaud, Ouspensky — even Plato). Blake's comments on this point may provide another key to our comprehension of Crane's reference to "apostle" and "Orators" in "Emblems of Conduct." In "The Marrige of Heaven and Hell," which Crane is likely to have read, as evidenced by a number of correspondences between it and "For the Marriage of Faustus and Helen" (correspondences, as we shall later see, that go beyond the similarity in title), Blake asserts that the "Priest-

[14]*Letters*, pp. 314–15.

hood" has exploited and perverted the writings of the true prophets, "the ancient Poets," who "animated all sensible objects with Gods or Geniuses / . . . Till a system was formed, which some took advantage of, & enslav'd the vulgar by attempting to realize or abstract the mental deities from their objects: / . . . Thus men forgot that All deities reside in the human breast."[15] The identification of the poet as the real communicator of inner spiritual truth connects nicely with the role of the artist in "Emblems of Conduct"; and the enslavement of the "vulgar" by religious systematizers matches well the enthralling of the "meek" by the "apostles."

Only "Bowls and cups," the archaeological remnants of an age that was spiritually alive, are left for our "adorations." In contrast to the purveyors of false faith, the true seer, the artist/wanderer reappearing in stanza three, pretends no such access to "spiritual gates." Knowing that the era of "summer and smoke" is past (whether this refers to an age of spiritual vitality, which interpretation I prefer; or, conversely, to the passing of the spiritual fakery of stanza one), the wanderer ceases his quest and takes "this spot of rest." He consoles himself with the contemplation of the vestiges, the reflections of a better time: the image of the "marble clouds," as they are reflected by and seem to "support" the sea, communicates a sense of analogical, derivative, insubstantial understanding—almost the mirrored "realities" of "Legend." The solidity of marble contrasts ironically with the vaporous quality of the clouds. The artist is left with shadows and inversions of the spiritual pillars of a better age—materials, along with the "uneven valley graves" and "Dolphins . . . arching the horizons," which can only "build memories of spiritual gates." Crane several times links his creative ability to his "faith." He says that "any true expression must rest on some faith in something"; and he characterizes the age in despairing terms: "the spiritual disintegration of our period," "a culture without faith and conviction," "These Godless days!" In a more hopeful mood, Crane talks about a "transition from a decayed culture toward a reor-

---

[15]*Blake: The Complete Writings with Variant Readings*, ed. Geoffrey Keynes (London: Oxford University Press, 1972), p. 153.

ganization of human evaluations" that would require a new language of "spiritual conviction" to express.[16]

There "was finally borne a chosen hero," but not one who could reopen the original "spiritual gates." It is almost pure guess, but the chosen hero could be the successor to the visionary who knows even better than his mentor that dolphins' arches, though lovely in their proportion and grace, are not to be mistaken for the primordial "arches," the "spiritual gates," which can never again be entered. He is not one who will cleave and burn as in "Legend," but an almost stoical, emotionally removed observer.

One might wonder why the last of the three theme-setting poems of *White Buildings* would be the least hopeful in terms of actual rather than imagined or remembered experience of the Ideal. Why would Crane not have built up to the more promising (and chronologically last written) affirmation of really entering into the "bright logic" in "Legend"? After all, the second half of *White Buildings* and *The Bridge* demonstrate that Crane did not finally decide his "spiritual gates" could only be found as in the artifacts of Yeats's Byzantium or Keats's Grecian Urn, although the "memories" of "Emblems of Conduct" bear close resemblance to the purely imagined ideals of these two magnificent romantic poems. If, however, we see "Legend" as the keynote for the entire collection, then it must have the more prominent position of first poem in the collection, and "Emblems of Conduct" can be taken as a minor keynote to the eleven poems that follow it. From "My Grandmother's Love Letters" to "Repose of Rivers" there is a subsidiary or preliminary theme—the theme, as stated previously, of the ideal lost or grasped at or preserved only within an artifice of the imagination. There is not until after "Paraphrase" any direct experience, however agonized, of the "pure possession." The "key" to the "spiritual gates" is not "ready to hand" until the flame is entered in "Possessions."

Up to this point, there has been a hint in the use of such terms as "symphony," "movement," and "keynote" that *White Buildings* has

---

[16]The origins of the previous five quotations are, in the order of appearance: *Letters*, pp. 264, 323, 259, 319; "General Aims and Theories," *Poems*, p.218.

at least some resemblance to a musical composition. Crane was an enthusiastic appreciator of music, both classical and jazz—though his appreciation of jazz has been understandably more emphasized because of his attempt to adapt jazz rhythms to his poetry. Although he did not become very familiar with Brahms' and Beethoven's symphonies until after 1928,[17] he was already quite appreciative of some other masters of the sonata or symphony forms: "For without . . . my Victrola with its Ravel, Debussy, Strauss and Wagner records—I am desolate."[18] Crane was for a period (1921–1922) acquainted with Ernest Bloch and his circle of friends about the Cleveland School of Music.[19] With his enormous assimilative powers, Crane could have learned from this coterie what he needed to know technically about the music with which he was already quite saturated—toward an application of those techniques to his poetry.

Crane was thinking rather early about *The Bridge* as having symphonic qualities. In 1923, three years before the publication of *White Buildings* and before more than a dozen lines of *The Bridge* were completed, he explains to Gorham Munson, "The form will be symphonic, something like 'F and H' with its treatment of varied content."[20] In his later letters, Crane refers at least three more times to the symphonic nature *The Bridge* will have.[21] Obviously, Crane was not talking about *White Buildings*; and, though he did think of "For the Marriage of Faustus and Helen" along with *The Bridge* as "symphonic," he did not ever speak specifically about *White Buildings* as having a symphonic character or structure. But one might contend that the symphonic mode employed deliberately in *The Bridge* was applied, if not consciously, as surely to *White Buildings* because Crane naturally thought of and instinctually composed poetry as analogous to music. The evidence is, once again, in the collection itself, the form of which can be analyzed by the use of musicological terms and concepts. A brief overview of the symphonic structure of

---

[17]*Letters*, p. 316.
[18]*Letters*, p. 108.
[19]*Letters*, pp. 66, 78.
[20]*Letters*, p. 125.
[21]*Letters*, p. 232 (two separate references to the "symphonic" quality of *The Bridge* on this page, one to his mother, the other to Waldo Frank), p. 241.

White Buildings here will further serve to demonstrate the book's unity.

The symphony, or sonata for orchestra, is an extended musical composition comprising usually four movements, which are distinct but thematically related pieces of the whole. There are some symphonies written in only one movement and others in as many as seven or eight. The first movement of a symphony usually consists of an exposition, development, and recapitulation. The exposition is the first statement of the work's main theme and may also include the statement of a secondary and perhaps contrasting theme. Between the statements of the main and subsidiary themes, there is a "bridge" passage connecting the two. This first movement then goes on to develop and restate the theme, which is further amplified through the remaining movements of the work.

This schema for the symphony is only typical, not a required formula. Some composers deviate markedly from its program. I think Crane, when utilizing the symphonic form for *White Buildings*, took liberties with it that would have been normal for a composer of music. And there are, of course, limitations to such an analogy as this. *White Buildings* is poetry not music; not even two symphonies can be compared except in certain aspects, and I would not want to force this comparison beyond its primary purpose of explaining the integrity of the collection's theme and design by analogy.

Instead of incorporating the statements of the primary and secondary themes as part of the first movement, Crane gave them independent status as an introduction, not an unheard-of practice among composers. The statement of the overall theme of *White Buildings*, as has been shown, is made in "Legend," and "Emblems of Conduct" is the expression of the collection's subsidiary and related theme. "Black Tambourine" is an ideal "modulating bridge" because the "mid-kingdom" protagonist hangs suspended between the generative burning of "Legend" and the sterile memories of "Emblems of Conduct."

Because of this removal of the exposition from the first movement to give it the status of a separate introduction, the poems from "My Grandmother's Love Letters" to "Repose of Rivers" would constitute the first movement but be limited to the development not of the primary theme of "Legend" but of the secondary theme of "Emblems of Conduct"—and would carry the same lamentational tone.

The next six poems, from "Paraphrase" to "Recitative," make for a second movement variously developing the more affirmative aspect of the collection's theme introduced in "Legend." "For the Marriage of Faustus and Helen," like the third movement in a classically structured symphony, would serve as a restatement and recapitulation of the composition's primary and secondary themes; and "Voyages" would function like the concluding fourth movement or "coda," which, while advancing the general theme, takes a new direction in its interpretation of that theme.

Because the symphonic design of *White Buildings* cannot be proved but only suggested, and because a more detailed application of the principles of sonata composition would be even more conjectural, this analogy will not be more specifically worked out but the musicological terms and concepts explained here will be utilized to further delineate the book's thematic and structural integrity.

III

But Echoes

In "Chaplinesque" the poet begins:

> We make our meek adjustments,
> Contented with such random consolations
> As the wind deposits
> In slithered and too ample pockets.

"Chaplinesque" stands at the center of an eleven-poem cycle and sounds again a "minor key" heard first in "Emblems of Conduct." Though the poem ends on the positive note of "Legend," the "memories of spiritual gates" the "wanderer" settles for in "Emblems of Conduct" become the resigned "adjustments" and airy "consolations" with which the tender tramp must be "contented" in "Chaplinesque."

From the "Old keys that are but echoes" in "My Grandmother's Love Letters" to "that memory all things nurse" in "Repose of Rivers," there is an almost exclusive preoccupation with a beauty, a goodness, a purity, the poet cannot touch or can only imagine or, having lost, can only remember. It must be reemphasized that none of these eleven poems is a stereotype of nostalgic sentiment. Each is an exquisite study of an Ideal conceived in strikingly different images and within uniquely varied contexts. Each poem does, however, partake of a certain aspect of the poet's sensibility—the more traditionally romantic sense of wonder at and desire for an unattainable perfection. Crane, or any poet, could

surely recognize the kindred contents of a cluster of his poems
that would constitute a natural grouping in a book even though
the separate poems were not deliberately composed for that
purpose.

This grouping may, in fact, represent a stage of Crane's artistic
and intellectual development: none of these eleven poems was
composed later than 1923 whereas all the poems of the second
half of the volume were completed after 1923. It is not necessary
that the structure of this collection represent actual phases of
Crane's artistic growth. Crane was after neither biographic nor
psychographic order ("North Labrador" was written in 1917 and
appears as the thirteenth of the thirty poems in *White Buildings*);
his intention was to give his book thematic and aesthetic integrity.
This relatively chronological order, however, does demonstrate
that the artistic order also follows the pattern of an evolving
consciousness as it obviously parallels, approximates, even simu-
lates, the organic growth of the poet's sensibility. This would
explain, too, the comparatively lucid style of these poems in the
book's first half. Though providing an aesthetically neat counter-
poise and prelude to the relative opacities of such poems as
"Passage" later in the book, they reflect the earlier, looser idiom of
Crane's poetry that predominated before "For the Marriage of
Faustus and Helen" (begun in 1923).

A closer examination of each of the poems in this sequence
should reveal how they are of one brilliantly variegated but single
cloth.

In "My Grandmother's Love Letters," the protagonist of the
poem encounters a fragile "memory" in the discovery, in "a
corner of the roof," of the letters of his "mother's mother," which
are "brown and soft, / And liable to melt as snow." He realizes the
extreme care with which he must approach such a delicate relic
for "It is all hung by an invisible white hair. / It trembles as
birch limbs webbing the air." Then the speaker asks himself if he
can enter into the spirit of these letters and know it as his grand-
mother did, "Are your fingers long enough to play / Old keys that
are but echoes . . . ?" He does not answer this question; but
reflecting on his own loss of the innocence these letters represent
("Yet I would lead my grandmother by the hand / Through much

of what she would not understand"), he can only "stumble" be-
neath the "gently pitying laughter" of the rain. And so, pitifully,
he cannot hope to repossess such a love, "To carry back the music
to its source," for there is only "room for memory" in this achingly
nostalgic vignette—which, in its subdued simplicity and re-
strained eloquence, so gracefully avoids the sentimentality such a
subject invites.

The imagery of the poem contributes to a sense of expanse and
frailty, distance and solubility. "In the loose girdle of soft rain"
there is indeed "much room for memory"; but there is an im-
passable vastness to the gulf between the speaker and
"Elizabeth's" girlhood love. And there is a brittleness to the "si-
lence" that shatters at his stumbling step, an unreality to the music
that seems to evaporate at his touch. The first "emblem" has been
struck: the incommunicability of another's initiation into love, the
blessed naivete (his own or his grandmother's) that cannot be
retrieved, but only remembered—not possessed.

In "Sunday Morning Apples," which follows "My Grand-
mother's Love Letters," there is a brusque change of voice. The
wistful tone of "My Grandmother's Love Letters" is clashed upon
by the more assertive acclamation of the mystical significance of
an arrangement of apples. The poem, addressed to Crane's
painter friend William Sommer, is actually a proposal to the
artist to paint a still life of the apples—"Put them again beside a
pitcher and a knife." But it is what the proposer sees in the apples
that provokes the exhortation; for, meticulously observed and
placed within their context, they "toss you secrets," these "Be-
loved apples of seasonable madness / That feed your inquiries
with aerial wine." And poised properly, seen essentially, the ap-
ples become "full and ready for explosion." This happens
through a kind of intoxication ("aerial wine"), perhaps the "di-
vine madness" Plato ascribed to poets and the influence of which
will be more fully explored in my analysis of "The Wine
Menagerie."

"Sunday Morning Apples" opens with the reflection that au-
tumn is imminent and that in the lineaments of nature at this
season are found the "purposes," the "rich and faithful strength
of line," that inform Sommer's art. Then, turning his attention to
an apple, the observer declares that the "ripe nude with head /

reared" challenges even the beauties of spring. The following images provide as concentrated an example of Crane's "logic of metaphor" as can be found in as many lines of his poetry. The "realm of swords" into which the apple lifts itself can only be found in the imagination. I think of shafts and blades of light that clash with and perhaps split "her purple shadow / Bursting on the winter of the world / From whiteness that cries defiance to the snow." The color of the apple is crossed with its shadow, and its brilliance — its deep-red skin and white flesh — is expressed synesthetically in tactile ("Bursting") and auditory ("cries") terms.

The dynamics of this Craneian mode is intensified in the collapse of the apple image and the leaping to another, seemingly unrelated, set of observations. Against the picture of the brashly nude apple, "A boy runs with a dog before the sun, straddling / Spontaneities that form their independent orbits, / Their own perennials of light. . . ." There is no purely rational connection here, but there is an imaginative and therefore "logical" one between the apple and the boy — and it is a simple one: the boy and the dog gamboling in the sunshine form as exquisite a picture as the apple; they are as poised and unlabored ("straddling / Spontaneities") and distinctly themselves ("their independent orbits") and as miraculously charged with power and beauty ("Their own perennials of light") as the apple. This third stanza, then, is an analogy, another example of the lovely abundance "In the valley where you live / (called Brandywine)."

The technique used by Crane here is, however, more than analogical or freely associative. It compares well with a method used and explained by James Joyce — one of Crane's favorite authors with whom he became acquainted as a youth (see Crane's essay, "Joyce and Ethics," published in 1918). Joyce's well known literary technique of juxtaposing two "minor epiphanies," realizations or revelations, in preparation for a "major epiphany" can be profitably applied to "Sunday Morning Apples." The observer experiences two "minor epiphanies" in apprehending the aesthetic dynamics of two independent but similarly striking phenomena. These two manifestations prepare the observer for and, by their interaction, give birth to the third, consummate, or "major epiphany" witnessed in the last two stanzas: a deliberate arrangement of apples "beside a pitcher with a knife." What the poet gets here is not a mere impression but an intimation of the hidden and fundamentally spiritual nature of reality with which the apples are ready to burst. He catches "secrets," grasps inarticulate answers, and communes of the "aerial," the sublime "wine" that "feeds" his thirst for what Gerard Manley Hopkins called the "inscape" of things.

This poetic apprehension of the spiritual essence of things is more explicitly discussed in several of Crane's prose pieces. In "General Aims and Theories," he eschews any basic identification with impressionism because the impressionist "is really not interested in the *causes* (metaphysical) of his materials, their emotional derivations or their utmost spiritual consequences."[1] And in a letter to the photographer Alfred Stieglitz, Crane declares his identification as an artist with life: "But in the true mystical sense as well as in the sense which Aristotle meant by the 'imitation of nature.' "[2] Critic Sherman Paul feels it was through Stieglitz and also Waldo Frank that Crane came to discover "spirit in the materials of the immediate world."[3]

Crane did not have to learn this profound ability to, as R.W.B. Lewis puts it, "perceive the divine shape in the physical universe, to read the ideal in the actual."[4] But it is always interesting to find a corroboration and possible source for a poet's idea in an author known to have influenced him: "Each precise object or condition or combination or process exhibits a beauty," Crane's "Meistersinger" Walt Whitman affirms, ". . . the poets of the kosmos advance through all interpositions and coverings and turmoils and stratagems to first principles";[5] or "If he breathes into anything that was before thought small it dilates with the grandeur and life of the universe."[6] Though Hyatt Waggoner feels that temperamentally, "Crane had more in common with St. John of the Cross than with Whitman" (with which I agree), he thinks that, like Whitman or Emerson, Crane "has found the Absolute everywhere."[7]

---

[1]*Poems*, p. 220.
[2]*Letters*, p. 139.
[3]*Hart's Bridge* (Chicago: University of Illinois Press, 1972), p. 63.
[4]Lewis, p. 333.
[5]Whitman, "Preface 1855," p. 723.
[6]Whitman, "Preface 1855," p. 715.
[7]Waggoner, p. 507.

The protagonist has clearly glimpsed spiritual significances, but he has not wedded them to himself. Though approached much more positively than in "My Grandmother's Love Letters," they are as yet potentialities, "*ready* for explosion" (italics mine). They are, however well observed, not yet "snared" as they will later be in "Possessions." Though there is a transfiguration of the object, there is no commensurate transformation of the observer; there is not a complete transubstantiation of knower and known. The focus is on "The apples, Bill, the apples!"; whereas the focus from "Paraphrase" on will be on the protagonist of the poems who, having seen the numina of things, is himself transfigured. "Sunday Morning Apples" belongs where it is placed in *White Buildings*. Whatever transmutation of reality it depicts, it is, after all, an artifice, a still life.

"Praise for an Urn" snaps us back to the elegiac mood and style of "My Grandmother's Love Letters" and is literally an epitaph for the death of Crane's close young friend Ernest Nelson. There is once again the sense of an irreversible loss of beauty as in "Emblems of Conduct" and of the perishability of love as in "My Grandmother's Love Letters."

The first stanza is a brief description of his friend as he remembers him. He characterizes him as "kind" and as embodying a beautiful balance of two opposite sensibilities: the delicate sensitivity that sees through tragedy in "The everlasting eyes of Pierrot" (the sorry-eyed, white-clad stock figure of French pantomime) and the earthy robustness of the gigantic indulger, "And, of Gargantua, the laughter." Such a perfect synthesis, such a poising of antitheses, is rare and, like all ideals, vulnerable. Crane called Nelson "a true Nietzschean" and so must have thought of him as containing within himself the Nietzschean balance of the Apollonian and Dionysian visions achieved only by a select few in the history of the arts. (Nietzsche's ideas on the Apollonian and Dionysian visions, set forth in *The Birth of Tragedy*, will be defined as their influence on Crane's poetry is examined in succeeding chapters of this study.)

In the second stanza, the speaker remembers Nelson's dying "thoughts, delivered to me / From the white coverlet and pillow" as "inheritances" that are as nearly subject to dissolution as life itself, "Delicate riders of the storm." He remembers too how "The slant moon on the slanting hill"—in its inevitable signification of transience, of passage—"moved" him and Nelson to a momentary penetration of the mystery of time/eternity, "presentiments / Of what the dead keep" . . . a rare privilege of those "living still," to come to "such assessments of the soul." The tick of the "insistent clock" in the "crematory lobby" reaffirms what they had learned of eternity while it teases the speaker back into time and a recollection of more temporal preoccupations, "Touching as well upon our praise / Of glories proper to the time." Nothing holds for the bereaved speaker, not his beloved friend, not his friend's parting words, not their brief dwelling within the mystery. Or these are held only in memory, and then but precariously.

The speaker is not consoled for, "having in mind" his friend's "gold hair," he "cannot see that broken brow." What his friend's "broken brow" signifies could only be told by Hart Crane—if indeed he wished to attach any single significance to the image. We can only conjecture about what the "broken brow" and the equally stymying following lines mean: "And miss the dry sound of bees / Stretching across a lucid space." The obvious meaning to me is, to paraphrase: refusing to focus on the death, the "broken brow," of his friend, the speaker drifts into reverie in which he lamentingly recalls, misses, a particular place they had both observed ("a lucid space"), a special moment they had shared, animated by the "buzz" of their conversation—a time of light and life.

Whatever the exact meaning of these images, the grieving protagonist has made no treaty with time and transience though he admits its victory. For, in the last stanza, he consigns this epitaph ("these well meant idioms") to be scattered and "lost" like the ashes of his friend into the "suburbs," the "smokey" enclave of obtuse Philistinism that had forced an "exile guise" on the sensitive Nelson. This reading can be supported by Crane's comment after Nelson's death in Cleveland: "He was one of the many broken against the stupidity of American life in such places as here."[8] The word "broken" here might also explain the "broken brow" above. The elegist then concludes, "They are no

[8]*Letters,* p. 93.

trophies of the sun"—these reflections will be no more enduring or triumphant over time than the life they commemorate. In the same resigned spirit of "Emblems of Conduct," the protagonist is left with no more than the dead "emblem" of an urn—with no more than memory tinged by regret.

"Garden Abstract" seems at first glance to violate the theme of the first movement of *White Buildings* and leap prematurely to the complete communing with the holy in the book's second half—in the subject's, Eve's, actual conjugation with the object of her desire. Eve is portrayed as fixed upon "her desire," an apple, which in its "Shining suspension" is the very image of all she could ever aspire to, the "mimic of the sun." Abruptly, she is imprisoned by the tree's "green fingers," which, having "caught her breath up" and "her voice," render her "Dumbly articulate" and blurred, disoriented—with unmistakable erotic overtones. (In a letter to Matthew Josephson, Crane admitted the "phallic theme" of his poem.[9])

In the second stanza, the communion with the desired is intensified and climaxed in her becoming one with the tree through a coital embrace (with a likely play on the word "comes"), "And so she comes to dream herself the tree / The wind possessing her, weaving her young veins." The orgasmic metaphor is carried through the next line in which she is held "to the sky and its quick blue." The word "quick" is the pivotal one here: beyond its superficial and common denotations of "alive" or "swift," it connotes—and the erotic context would bear these connotations— "intense," "fiery," "shifting," and, in its archaic sense, "pregnant." It is not nature that is inseminated; it is Eve. But in the sense that the sky is fecund, "quick" with life, it may be seen as potent to impregnate and therefore itself "pregnant." It is, however, characteristic of Crane's "logic of metaphor" to cross the wires of images and attribute the accepted quality of one aspect of the image to one of its other aspects. However the "quick blue" is explained, its effect is the absorption of Eve's frenzy, "Drowning the fever of her hands in sunlight." The sun that was but mimicked by the yearned-for apple is now the solvent of her desire, and she the recipient of its generative powers (in mythological lore through the middle ages the sun was said to

[9]*Letters,* p. 37.

have impregnating powers). And she in her ecstasy is transported, fulfilled by her commingling with the apotheosized sun, "She has no memory, nor fear, nor hope / Beyond the grass and shadows at her feet." Though Crane inverts and takes other liberties with the story in Genesis, in which Eve's partaking of the fruit of the Tree of the Knowledge of Good and Evil is her fall, the sense of aspiration to complete felicity by the assumption of divinity is similar.

In "Garden Abstract" one seems to find the desire consummated, rather than thwarted or merely whetted as in the previous four poems. But closer examination reveals a number of factors that warrant the placement of this poem in this cycle. First of all, the poem is an "abstract," which in its general sense suggests an idea transcending any concrete realities, and in its specific use within the graphic arts refers to a composition of lines and colors having relationship only to each other without representing any identifiable object. Perhaps nothing in art is more artificial than an "abstract" that is not intended to communicate any object or experience beyond the purely imagined. The poet's discovery of the fullness of life — his tasting of the "new and scattered wine" in "For the Marriage of Faustus and Helen" and his hearing of the "unbetrayable reply" in "Voyages" — although imagined, as all poetry is, refers to actual observations and actual experiences of the protagonist. These two poems, given their highly fictive character as works of art, read like recordings of factual events heightened and shaped, *re-created* — not utterly created — by the imagination. In the case of "Voyages," we have, of course, documentation in Crane's letters of the intense love affair out of which the poem came. Not that a poem must derive from an identifiable experience, but "Garden Abstract" is relatable to no experience of the Ideal beyond a purely conceived one, nor is its protagonist the speaker of the poem so that there is no direct involvement by the poem's speaker with the Ideal. Crane acknowledges the poem's impersonal voice in a letter to Gorham Munson: "Of course the theme was pure pantheistic aestheticism, — and I suppose they would say that it was too detached from life, etc."[10]

Certainly "Garden Abstract" is a valid and meaningful poem,

[10]*Letters*, p. 40.

but as a pure artifact, as an abstract, aesthetic study (of no matter how carnal or consummate an activity), it properly belongs with the anticipatory, contemplative poems of the first part of *White Buildings* — not with the actual "cleaving" and "burning" of the collection's latter part. Though the desire of the protagonist is real enough, its fulfillment, her conjoining with the tree by becoming the tree, is a dream. Her possession of (or by) the "quick blue" is a fantasy within a figment. The poem does, however, contribute directly to the larger theme of the book for it "pictures" a union with the blessed, the holy, which will elevate the postulant to where there is "no memory, nor fear, nor hope" because all felicity will be wound into that transport. Such will be the "bright logic" as yet but "portrayed," not yet possessed, in "Garden Abstract."

"The lover's death, how regular . . ." the poet begins, almost casually, in "Stark Major" and goes on to describe what appears to be a final parting of lovers, "the time of sundering." We have that same song of the expiration, the elusiveness, of love or anything cherished, keynoted in "Emblems of Conduct," sounded again, but on a "starker" note. The hard obtrusion of this stronger, major key, though harmonious within the poem, imposes an unsettling but appropriate variation with the dirgelike commemorations and mirrored visions that dominate the sequence. The experience is less a recollection or projection of the Ideal and more an almost brutal fronting of the desperate condition without it. The word "stark" carries connotations from "strong" to "harsh" to "barren" or "dead" — all of which fit the context in that the theme of the poem is a "stark," direct study of emotional barrenness, of love's death.

But how "regular" is this close of love, against the background of the sound of the lover's departure — the "lifting spring" of the door latch and the first bare traces of dawn's light ("starker / Vestiges of the sun that somehow / Filter in to us before we waken")? It is the soft and silent time of twilight, not yet the more blatantly revealing light of midday, "that heat and sober / Vivisection of more clamant air"; the lover's desertion of his pregnant mate is shrouded, muted, by dawn's dimness. But though he has been spared the "Vivisection" of daylight, he will forsake the comfort of "hands joined in the dark" that can soothe, "answer," the enervating effects of the day's clamor, "After the daily circuits of its glare."

The protagonist, whose love has died, whose emotions have been emptied, looks with tender envy upon the woman whose passion, unstinted, he could not match. She is alive in her love, full of potential for joy or sorrow:

> Beneath the green silk counterpane
> Her mound of undelivered life
> Lies cool upon her—not yet pain.

She will not guess he is escaping her "cries" and "ecstacies" and, waking to his stealthy descent of the stairs, will laughingly call after him and, it would seem, wonder at his "answering her faint good-byes." The dying lover "Will find the street, only to look / At doors and stones with broken eyes"—only to be faced with the hard truth of his own emotional sterility and rigidity. And so he is to "note" (an appropriately detached type of observation) his own spiritual demise and know that even her memory can recall a more vital partaking of life—"in cries, in ecstacies"—than he can "ever reach to share."

The experience of the cooling of love's ardor (or of unrecipro-cated ardor, or of the inability to love) is, though treated uncom-monly here, familiar enough; but in the context of *White Build-ings*, the poem takes on a greater thematic significance. To reiter-ate, it continues and provides a heavy variation upon the sub-theme of missed beatitude and carries forward the persona of the stoical, disengaged "wanderer" of "Emblems of Conduct" or the "mid-kingdom" misfit of "Black Tambourine." This is not yet the stepping of the legend into noon; the emotional paralytic of "Stark Major" flees, cannot abide, his partner who can cleave and burn, who does spend out herself again and thereby wins the "bright logic." Though the poem does not bring the lover through tragedy to the "fervid covenant" the lover enters through his wrecked love in "Voyages," the premise for such a transubstantiation of the poem's protagonist is established. It is through such anguishing experiences as that of "Stark Major" that the protagonist of the book's second part will find "The secret oar and petals of all love" ("Voyages IV"). An important difference between "Stark Major" and "Voyages" is that the protagonist of "Voyages" is the lover whose passion is unrequited rather than the "lover" of "Stark Major" whose passion is choked. The proper place for "Stark Major" is in this cycle in the first half of the collection.

Of "Chaplinesque" (written late in 1921), Crane reveals in a letter to Gorham Munson, "I like the poem as much as anything I have done."[11] And in another letter, to William Wright, he places the poem's subject, Chaplin, "with the poets" and explicitly identifies the poem's theme: "Poetry, the human feelings, 'the kitten,' is so crowded out of the humdrum, rushing, mechanical scramble of today that the man who would preserve them must duck and camouflage for dear life to keep them or keep himself from annihilation."[12] We did not need to have Crane tell us the point or to emphasize the importance of "Chaplinesque"—especially in relation to his earlier, pre-1923 verse. Such an authorial comment, however, has a way of efficiently focusing our attention.

The most gracious things are also the most vulnerable, the most difficult to grasp and preserve, we are reminded; and their devotee, as we learned in "Black Tambourine" and "Emblems of Conduct," is as vulnerable—subject to banishment, to tramp a "mid-kingdom." The "relentless caper" of "Legend" is danced deftly enough by Charlie in his "fine collapses" and "pirouettes," in his keeping of the "bright logic," in his holding of "the heart." But, like the visionary of "Legend," he pays the price in "random consolations" and "too ample Pockets" and "the doom of that inevitable thumb / That slowly chafes its puckered index toward us"—the "bum's rush" gesture of the omnipresent cop, officialdom, which cannot abide the seeming vagrancy of the artist.

"Chaplinesque" is not a duplicate of "Legend," "Black Tambourine," or "Emblems of Conduct" any more than they are of each other. But in its unique way, at the center of a largely somber evaluation of the Ideal, it recollects the lot of the pursuer of evanescent goodness and beauty and carries the theme forward. It does not excuse the visionary from involvement (despite the stoical stance of the artist in "Emblems of Conduct"):

[11]*Letters*, p. 69.
[12]*Letters*, p. 68.

For we can still love the world, who find
A famished kitten on the step, and know
Recesses for it from the fury of the street,
Or warm torn elbow coverts.

Just as the speaker of "Legend," truth's tramp must not "match
regrets" but "to the final smirk / Dally the doom" of the Philis-
tine's "dull squint" — humoring his myopic persecutor and feign-
ing whatever "innocence," "surprise," or "obsequies" — using
whatever dissemblings will deliver him from "all else but the
heart." Though his task is "no enterprise" but a "game" that
"enforces smirks," the cynicism incipient in "Emblems of Con-
duct" and pointed to here is not cultivated because "we have
seen / The moon in lonely alleys make / A grail of laughter of an
empty ash can."

The agile "sidestep" and "pliant cane," the evasions of the
eternal fool, are eclipsed by the liquid moon and its transfigura-
tion of a waste can into the holy grail — the sacred chalice of
felicity. In the purest example of transubstantiation in *White
Buildings* since "Legend," this beatific experience is characteristi-
cally not separable from even the crass elements of the quoti-
dian — alleys or ash cans — and can, *must,* be heard in and through
the welter of the very things that obscure its being ("through all
sound of gaiety and quest"), in the famished cry of "a kitten in the
wilderness." R.W.B. Lewis sees this as "the act of transfiguration,
the act by which a poetic vision transforms the object it con-
templates, by seeing . . . the miraculous in the common and near
at hand";[13] and he sees this transfiguration extended to the ob-
server through "an immense inversion of values whereby the
humble shall be exalted."[14]

Because the breakthrough is made in an unmistakable trans-
mutation of vision, because, in the tramp's mute devotion to "the
heart," there is a perfect obedience to the dictum of "Legend" to
enter the "flame," one might consider the poem to have been
better placed with "Possessions" and "Voyages" later in the collec-
tion. Like "Legend," which it hearkens back to, we can read
"Chaplinesque" as a glowing signal of how the Ideal will be

[13]Lewis, p. 78.
[14]Lewis, p. 79.

embraced as the book develops. But just as "Legend" points the way and therefore rightly opens rather than closes the collection, "Chaplinesque" is another indicator of the way; the truant hero is another image, artifice, if you will, drawn from yet another artifice, the movie *The Kid,* which inspired the poem.

All poetry is fiction and emblematic in that sense; but as was pointed out in the discussion of "Garden Abstract," we do not yet have, even in the transfiguration of the protagonist and his world, a direct experience, by the *first-person* protagonist and speaker of the poem, of the transubstantive vision. Every poem from "Paraphrase" on (with the exception of "At Melville's Tomb") is spoken by the protagonist in the first person, as *he experiences* transformation. ("Paraphrase" itself provides such a transformation of the speaker/protagonist through the use of the impersonal pronouns "one" and "you" instead of "I." The "we" of "Chaplinesque" identifies the speaker with the poem's protagonist but does not communicate the personal immediacy of the experience that we get in "Paraphrase.") "Chaplinesque," *White Buildings,* has not yet translated the "legend"—it continues as a "mirror" of those "realities" that will become the "perfect cry" of a "constant harmony" after "Paraphrase."

As indicated earlier, "Chaplinesque" does more than rest at the center of the eleven poems that form this unit in *White Buildings.* To repeat, while recalling the outcast condition of the "artists" of "Black Tambourine" and "Emblems of Conduct," with "Legend" it also prefigures what will be the theme of the book's major movements. The five poems in this movement after "Chaplinesque" are more spare, even less compressed than the five relatively open poems preceding it. It is as though the melancholy, romantic mood of this movement were thinned, reduced to its purest form in preparation for, in anticipation of, the whelming of the more forceful movement after "Paraphrase."

A *pastorale* is a musical piece with a pastoral subject. The next poem in this sequence, "Pastorale," reinforces the musical conceit implicit in "Stark Major." The subject of the poem is indeed nature, but there is an ironic implication in the title, for this is nature just at the moment of the year's death, beyond even the brilliance of autumn and its "Already fallen harvest." "No more violets" are the speaker's first words, "And the year / Broken into smokey panels"; he is aware of time's smouldering consumption and breaking of what he thought would endure. He misses the youth and promise, the ebullience and romance, of summer, "What woods remember now / Her calls, her enthusiasms." For "That ritual of sap and leaves / The sun drew out, / Ends in this latter muffled / Bronze and brass"; and at this brown and breathless, almost funereal season, "The wind / Takes rein."

But the speaker seems not to have learned the lesson of fall; for, in spite of what he knows, he tries to salvage a "dusty" souvenir, a token "image" of what the woods cannot even remember. And so, he chides himself, "Fool— / Have you remembered too long . . . ?" He asks himself if there was "too little said / For ease or resolution"—had he spoken enough, done enough, seized the day of "Summer scarcely begun" so that he could now rest easy that he had run the complete course to resolution. "And violets, / A few picked, the rest dead?" is the resonating and disturbing question with which he is left.

"Pastorale," given the return to the Imagistic idiom characteristic of his earlier poetry (such as the poem that follows it, "In Shadow," written in 1917), and given its free verse form, has a conventional, almost Tennysonian flavor about its rhetoric. The poem provides a singularly uncomplicated lament, a traditional "complaint"—which rounds out well the elegiac movement in which it appears, continuing the contemplation of that evasive felicity.

If "summer and smoke" are not past—as they are in "Pastorale"—they are passing in the following poem. "In Shadow," which continues to focus on fleeting time as the corrupter of the Ideal, is yet another "emblem" bespeaking receding "spiritual gates." "In Shadow," in comparison to "Pastorale," has an upbeat quality in tone and content—consistent with Crane's tendency in *White Buildings* to alternate between gravity and alacrity.

The realm of the action is a "shadow," another suspension in another "mid-kingdom." In the first stanza, the sense of transience in the "late amber afternoon" is met in the subject by confusion "among chrysanthemums" as she, or her "parasol," "swims" like a "pale balloon, / Like a waiting moon." Although amber is the only color mentioned, one gets an inevitable if indefinite sense of color in the images of the chrysanthemums, parasol, balloon, and moon. We have another richly toned abstract resembling "Garden Abstract."

The subject's frailty, her vulnerability to time, are further established in the second stanza: "Her furtive lace and misty hair," which, crossing "Over the garden dial" (the inexorable indicator of time's passage), "distill / The sunlight" by which she is very nearly sublimated—as she is in a sense dissolved by the shadow into which she again withdraws.

And then, in stanza three, "Gently yet suddenly," she is absorbed by the advancing night as "the sheen / Of stars inwraps her parasol." Into this "green / Twilight" the speaker of the poem enters as "She hears my step . . . / . . . stiller than shadows, fall." The placement of the word "fall" at the end of the last line of this stanza gives it obvious thematic significance in the poem while it reverberates with the "fallen harvest" of "Pastorale." The entrance of the observer punctures the suave, if ominous, image of the subject being swallowed by time in his urgent recalling her to time (like the "insistent clock" of "Praise for an Urn"), "Come, it is too late,—too late / To risk alone the light's decline: / Nor has evening long to wait." It is as though time had confused, then seduced, and very nearly "taken" her before the speaker seeks to rescue her from night.

The poem ends in darkness, literally and figuratively, as we do not learn her answer to the proposition: "But her own words are night's and mine." We are left with an implicit question: what is her (the) answer? It is the same question asked at the end of "Pastorale" and in a sense implicit in the hung fire at the ends of most of the poems in this sequence: how do we live with the relentless encroachment of "shadow" . . . how do we cross the impossible chasm, how do we actualize the blessed hope we can scarcely imagine or remember?

"The Fernery" provides no answer but rather gives the screw another turn by confounding the question in the speaker who sees himself "a nephew to confusions." The subject of this poem is not the frail nymph flirting with shadow as in the previous poem, but a gray-haired, bespectacled aunt "composed / To darkness." Contrary to fearing the "light's decline," she has become resigned to its absence and shrinks from its presence—with no interest in what it illuminates. "The lights that travel on her spectacles / Seldom, now, meet a mirror in her eyes": her glasses serve as a screen, a reflector of light, behind which her eyes are lowered, not "meeting," receiving as a "mirror" might, the visual stimuli that impinge upon her lenses. But if you "chance to lift a shade / Beside her and her fernery," if you happen to cast some light in her direction, you witness ("follow") her contraction from the glare in the compression of her mouth and the formation of taut lines around it, "The zigzags fast around dry lips," which make a "wreath of sudden pain."

The disquieting picture of this woman delivered over (or surrendered to) everything opposing life and hope throws the observer into reflecting on himself. Looking ironically at the "fresh sunlight" that "splinters humid green"—and contrasts so resoundingly with the "dry lines," "darkness," and "pain" of his aunt—the speaker sees himself though younger, an heir, a "nephew" to her darkness, her "confusions / That sometimes take up residence and reign / In crowns less grey." And he admits himself a sharer in the bitterness and despair she has so neatly domesticated under her "merciless tidy hair!"

For an earlier poem, "The Fernery" (1920) is unusually thick in its "logic of metaphor," making paraphrase such as I have done both difficult and a little conjectural. Confident, however, that the poem is dealing with spiritual and emotional torpor, I would observe that "The Fernery" touches a much more dire chord than either "Pastorale" or "In Shadow," which are more concerned with the passage of love than with the death of a person's spirit. Not even "Stark Major," in which the emotional rigidity and spiritual demise of the protagonist is offset by the vitality of the abandoned woman, sounds as hopeless a note. Only the implicit compassion the speaker has for his aunt keeps the poem itself from despair. The identification of the speaker with the woman's despair, the sensitive, gentle description of her condition, evoke in me a response of sorrow—nothing like judgment or condemnation. Acceptance is love; and though there is no hope here for "bright logic" in the aunt's shunning the light, there is mourning for its loss, which will be blessed by its rediscovery as the "bright stones" of "Possessions." The potential despair of "Emblems of Conduct" is approached most directly, unrelievedly, and concen-

tratedly in this poem—but it is not confirmed. It is redeemed by
pity. Another symbol of the search—the most disheartening—is
given in this dark meditation upon that blessed state to which the
poet aspires and which is so powerfully present to us by its
absence.

I have suggested that in *White Buildings* Crane will finally find
the Absolute in and through time, in and through birth and
death—not in transcendence of them; but in this preludial seg-
ment of the book, the poet is more concerned with defining the
holy and with demonstrating its ideality. One way he does this, I
have proposed, is through the offering of an artifice, an incorrup-
tible construct, for our contemplation. "North Labrador" is such
an artifice in which the Absolute, if not embraced, seems perfectly
preserved—frozen. For in that "Land of leaning ice / Hugged by
plaster-gray arches of sky," there is "No birth, no death, no time
nor sun."

One is reminded again of W.B. Yeats's "Sailing to Byzantium"
where, because there is no generation, no procreation, there can
be no degeneration, no death—where all is contained in an im-
perishable gold "artifice of eternity." In "North Labrador" the
artifice is not literally a crafted object as in Yeats's poem (or again
as in Keats's "Cold Pastoral"), for the supernal beauty is caught
not in gold but in ice. But it is the quality Crane gives his subject
that makes it as much a fiction, as much an artifice, as Yeats's
Byzantium. That icy place "Flings itself silently / Into eternity"
where there is no decay, no transience.

"North Labrador" is a virgin who, in her "frigidity," is spared
the cycle of change and disintegration that is set in motion by
generation:

> "Has no one come here to win you,
> Or left you with the faintest blush
> Upon your glittering breasts?
> Have you no memories, O Darkly Bright?"

There is an ambivalence in this apostrophe keyed in the phrase,
"O Darkly Bright." It is the tormenting and familiar dilemma,
unresolved in this poem, that the perfection we covet, a far
fantasy till clutched, is defiled and finally killed by our very

possessing it. Though "dark" and unrealized in her cold virginity, the "bright" maiden has not been seduced from "eternity."

The question asked in stanza two is answered by "Cold-hushed" silence in the last stanza. There can be no answer where there is no life but "only the shifting of moments / That journey toward no Spring." Though spared the anguish of losing that for which we quest, we are given nothing—not even the ravage that we must eventually pass through to illumination. The penetration of the Absolute that was depicted in the artifice of "Garden Abstract," though a kind of stasis ("She has no memory, nor fear, nor hope") resembling the inertia of "North Labrador," is a dynamic transportation through time by communion with the Divine—the result being fulfillment, peace, repose. "North Labrador" as imagined by Crane is neither dead nor alive; there is no resolution of tension, no achievement of equilibrium, only the proposition, admittedly enviable in a world of transience and pain, never in a sense to have been.

The image is strangely beautiful, "Darkly Bright" to repeat Crane's appellation, and not to be received negatively. It is the crystalline emblem of "spiritual gates," which can never be entered for they never have been. It is the negative, polar counterpart of the "bright logic," for its cold flame grants no "kisses." This contemplation of absolute nothingness as an alternative to our aching for absolute being has its attraction and provides a necessary facet of, a valid refraction through, the "bright stone" of ideality as we approach the last poem in this cycle.

This is the seventh poem in this series given to the embodiment of the Ideal in a female figure. We can see here Crane's proclivity to project the Ideal through or find it in the feminine—an imaginative technique that becomes most pronounced in the later apotheosis of Helen in "For the Marriage of Faustus and Helen" and in various other feminine metaphors, especially "Powhatan's Daughter," in *The Bridge*.

Crane has already shown us from "Emblems of Conduct" that one of the sanctuaries of the Ideal is memory. At least seven of the eleven poems discussed in this chapter deal in some way with memory. "Repose of Rivers" is a remembrance of childhood, wooded haunts awakened in the speaker by the sound of the monsoon where the Mississippi meets the Gulf:

> The willows carried a slow sound,
> A sarabande the wind mowed on the mead.
> I could never remember
> That seething, steady leveling of the marshes
> Till age had brought me to the sea.

The tempo of this opening stanza, remarkably mimetic of the rush of wind over land, is as stately as the "sarabande" it describes—which eases the reader softly from the stunning chill of "North Labrador." But in keeping with Crane's practice of shifting pace, the speed of "Repose of Rivers" gradually accelerates and the mood is intensified toward the epiphany of the closing couplet. The poem's persona is never more excited than to be vigilantly responsive to and grateful for another of nature's "tossed secrets"; and the speaker is not nearly so expansive as the imperative observer in "Sunday Morning Apples." There is nothing of the "brazen hypnotics" we will find at the same kind of discovery in "For the Marriage of Faustus and Helen." "Repose of Rivers," in its tranquil ascent, does, however, lift the reader from the depression of "The Fernery" and from the quiescence of "North Labrador."

It is in memory, the poet tells us in the fourth stanza, that "all things nurse"; for in its haven are fed, kept alive, what would otherwise perish—our most cherished revelations. And the speaker does remember, goes back to, the intimations he had received at play in hills and by stream and pond. He shares the secrets by offering us the very images in which he had found them—trusting we too will find them. Through stanzas two and three, we have the cabalistic catalogue:

> Flags, weeds. And remembrance of steep alcoves
> Where cypresses shared the noon's
> Tyranny; they drew me into hades almost.
> And mammoth turtles climbing sulphur dreams
> Yielded, while sun-silt rippled them
> Asunder . . .

One gets a sense of having entered the mystery of a charmed, an infernal and supernal realm, "hades almost," in the dreamy commingling of light and dark, in the hiddenness of the place, and in the preponderance of the funerary cypresses. And ponderous turtles, "Mammoth," primordial one might infer, slip as though from trances down sulphur-yellow banks into the "sun-silt" below—adding to the primal, the pristine, character of the scene.

"How much I would have bartered!" the speaker exclaims in stanza three: what he would have given to have more than just the memory of what he had touched upon there and in the "black gorge":

> And all the singular nestings in the hills
> Where beavers learn stitch and tooth.
> The pond I entered once and quickly fled—
> I remember now its singing willow rim.

The music he had heard, it seems, portended too much—more than he could then endure or comprehend.

And finally, resigned to the mere recollection of these things, he is almost contented to "nurse" in his memory their mystical import against their desecration by the filth spewed from the stacks of urban industry, "With scalding unguents spread and smoking darts." But then, "After the city that I finally passed," he says, with no indication that he was either seeking or expecting, "At gulf gates":

> I heard wind flaking sapphire, like this summer,
> And willows could not hold more steady sound.

There is another fusion of two distinct but parallel experiences— two "minor epiphanies"—to produce a "major epiphany," as in "Sunday Morning Apples." What he could not rightly respond to or apprehend in his youth he receives now as the fruition of the seed of wisdom planted then. The sound of the monsoon "flaking" the Gulf's blue water is more than just physically sustained, "steady." It is metaphysically constant, as revelatory and dependable, as salvific, as what the wind spoke through the willows of his youth—only better apprehended.

Memory is not discarded. It has done its work and will, we know, serve the poet again; but the persona in *White Buildings* no longer needs to find his sole solace in memory. What the observer sees is not artifact either. It is a direct experience of transubstantial vision. The last two lines of the poem break this movement's pattern of lament, revery, and artifice through which that "steady sound" could only be heard vicariously or in echoes. The transformation of the vision is not as far reaching or radical as it will be after "Paraphrase," but it is real. Curiously, it does not come through the expenditure of self foretold in "Legend"—at least that immolation, that "burning," is not made explicit here. It is a gratuitous, a purely graced, transfiguration, not characteristic of most of Crane's poetry in which the price is always paid by passage through deprivation and destruction—as it will be from this point on in *White Buildings*.

Yet it is right that before the experience of annihilation in "Paraphrase" and the immolation of "Possessions" whereby the "bright logic" is earned, that there be one purely given glimpse of its essence—which is also an apt close to a cluster of "emblems" that could not kindle but could only mimic or recall or yearn for the "bright logic." The "gulf gates" of this poem are more than just "spiritual gates" remembered. If they are not yet thrust open, they are found and the "key" made "ready to hand" for entry in "Possessions."

Toward our understanding of the structural design of *White Buildings*, it would be beneficial to ask with what "movement" in *The Bridge* this movement (with eleven variations) might be compared? It was already suggested that the opening three poems of *White Buildings* provide a symphonic-like introduction for the book's entire theme and scope, and that the "Proem" and "Ave Maria" sections provide the same expository function for *The Bridge*. In the same way, I hold that, for more than just its parallel position to "Powhatan's Daughter," this sequence keynoted by "Emblems of Conduct" corresponds to "Powhatan's Daughter" as the book's first movement after the introduction.

"Powhatan's Daughter," tied together by the single trope of the land as woman as Ideal, is an examination in all its ramifications of the blessed truth sought and finally reached through "The Tunnel" in "Atlantis." The "myth of God," posited in the "Proem" and prayed for as "the Chan's great continent" and "one shore beyond desire" in "Ave Maria," is defined and explored—not reached— in "Powhatan's Daughter." The map is drawn to be followed through the later sections of *The Bridge*, after "Cutty Sark." In "Powhatan's Daughter," the speaker surveys the experience of the Ideal, the nameless Woman, as she is known by others who have loved her (the speaker of "The Harbor Dawn"), tarried with her ("Van Winkle"), touched her ("The River" hoboes), been consecrated to her (Maquokeeta of "The Dance"), and been born to her (Larry of "Indiana"). Similarly in this first movement of *White Buildings*, the poet contemplates the elusiveness and instability of the ideal and is able to fix it only in artifacts until the last two lines of "Repose of Rivers."

There are important differences in content and texture between these two sequences, which are obvious, but in terms of their surveying a truth known only by analogy or in memory, a truth that will be directly apprehended by the persona later in the collection, both cycles are identical. Though there is a greater sense of hope and promise in "Powhatan's Daughter" than in this first movement of *White Buildings*, in both movements there is a prefatory quality of anticipation and examination, spoken in a subjunctive mood of vicariousness. It is not, for example, the poet/persona who delves "death's best" in "The Dance," but Maquokeeta; and it is not the speaker who discovers the "grail of Laughter" in "Chaplinesque," but the clown. It *is*, however, the poet/persona who directly receives the "Kiss of our agony" in "The Tunnel" and personally hears the answer "in the vortex of our grave" in "Voyages II"—both poems coming as parts of corresponding later movements in their collections.

IV

New Thresholds

In his "General Aims and Theories," Hart Crane defines the purpose, the nature, of his poetry:

> Its evocation will not be toward decoration or amusement, but rather toward a state of consciousness, an "innocence" (Blake) or absolute beauty. In this condition there may be discoverable under new forms certain spiritual illuminations, shining with a morality essentialized from experience directly, and not from previous precepts and preconceptions. It is as though a poem gave the reader as he left it a single, new *word*, never before spoken and impossible to actually enunciate, but self-evident as an active principle in the reader's consciousness henceforward.[1]

We have seen that Crane's poetry generally, and *White Buildings* specifically, is an unrelenting quest for what Crane calls here "innocence . . . absolute beauty." In "Legend" the "bright logic" is to be "won" by an entry into the "flame"—by what is explained above as "spiritual illuminations . . . essentialized from experience directly." In the preceding sequence from "My Grandmother's Love Letters" to "Repose of Rivers," these "spiritual illuminations" could only be mournfully recalled or depicted, projected through pure constructs of the imagination; they were not yet (except at the end of "Repose of Rivers") "directly"

---

[1]*Poems,* pp. 220–21.

experienced—though the blueprint for "essentializing" them from experience was drawn.

It was suggested that this "new *word*," prefigured in "Legend" and desired, defined, in the book's first movement, does not become the "active principle" Crane speaks of above until after "Paraphrase." But passing through that "white paraphrase," this second movement of *White Buildings* will now give us the unpronounceable "new *word*" in the "bright stones" of "Possessions," in the "perfect spheres" of "Lachrymae Christi," in the "glittering abyss" of "Passage," in the "new anatomies" of "The Wine Menagerie," and in the "ensign of our will" of "Recitative."

These five poems, though sharing one motif, are strikingly different variations upon it. They are like the distinct refractions of color on a spectrum, each a reduction from the same white light, each on a continuum one from the other, but none covering the full scope of the spectral band. It is left to "For the Marriage of Faustus and Helen," the next movement of the collection, to contract these separate colorations into Helen's "deep blush." We do not, however, have to wait for Helen's "Reflective conversion of all things" to enter her "eventual flame"; once we are "hollowed," emptied for its reception in "Paraphrase," we are given the "bright logic" actualized in these five self-contained, brilliant strains. Nor does *White Buildings* return again to the stoically contemplated "emblems" of "Spiritual gates." We now cross "New thresholds" and pass through these "gates" to find "the inclusive cloud." But this bargaining of "innocence," or what Crane calls an "improved infancy" in "Passage," can be had only by an immersion in experience; even, as Crane says it in "Possessions," by way of immolation—"in sacrifice (the direst)."

Each of these intense lyrics moves to its separate epiphany through some form of agony or dismay or embracing of the human condition to the achievement of "salvage" in the last poem, "Recitative." "Paraphrase," as the poem that brings us down into the dark night from where we can begin to find illumination, leaves us "stunned in that antarctic blaze" of annihilation. We must be "Wounded by apprehensions out of speech" before our "fixed stone of lust" will be transmuted into "bright stones wherein our smiling plays" in "Possessions." Until with the "Nazarene" of "Lachrymae Christi" we have been crucified to the "perfidies of spring," we will not accede to Dionisus' "Unmangled target smile." Our memories cannot be broken and we be freed to gaze on "unpaced beaches" unless we submit to time, agree to be "turned about and back" in "Passage." It is by fronting the violence and sordidness and sadness of "The Wine Menagerie" that "new purities are snared." Nor will the "fragment smile" of "Recitative" be healed, the "nameless gulf" be bridged, unless we "leave the tower" and "walk through time with equal pride."

Elizabeth Jennings, in her study of mysticism, sees Crane's acceptance of and passage through the quotidian as consistent with the mystical tradition:

> Every poem Crane wrote was a wholehearted plunging into experience and, above all, a willingness, even a passion, to surrender. It is this willingness, together with his often repeated desire for loss of self in some transcendent experience of being, that brings him in line with the more orthodox mystical seekers after God.[2]

Though I would quibble with Jennings's use of the word "transcendent"—for, as I explained in my "Introduction," I see Crane's God as less transcendent than immanent, incarnated within the sensible—her linking him with a classical spirituality accords well with a line of argument I will be following: Crane's movement toward the holy parallels rather closely the western contemplative practice, typified in *The Spiritual Exercises* (1548) of St. Ignatius of Loyola, to use the sensorial, to get as vivid a physical image of a biblical scene or situation, for instance, as the imagination will permit (what St. Ignatius calls "application of the senses") toward an appreciation of the spiritual significance of the object of contemplation—and finally toward illumination and communion with God. Unlike the non-Christian, eastern contemplative tradition, which is truly transcendent as it seeks union with God by a negation of the senses, St. Ignatius is an incarnationalist in his spirituality, and so is Crane.

There is no evidence that Crane even knew of, let alone read or practiced, *The Spiritual Exercises* as had Gerard Manley Hopkins, whose poetry exhibits an almost identical incarnational spirituality and who as a Jesuit priest would have daily practiced the

<hr>

[2]*Every Changing Shape* (Philadelphia: Dufour Editions, 1962), p. 224.

Ignatian method of prayer. Crane's poetry simply corresponds to
this approach to the holy, which is, after all, larger than the
Ignatian tradition—its most representative and best known for-
mulation. This point is made here not to authenticate but to
clarify the nature of Crane's spirituality and to demonstrate its
classicism. There is a fundamental difference in attitude between
an orthodox Christian using the incarnational method of prayer
to better know his revealed Incarnate God and an artist seeking
through his poetry to incarnate the Divine, searching for the very
revelation itself—"the very 'sign manifest' on which rests the
assumption of godhead," to quote again the words of Crane.

White Buildings, having leapt from mere "echoes" to the "steady
sound" at the end of "Repose of Rivers," now sustains that "steady
sound" as it is "instressed" (to use Hopkins' companion coinage to
"inscape") from the quotidian as the "perfect cry" anticipated in
"Legend." "Anguished, the wit that cries out of me," the poet says
in "The Wine Menagerie"; and such has been and such will be the
mode of *White Buildings*—but now the mood, the timbre, will
move from elegiac to austere.

"Paraphrase," to repeat, is the axis, the fulcrum of *White
Buildings*—the pivot upon which the theme of the book turns and
the point from which the collection takes definitive direction and
accelerated pace. But as with all turning points, the way up is
down, the way to light is oblivion, the way to hope is despair, the
way to the Word is silence, the way to life is death. As the descent
to illumination, "Paraphrase" compares interestingly to the
paradoxical descent of Dante in his *Inferno* where in the pit of
hell's vortex, unable to bear the malevolent presence of Satan,
which is so nihilistic that we find there not fire but ice, stunned
between death and life he finds that, having reached the ex-
tremest depth, the only path left is ascent—through the cleansing
atonement of the *Purgatorio* to the beatific illumination of the
Paradiso. It is the archetypal story, told and retold, of passing
through the eye of death to new life—told again so uniquely by
Crane. It is that common fact of life that the way to felicity is
through pain. "Paraphrase" itself does not, of course, complete
this cycle of descent/ascent, but by its placement at the center of
White Buildings, it initiates the paradoxical process.

The poem opens abruptly in desperation, the protagonist hearing "at night" the "steady winking beat," the "Systole, diastole" pumping of his heart with an urgent "spokes-of-a-wheel" rhythm. "Rushing from the bed," he hears the repeated beat now metamorphosed into the monotonous pulse of a spent phonograph record; but it seems to be "wedged in his soul." The sense here, communicated so realistically through the "logic of metaphor," is of someone waking, heart pounding, to an unutterable fear that renders him nearly paralyzed. There is no remembered nightmare or any other assignable cause for this stark horror. It is as though the person were dying or had died, had slipped into the realm of nonbeing, which cannot be articulated.

After the shock and trauma of waking to this unspeakable terror passes, the protagonist collapses into a state of "purposeless repose" in the second stanza. Stilly, he notes how the "clever sheets / Lie guard upon the integers of life." The "integers of life" here refers to two things, the toes and perhaps fingers of the protagonist and the moments and hours, the days and years, of his existence, of which these mortal "digits" remind him. The word "clever" can only be taken ironically in its primary sense of "facile" or "ingenious," for how good a "guard" are "sheets" over the finitude of flesh and time? In the word's secondary meaning of "superficial," however, the sheets are quite literally the "clever," the specious and inadequate, protectors of his life. The attention then turns to "what skims in between" the sheets and his supine body and "uncurls the toe, / Involves the hands in purposeless repose." As usual, direct and sure paraphrase is not possible (or intended), but it is as though death came within a mortifying, airy medium to render the body lifeless.

Having witnessed himself "dying" in stanza two, the protagonist marks further his moribund condition in stanza three: "But from its bracket how can the tongue tell / When systematic morn shall sometime flood / The pillow—how desperate is the light / That shall not rouse. . . ." The comparison of the mouth to a "bracket" for the tongue intensifies the mood of stasis and prepares the reader for the "white paraphrase," the "bracketed," so to speak, merely parenthetical and parabolic statement finally made in stanza four. The phrase "systematic morn" complements and continues the notion of the measured regularity of time begun with the "spokes-of-a-wheel" chronometry of the first stanza and carried through the second stanza as "the integers of life." How can it be said, though, what it means not to arise to the light of another day? And "how faint the crow's cavil" to dead ears or to inexorable death who will not, cannot, listen to the bird's petty protestation. The crow itself, in its ancient symbology, comes as death's watchman.

The protagonist has been "stunned in that antarctic blaze" of annihilation, and his lifeless head, "unrocking to a pulse, already / Hollowed by air, posts a white paraphrase / Among bruised roses on the papered wall." What his "stunned" and "Hollowed" head says is left necessarily unsaid or as a "white paraphrase," for how can negation be spoken except inversely? This is an emptiness, a nullity, so substanceless it can only be "white," and so utterly devoid of life it can only be expressed ambivalently as an "antarctic blaze"—recalling the "Darkly Bright" bride of emptiness in "North Labrador." It is right, too, that the speaker "posts" his mute communication, for there is no vital or spoken message. It is a profoundly senseless last testament placed like a pointless poster among the printed likenesses of roses, "bruised," it would seem to me, as a reminder of time's "systematic" undoing of everything that has life. Such an experience of nullification can be expressed, as the poem's title suggests, only in paraphrase.

The explanation I give this poem is, as with most of Crane's poems, at best an approximation of the poem's meaning. Though I make no apology for engaging in the necessary business of explaining a poem as best I can for the purpose of interpretation, my inability to do more than talk about the poem as a philosophical comment on the question of nonbeing serves to demonstrate how Crane avoids ontological dialectic and draws us directly into the experience of death by subsuming the laws of dialectic under those of the senses and imagination as they interact in a semiconscious state by the "logic of metaphor." Philip Horton connects the poem with an actual experience Crane had and says it was written "after waking from a drunken sleep to the brilliant morning light with the impression that he was dead."[3] The point is that

[3]Horton, p. 174.

the reader of *White Buildings*, along with the persona of "Paraphrase," is taken down to absolute stillness, "Hollowed," almost in the biblical (and especially Pauline sense), by being emptied out, dying to the "old man" that he might "put on the new man"— "Invent new dominoes of love and bile" in the succeeding five poems and beyond to the book's end.

Unlike "The Fernery" and "North Labrador" of the previous sequence, the vacuity of "Paraphrase" is to be directly known by the reader whom the speaker of the poem addresses personally as "you." As one of the most intimately spoken poems of the book, there is no vicariousness or indirectness about "Paraphrase." It is a participation in the numbing metanoia of the persona that makes possible for the reader the same breakthrough the speaker/protagonist will have from "Possessions" on.

Samuel Hazo suggests that "'Paraphrase' borders on prophecy after the poet has paused to explore the true and false notions of time."[4] And so it does in its uncompromising proclamation of time's essence. The speaker here is not complaining about or lamenting time's ravage as in the previous movement. Nor is he contemplating the void through another's experience ("The Fernery") or as it is contained within an artifice ("North Labrador"); he has himself embraced the ultimate consequences of time and begun thereby to be transformed.

The ascent from "Paraphrase" begins with the first line of "Possessions." "Paraphrase" ends with a word without content, "a white paraphrase." "Possessions" opens with a promise, a hope: "Witness now this trust!" But we are not told immediately what this "trust" is and how it shall be realized. The poet first creates an ambience, establishes the situation: ". . . the rain / That steals softly direction." Reminded of the "loose girdle of soft rain" in which the book's persona heard "Old keys that are but echoes" of his grandmother's love, we might expect some similarly poignant discovery.

Indeed, a "key" is "ready to hand," which, we would surmise, should grant him passage to the "trust" fulfilled. He, however, holds the key, "sifting" it, fingering it, as though to question its

4Hazo, p. 41.

authenticity, its use. The word "sifting" can literally mean "questioning," but it can also imply a shaking, agitating action. Crane admitted, "A poem like 'Possessions' really cannot be technically explained. It must rely (even to a large extent with myself) on its organic impact on the imagination to successfully imply its meaning"—depending, he says, "on "inferential mention."[5] I have already acknowledged that untranslatable aspect of Crane's "logic of metaphor," but, once again, the critic seeking to interpret is faced with the need to produce some prose approximation of the poetic statement. For as R.W.B. Lewis observes, Crane was using the medium not for "description but in the act of transfiguration."[6] And it is that transfigured truth we must at least approach in discursive language.

The most obvious meaning of "key," as that which will figuratively unlock what has been heretofore closed to the protagonist, is perfectly compatible with the poem's premise of holding a "trust." But one is always invited with Crane's poetry to explore an important word's secondary or tertiary—or purely private—connotation suggested by the context. We learn that the speaker is sifting the key "One moment in sacrifice (the direst)." Some have suggested that the key is literally that which will gain the protagonist entry into his homosexual lover's apartment—a deviant act causing hesitancy, reflection. This reading is based on the third stanza, which seems to depict an inward debate as the protagonist guiltily, stealthily, goes to "make a man . . . / In Bleeker Street" (with a sexual pun on "make"). The poem would support such an interpretation, but there is another related meaning for these images that makes more sense to me. Returning to the first stanza, we have seen that the key is handled in the most desperate, the extremest "moment" of "sacrifice." I believe that the key is intended to have a phallic connotation and that the dire "sifting" refers to an autoerotic act repeated "Through a thousand nights" and through which "the flesh / Assaults outright for bolts that linger / Hidden." These words are suggestive of the spasm of the orgasmic moment; and "bolts," in addition to being "locks" that will be sprung by the "key," can also mean

[5]*Poems*, p. 222.
[6]Lewis, p. 44.

sudden "discharges" or "jets"—ejaculations. These "bolts that linger / Hidden" and are sought so desperately, so blindly—"O undirected as the sky / That through its black foam has no eyes"—could be the solitary moments of masturbation. And finally, the phallic image of the key is changed, in the last line of this first stanza, into another more explicit phallic term, "this fixed stone of lust."

If this poem is about masturbation, it is simply in keeping with Crane's above quoted intention as a poet to give "under new forms certain spiritual illuminations, shining with a morality essentialized from experience directly." For a poet who incorporates just about every other aspect of "experience" into his verse, autoeroticism as a subject or as a figure is inevitable—though it is, understandably, presented very subtly . . . "inferentially," to use Crane's word. Though a sensitive subject, masturbation provides a very apt figure for Crane's thematic purpose. The double conceit sustained through the entire poem is lust and sacrifice. A religious or ritual sacrifice is the offering of a victim, or a gift, to a god to gain a favor from or union with that god. The essential sign of the offering is the immolation, the slaying, of the victim or the oblation, the pouring out, of the gift. The autoerotic act (and sexuality generally) is intimately close to sacrifice in that it involves a kind of immolation and oblation, a kind of self-victimization with the end sought being a type of communion and peace.

Eroticism has always been a powerful and proper metaphor to express the relationship of the soul with the Divine—in the Song of Solomon, in numerous classical myths, and in such mystical works as "The Dark Night of the Soul" (the poem) by St. John of the Cross.

A prime symbol used in Scripture to represent Christ's relationship with His Church is the Bridegroom and the Bride. Though in this poem, the narcissism, the indulged lust—before it is purified and transmuted—produces only guilt and anguish, the use of sexuality, whether self- or other-centered (as in the previously discussed "Garden Abstract"), provides a very appropriate figure or vehicle to communicate humankind's desire for "pure possession" . . . which *is* what the poem is about.

The erotic conceit is continued into the next stanza: "Accumulate such moments to an hour: / Account the total of this trembling tabulation." What would be the "trembling" intensity of such orgasmic "moments" if fused into a single duration? The implicit answer seems to be, "not enough." For "I know the screen," the speaker says; he is familiar with the sexual fantasies projected, figuratively speaking, cinematically by the imagination—"the distant flying taps"—more phallic fantasies, it would seem, if you understand "taps" to mean spigots. But this does not satisfy his desperate longing; for he can also tell of the cutting anguish in this array of sensual, throbbing propositions: "And the stabbing medley that sways." The words of this second stanza create a mood of sexual arousal, of floating consciousness, and disorientation of the senses—but also of hope for a union (against the deathly, "stabbing" songs and images in his head) that will abide: "And the mercy, feminine, that stays / As though prepared." This "mercy," characteristically for Crane imagined in feminine terms, is the first indication in the poem that his "trust" is not in vain— that it awaits him, "prepared." For if not in, then through and beyond these "sacrifices" will the "possession" come. Or, in terms of "Legend," the book's keynote poem, "not ready for repentance," it is through "This cleaving and this burning" by "one who / Spends out himself again" that "the bright logic is won."

Several critics have suggested that Crane cultivated aberrative and immoral behavior as a means to the vision he sought. Certainly, in this poem and elsewhere, Crane includes experiences that might be considered sinful or perverted. But the question is whether he valued these things for their own sake or, taking them as undeniable if not desirable facts of his own experience and accepting the validity of the groping need for happiness that motivated them, the poet transformed them by the very anguish they caused into something pure and inviolable. On the basis of "Possessions," I prefer the latter approach. I think Crane's attitude toward his own "fall" was in a fundamental way Christian in that he used his "sin," his guilt and sorrow, as the very means by which he might enter the sanctuary. In the gospels, Christ repeatedly points out the need for persons not to be "righteous" but to admit their sinfulness and be forgiven, for the well need no physician, no redemption. In parable after parable and gesture after gesture, Christ insists on the need for spiritual poverty: in the story of the publican who, standing ashamed of his sins in the temple, cannot lift his head but leaves justified—rather than the Pharisee who stands before God recounting his good deeds; in loving and forgiving the notorious prostitute and saving her from a stoning because she stands obviously admitting and regretting her sin while those who would have stoned her feign decency.

One could turn to Walt Whitman for another analogue to and perhaps source for this paradoxical attitude toward "evil": "And I will show that whatever happens to anybody it may be turned to beautiful results" ("Starting from Paumanok").[7] But I do not think Crane would have said with Whitman, ". . . —and I say there is in fact no evil, / (Or if there is I say it is just as important to you, to the land or to me, as any thing else.)"[8] Crane's sense of evil is not Manichean, which considers evil an ontological necessity as an attribute of God; nor is it mayavistic, which considers evil an illusion. Crane's attitude toward evil is, as I have said, Christian and transubstantive. In short, the sordid is to be redeemed, not merely accepted—transformed into beauty through humility and love. This redemption of "sin" is not just a sublimation of psychic energy although it involves this. It is more than a redirecting of passion; it is the remaking, the transmutation, the transubstantiation of the sinner's intensity into love and joy without ever valuing the sin for itself.

In the next stanza the protagonist says, "And I, entering, take up the stone / As quiet as you can make a man . . . / In Bleeker Street." It is hard to know here whether the object of the speaker's lust has now become someone else, or whether he compares his autoeroticism to a similarly "quiet" or secret homosexual pursuit. While conceding, as I have, that the entire poem may be read as an affair with someone else, I still favor the interpretation of a sustained autoerotic conceit. Either interpretation, however, will bring us to the poem's point. The "key," the "fixed stone of lust," is now just "the stone" in stanza three and begins to be less phallically suggestive and more representative of the conflict upon which the protagonist is forced to reflect: the tortured aspiration for something more beatifying than his lust. As the poem de-

---

[7]Whitman, p. 23.
[8]Whitman, "Starting from Paumanok," p. 19.

velops, the image is metamorphosed, transmuted into the "bright stones" of the last stanza and it is thematically significant that the dominant image of the poem is "stone."

Earlier in this study, Crane's transfiguration of experience was compared to an alchemical transmutation of a base material into an invaluable material impervious to corruption. This might be done, according to the medieval lore of alchemy, by a discovery and proper application of the "elixir"—also called the "philosopher's stone." If the crucible were hot enough, the action violent enough, or the pressure intense enough, this "stone" could be produced and in turn produce an imperishable substance from even the corruptible stuff of mortal life. This alchemy furnishes a conceit complementary to and inseparable from the sacrificial metaphor. For as the poem progresses, along with the "stone," the protagonist is transmuted (unlike the medieval alchemist) as he is violently fired in his own crucible of desire and self-condemnation. Although not identifying the alchemical figure, M.D. Uroff says that in the poem "violence is a means to possession," which is found in the "imagination's violent power to wrest from experience a new and purified meaning."[9]

As stanza three continues, "still trenchant in a void," keenly, painfully aware of his own person though oblivious to what surrounds him and "Wounded by apprehensions out of speech," stung silent by his own guilt, he examines what the "stone" has come to embody—his sorrow, his frustration, his "sacrifice": "I hold it up against a disk of light— / I, turning, turning on smoked forking spires." It is as though he had become the stone and were impaled against the sky on the towers and steeples of the city where he rotates in his anguish, in the city's smoke, like an immolated victim, an oblation for the "mercy" he seeks. The lust has begun to be burned and pounded out and the "mercy" sought more accessible, for in his agony he is aware of a communion of sufferers, that his sacrificial altar rises out of "The city's stubborn lives, desires."

Before going any further, it would be good to look at some corroborating, or confirming, sources for Crane's alchemical

[9]*Hart Crane: The Patterns of His Poetry* (Chicago: University of Illinois Press, 1974), p. 8.

figure in "Possessions." Crane, we know, was quite enthusiastic about P.D. Ouspensky's mystical treatise, *Tertium Organum: A Key to the Enigmas of the World* (1920), which he read no later than 1922.[10] One attitude of the Russian mathematician/philosopher that might illuminate "Possessions" and clarify its alchemical motif is his belief in the transformational powers of love: "Perhaps it is an alchemical work of some Great Master wherein the souls and bodies of men play the role of elements out of which is compounded *a philosopher's stone, or an elixir of life,* or some mysterious magnetic force necessary to someone for some incomprehensible purpose."[11] But if the nature of that for which the transmutation takes place is "incomprehensible," its purpose for Crane is not; it is into joy that he wishes his "apprehensions" to be translated. Perhaps too this metaphor was inspired by Arthur Rimbaud's notion of poetry as the "Alchemy of the Word" by which is "recorded the inexpressible" in *A Season in Hell* (which Crane read as a youth).[12] Babette Deutsch feels that Crane did take and apply this "doctrine of Rimbaud" as his poetic technique and in fact saw himself too as an "alchemist of the word."[13]

"Beauty," Crane wrote Gorham Munson in 1920, "has most often appeared to me in moments of penitence and even sometimes, distraction and worry."[14] This comment describes perfectly the movement of "Possessions," which is climaxed in the last stanza. The "spires" upon which he is immolated become now the irreconcilable "horns" of his dilemma over his desire and his guilt for he cannot find the perfection he seeks in lust's indulgence: "Tossed on these horns who bleeding dies. . . ." Yet paradoxically, it is upon this brutal altar that the sacrificial death is accomplished, and through that death will be found the imperishable "bright stones"—but not until his "piteous admissions," his penitence, have been spoken, "spilt / Upon the page." Responding, one might say, to the call of "Legend" to utter the

[10]See Philip Horton's comments on when and with how much interest Crane read *Tertium Organum,* p. 136.
[11]Trans. Nicholas Bessaraboff and Claude Bragdon, introd. Claude Bragdon (New York: Vintage Books, 1970), p. 151.
[12]*A Season in Hell* and *The Illuminations,* trans. Enid Rhodes Peschel (New York: Oxford University Press, 1973), p. 77.
[13]*Poetry in Our Time* (New York: Henry Holt and Company, 1952), p. 316.
[14]*Letters,* p. 46.

"perfect cry," the protagonist must acknowledge the futility, the emptiness, of his lust "whose blind sum finally burns / Record of rage and partial appetites." Then, as though the transubstantive power were contained in that spoken Word, the "stone of lust" is instantaneously transfigured into the "pure possession" through the creative destruction of "the white wind" that will "rase / All but bright stones wherein our smiling plays." Vincent Rago sees in this transfigurative power of language "an effort in words not only to say something but more than that, to *do* something, even to *turn into* something."[15] This "pure possession" is not had, as I have repeatedly said, by transcendence or stoicism, but by a beatification of the flesh, an alchemical firing, an "instressing" of carnal desire until it is transubstantiated into its incorruptible, spiritual essence as it is incarnated in the person of the protagonist. Perhaps the "bright stones," newly possessed, might be more fully understood by reference to a passage in the Book of Revelation: "To him that overcometh will I give . . . a white stone, and in the stone a new name written, which no man knoweth saving he that receiveth it" (2:17)—again, Crane's "new *word*, never before spoken and impossible to actually enunciate. . . ."

There is a most interesting prose equivalent to this poetic statement of "Possessions" in one of Crane's letters. Confiding in Waldo Frank about his love affair that would finally lead to his writing of "Voyages," he says:

> I say that I have seen the Word made Flesh. I mean nothing less, and I know now that there is such a thing as indestructability. In the deepest sense, where flesh became transformed through intensity of response to counter-response, where sex was beaten out, where a purity of joy was reached that included tears.[16]

The use of Hopkins' words "inscape" and "instress" to explain Crane's poetry is intended as more than just comparative, for these words uniquely identify a dynamics of vision essentially the same as that of Gerard Manley Hopkins. Crane did not discover Hopkins' poetry until 1928, four years after "Possessions" was written; so my purpose is to point out a kindred vision, not to

---

[15]"The Vocation of Poetry," *Poetry*, 110 (1967), 341.
[16]*Letters*, p. 181.

trace a source. In a letter effusively praising Hopkins ("I've never been quite so enthusiastic about any modern before"), Crane himself acknowledges their similar sensibility: "I am not as original in some of my stylisms as I had thought I was."[17] Hopkins' poem "The Windhover," for example, follows the same course as "Possessions" in its arrival at epiphany. From the meticulously careful observation of a falcon springs, as though spontaneously, an apprehension by the poet of the nature of his Incarnate God. This process is both a collapse of the sensorial (in Crane's poem it would be the sensual) and a fusion with and transmutation unto the spiritual, the Divine:

> Brute beauty and valour and act, oh, air, pride, plume here
>   Buckle! AND the fire that breaks from thee then, a billion
> Times told lovelier, more dangerous, O my chevalier!

From the "instressing" of the bird's "inscape," its *haecceitas* (a word used by Hopkins' favorite Church Doctor, Duns Scotus, to mean "thisness"), the poet leaps to an "instressing" of his Incarnate God. In the same way, the "inscape" of the protagonist's "rage and partial appetites" having been unflinchingly "instressed" by Crane, they too suddenly "buckle" with/under the "pure possession."

One last image remains to be explained—the most important figure in the poem—"The inclusive cloud / Whose heart is fire shall come." There is a propriety to the image as it incorporates the idea of beatitude "essentialized" out of experience, the "fire" at the heart of things. The inclusiveness of the "cloud" suggests both the consummate completeness of the "possession" and the fullness of life from which these "bright stones" will be extracted. But the full import of the image cannot be known until we recognize its likely origin in the Bible:

> And the Lord went before them by day in a pillar of a cloud, to lead them the way; and by night in a pillar of fire, to give them light; to go by day and night: He took not away the pillar of the cloud by day, nor the pillar of fire by night, from before the people [Exodus 13:21–22].

---

[17]*Letters*, p. 317.

If we accept the source of this figure, "the inclusive cloud / Whose heart is fire," as being the symbol of God's presence to the Israelites by which he led them out of the bondage of Egypt and into the liberty and gladness of the Promised Land, then the theme of "Possessions" takes on an added dimension. The "trust" of the first line may be seen as a promise, a "covenant," of deliverance from the bondage of introverted lust (whether homosexual or autoerotic), its agonizing "horns" and "partial appetites." "The pure possession, the inclusive cloud / Whose heart is fire," becomes (along with the "bright stones") the salvation of a lost person and is, in a sense, "the mercy, feminine, that stays / As though prepared."

"Possessions" ends in the future tense; this consummation "shall come." The aspiration of the poem is not tentative or impeded and indirect as are the longings of the poems in the previous sequence. There is a direct, personal grasping of the Ideal here, a passing through "spiritual gates." But it as though the gates were just entered and the "Promised Land" surveyed from the portal—the richness of its life, its freedom, not yet fully explored. This could also be compared to the protagonist of *The Divine Comedy,* newly emergent from hell and purgatory, gazing on the paradisiac panorama of ever intensifying spheres of light and bliss with God at its center. Crane did well to place "Possessions" after the descent and purgation of "Paraphrase" and at the entry way to the abundant intimations of the holy given through the rest of *White Buildings*.

It is appropriate that the "trust," the covenant of "Possessions," be followed by a prayer of praise and petition—a hymn to seal the pact, the promise of "pure possession." Though beginning with what appears to be only intense observation, "Lachrymae Christi" does gather to such a prayer. In this respect, the poem resembles very much the Psalms of Scripture in which the poet often begins in meditation, an assessment of the situation—be it the glory of the Lord's creation or the psalmist's own suffering or the history of Yahweh's great works—and is moved by these considerations to a proclamation of God's greatness or a heartfelt petition for deliverance or a joyous song of gratitude for God's favors. "Lachrymae Christi" follows the same psalmic pattern, which also represents the schema of Crane's mature poetry, to go from restrained (if often tensed) rumination and description to worship or prophetic exclamation. R.W.B. Lewis also regards this as a general tendency in Crane's poetry, noting that " 'Ave Maria' . . . divides, as so many of Crane's poems divide, into a meditation and a prayer."[18] This evolution through sensation to illumination is, we have seen, analogous to the Christian contemplative tradition represented by *The Spiritual Exercises,* and it is the necessary mode of the incarnational/transubstantive vision. The title, "Lachrymae Christi," translates literally "Tears of Christ," but it is also a type of wine produced in Italy. Perhaps the implicit reference to wine is intended as a eucharistic prefigurement of the sacrificial rite with which the poem ends. If the Christ of the title prepares us for a blessing, these "tears" also alert us to the agony through which it will come.

Though the poem is spoken in the first person, "Lachrymae Christi" is slightly less personal than the rest of the poems in this second movement for its focus is on Christ/Dionysius rather than on the speaker. But it is not a return to the vicariousness of, for instance, "Chaplinesque." The speaker of "Lachrymae Christi" is not observing another as he is graced in finding the "grail of laughter"; he is himself graced directly by receiving from the "Nazarene" the "grail / Of earth again."

Friedrich Nietzsche was one of the first authors to profoundly affect Crane (see Crane's essay, "The Case Against Nietzsche," published in 1918), and traces of the influence of *The Birth of Tragedy* can be found throughout Crane's poetry—especially in "For the Marriage of Faustus and Helen." An angle of approach to "Lachrymae Christi" is suggested by Nietzsche's assertion that "with the potent coming of spring that penetrates all nature with joy, these Dionysian emotions awake, and as they grow in intensity everything subjective vanishes into complete self-forgetfulness."[19] This is precisely what happens in "Lachrymae Christi" with the poet's entry into the mystery represented by Dionysius.

[18]Lewis, p. 258.
[19]*Basic Writings of Nietzsche,* trans. and ed. Walter Kaufmann (New York: The Modern Library, 1968), p. 36.

In stanza one, almost as a backdrop if not as an integral part of the natural scene of spring, Crane describes factories as they have been strangely, "Whitely," transformed by the "benzine / Rinsings from the moon." The fluid moonlight—compared appropriately in this industrial context to a petroleum distillate—is said to "Dissolve all but the windows of the mills," which naturally reflect its glow and are not obscured in shadow with the rest of the structure. In this surrealistic picture with only the watery white panes visible through the night, the occasional configuration of the solid hardware of the mills can be noticed but only where a window has been left partially open: "(Inside the sure machinery / Is still / And curdled only where a sill / Sluices its one unyielding smile)." The image of curdling is created by the slick metallic surfaces reflecting the moon's "benzine / Rinsings," and the slight aperture above a window sill "Sluices," spills in, the liquid, "unyielding" smilings of the moon.

Stanza two jumps immediately to a consideration of the animate signs of spring, and there is nothing else said of factories. There is, however, a connection between these two apparently disparate observations, and the rationale for it will be found once again in the "logic of metaphor." Their association is also related to the epiphanic medium of discovery discussed in some detail in relation to "Sunday Morning Apples" and "Repose of Rivers." Having "essentialized" the mysterious nature of even a contrived object, caught its "inscape" through an altercation of normal perception (more on this in the treatment of "The Wine Menagerie"), the poet is prepared to similarly "instress" the "Perfidies of spring"—both "minor epiphanies" fusing into the "major epiphany" at the end of the poem in the supernaturalized knowledge of the "Unmangled target smile" of Christ/Dionysius.

One might wonder why Crane chose machinery, rather than another natural object as he did in "Sunday Morning Apples," for his "minor epiphany." A statement by Crane in his essay "Modern Poetry" (1930) reveals an attitude toward the machine that explains its presence in "Lachrymae Christi," in "For the Marriage of Faustus and Helen," and its prominent role later in *The Bridge* and defends Crane as well against the charge of worshipping technology for its own sake:

For unless poetry can absorb the machine, i.e., acclimatize it as naturally and casually as trees, cattle, galleons, castles, and other human associations of the past, then poetry has failed of its full contemporary function. This process does not infer any program of lyrical pandering to the taste of those obsessed by the importance of machinery; nor does it essentially involve even the specific mention of a single mechanical contrivance. It demands, however, along with the traditional qualifications of poet, an extraordinary capacity for surrender, at least temporarily, to the sensations of urban life.[20]

This "surrender," Crane goes on to say, must produce, "as spontaneous a terminology of poetic reference as the bucolic world of pasture, plow, and barn."[21] The seeming shift from one closely perceived object in stanza one to another very different set of perceptions in stanza two is not so much a shift as it is an analogy. There is a natural continuum of sensibility from the mill to nature as the observer pierces through to the pith of both. But there is a contrast too, for the factory machines are "still" and "curdled" showing none of the dynamic signs of spring in the next stanza. The vitality and mortality of spring together clash sharply with the inertness and inanimateness of the machine, but the contradistinction serves to clarify and heighten the essence of both. The shock of the contrast sensitizes the reader to the deepest significance of the sacrament of spring.

The paradox of spring—violent in its beauty, deathly in its births—is established abruptly in the second stanza: "Immaculate venom binds / The fox's teeth, and swart / Thorns freshen on the year's / First blood." If the fox can deal death, still its "venom" is spotless, blameless; the word "immaculate" might even suggest that it is holy. And the dark "thorns" that draw the new sap, "the blood," of life seem in their very emergence into life to be readying for the kill. And "From flanks unfended," from the vulnerable land, "Twanged red perfidies of spring / Are trillion on the hill." The alliteration and assonance of these lines lend music and added irony to the slaughter implicit in these births, these

[20]*Poems*, pp. 261–62.
[21]*Poems*, p. 262.

"perfidies." The inseparability of life and death in the cycle of nature would be enough to explain the strong paradox here; but the paradox is larger, mystic, and supernatural. The "Thorns," "blood," "flanks unfended," and "red perfidies" or betrayals all allude to the crucifixion of Christ and give "paschal" significance to the sacrifice of spring consummated at the end of the poem.

In the midst of this sacrificial bleeding and treachery, we have the old rites and wisdom sung anew: "And the nights opening / Chant pyramids"; and we are renewed, healed of the lies that have blinded our eyes as the "nights" continue to "Anoint with innocence,—recall / To music and retrieve what perjuries / Had galvanized the eyes." Through immolation, we are given back the primal song.

As the tempo is augmented in stanzas four and five, we learn what it is from which nature takes her song: "Thy Nazarene and tinder eyes," which "chime / Beneath and all around / Distilling clemencies." The mercies granted, "chimed," by these eyes are "distilled," rarified out of the rude immolations of spring like the quintessence of prayer that will arise from a sacrificial fire—an analogy suggested by the "tinder" eyes of Christ (with a play on the word "tender"). The Nazarene's eyes, merely flammable here, will become ablaze with grace and prophecy in stanza seven as His immolation is carried out. Even the lowest life forms emulate the saving music of these "eyes": the "worm's / Inaudible whistle, tunneling / Not penitence / But song, as these / Perpetual fountains, vines." The "penitence," the self-recrimination of "Possessions," has been passed through, "rased"; the sacrifice is no longer "dire" but beyond condemnation and is now to be celebrated in song.

For the purpose of explaining Crane's contorted syntax above, I inverted the order of the lines. "Thy Nazarene and tinder eyes," of course, comes after stanza four and stands alone as a one-line stanza. This gives obvious importance to the phrase and also marks emphatically the movement from meditation to prayer. After this direct address, the poem shifts back to reflection in the parenthetical observations of stanza six. It is as though the speaker were poising his ardor, clarifying and justifying his faith, for the eruption of praise and petition in the last three stanzas:

(Let sphinxes from the ripe
Borage of death have cleared my tongue
Once and again; vermin and rod
No longer bind. Some sentient cloud
Of tears flocks through the tendoned loam:
Betrayed stones slowly speak.)

In stanza six, more Egyptian artifacts, "sphinxes," complement the "pyramids" of stanza three as oracles of mystical truth. The sphinxes, as funerary emblems, are said to "have cleared" the poet's "tongue" because they grant the eternal wisdom gained only through death, which is here called a "ripe / Borage," a fruitful store of healing power (borage is a medicinal herb). The word "Let" poses a problem for interpretation because it is apparently used as an adjective describing the sphinxes, and its exact meaning is unclear inasmuch as "let" is virtually never used as a past participle. Its closest synonym in this context would seem to be "released," which would suggest that the sphinxes, as emblems of renewed vision, have been "let," spawned, so to speak, by the rite of death celebrated here.

Crane probably picked up P.D. Ouspensky's notion that the sphinx was a mystic sign of "higher consciousness"—that its gaze pointed the way to the eternal dimension, and that the pyramids, by their placement and form, were mathematical keys to occult knowledge.[22] In this poem, even if one did not know their potential origin, these figures are clear and understandable symbols of spiritual insight. Though it is through death, sacrifice, that such illumination will come, there is no decay or oppression about death—no "vermin" or the "rod" of law to "bind." This death will bring life and liberation; these "tears" will seep as a life breath ("sentient cloud"), a life blood, into the body of earth, "the tendoned loam"—into the core of "betrayed" reality to make even "stones slowly speak." Here too, it is impossible to know if Crane had in mind the gospel account in which Christ rebuked those embarrassed by the jubilant cries of his followers at his entry into Jerusalem four days before his betrayal and execution: "I tell you that, if these should hold their peace, the stones would immediately cry out" (Luke 19:40). Recognizing the tenuous,

---

[22]Ouspensky, passim.

though plausible, connection of the poem's speaking stones with this scriptural image, we can certainly sense the cosmically generative force of spring's, of Christ's, sacrificial rite in its vitalization even of inanimate things. We have an echo too of the "fixed stone of lust" transfigured in "Possesions" to the "bright stones" of revelation and gladness.

This last qualification made, the speaker soars into a blessing of the divine victim:

> Names peeling from Thine eyes
> And their undimming lattices of flame,
> Spell out in palm and pain
> Compulsion of the year, O Nazarene.

The "Names" that the Nazarene's eyes now speak through their brilliant, constant, and many-faceted flame are the prophetic truths, the oracles, the divine wisdom prepared for through the previous stanzas. They are each. to quote once again Crane's principle, "a single, new *word,* never before spoken and impossible to actually enunciate." For this reason, the Word must be glared out rather than pronounced, and what it tells can only be read in Christ's pierced "palm" and in "pain." These "Names" tell of the "Compulsion of the year," which is to die that it might live, pass through anguish to bliss. It tells us to imitate spring, enter into the sacrifice represented by Jesus and embrace this "crucifixion" by which we will have a renewed life. I do not believe "Lachrymae Christi" is an evangelical call; I do not believe Crane was talking literally here of Christ as a personal savior. Christ is at least in part a personification of nature and, in fact, loses his identity to Dionysius in the last stanza. But psychologically, if not theologically, what the speaker seeks in sacrifice, which he finds at the metaphysical heart of reality, is exactly what a Christian would seek in the cross—redemption, a transfiguration of suffering into beatitude, a new vision, a new birth—reunion with God.

And now the supplication is made in stanza eight that the Savior, undiminished and bright even as he hangs on his dark and fragile cross of branches, bend to bless him: "Lean long from sable, slender boughs, / Unstanched and luminous." The speaker then begs this favor: "And as the nights / Strike from Thee perfect spheres, / Lift up in lilac-emerald breath the grail / Of earth again." He asks to be given the gift of seeing unbroken circles of holiness and to taste, commune again with, the "grail," the sacrament, of life—true to its earthy-sacrificial nature, the crucifixion at its core. The color "lilac-emerald" suggests the first lights of dawn, the easter-resurrection arising out of the night's, the season's, holy violence that has "struck" from its Victim perfection.

The Victim/Savior is still petitioned and adored in the last stanza, but he is now Dionysius. In the surrealistic manner already established and sustained in the poem, the "grail," the morning light, which is raised, breathed from the tree of life, is now "Thy face / From charred and riven stakes, O / Dionysius." The crucifixion is metamorphosed into the death of Dionysius. There is a resemblance to the cross ("the sable, slender boughs,") in the "charred and riven stakes," but these seem more the support poles in a vineyard, as the introduction of the person of Dionysius might suggest. Though the figure has changed, the focus, the sense of the poem, has not. Dionysius is the god of fertility or wine, but like Jesus in his bringing fruitfulness, in his granting "new life," he must lay down his life, be immolated. Given the obvious and important differences between Christ and Dionysius, they are often linked in the archetypal mind as gods of tragedy—the classic sense of "tragedy" as it brings rebirth. Why the stakes should be singed and cleft is hard to say. We can surmise that Crane saw Dionysius's sacrifice as a violent act of hacking and burning carried out appropriately with the wine god tied to vine supports. There are many versions in myth of how Dionysius dies, but he is usually torn to pieces, symbolic of the pruning of the vines he bequeathes. The point is that Dionysius was, in a certain sense, to the ancient Greeks what Christ is to Christianity—the scapegoat, the sacrificial victim with whom humankind can identify and to whose sacrificial act all nature conforms—and upon whose resurrection his devotees depend for renewal.

Crane, in another context, was quick to notice basic correspondences between Christian and non-Christian rites and beliefs. Later in Mexico he happened to witness the annual Feast of the Virgin in Guadalupe and commented, "The figure of the Virgin of Guadalupe miraculously unites the teachings of the early Catholic missionaries with many survivals of the old Indian myths and pagan cults. She is a typical Mexican product, a strange blend of Christian and pagan strains."[23] From this immolation of nature, of Christ, of Dionysius, comes, then, the "Unmangled target smile," the fullness of the gift granted first in "Possessions" as that "wherein our smiling plays" and which we will see again in the "Half-riant" eyes of Helen. This "smile" is "Unmangled" by its ordeal; it is paradoxically made whole by and born out of tragedy, and represents the apogee, the "target," the perfect orb, of all we could want.

"Lachrymae Christi" is not just a poem about coming to felicity through pain, although it confirms that truth. The paradox goes deeper. For some, peace is found through pain, but by way of a transcendence of pain, by finding, beyond tragedy, a peaceful place removed from the tragic springs of sorrow—a form of stoicism. For Crane, and I might add for the Christian whose attitude in this respect the poet's parallels, experience is an ongoing tragedy but also a sustained redemption through an incarnation of supernal beauty and sacrificial love. The discord and agony at the center of things is not escaped; it is "instressed," then transmuted, so that the very substance of its sorrow and dismay is transubstantiated into a vision of concord and repose. These "tears" are "flames" of transfiguration. This is the "Unmangled target smile" vouchsafed from the very altar of immolation. Nietzsche, in *The Birth of Tragedy*, says something that likely provided Crane with the seed for the central conceit of "Lachrymae Christi": "From the smile ofDionysius sprang the Olympian gods, from his tears sprang man."[24] In that "Unmangled target smile" is the signal that the poet has passed through redemptive tears to a share in divinity. Though the poet has shared in the sacrifice, earned the vision, there is a sense in which the blessing is simply given, unattainable except as it is granted, as Crane puts it in his last poem before his death, by "that tribunal monarch of the air."

Walt Whitman speaks in his poetry of the "Passage indeed O soul to primal thought."[25] This line well describes the theme and

[23]*Letters*, p. 391.
[24]Nietzsche, p. 73.
[25]Whitman, "Passage to India," p. 418.

thrust of the next poem in *White Buildings*, "Passage." From the "trust" of "Possessions" to the partaking of the "grail / Of earth" in "Lachrymae Christi," this second sequence now offers "an improved infancy" in a further amplification of vision. As with the first three poems of this movement, the "passage" must be through some form of dying; here the forward step comes only after being "turned about and back" in time. Though there is deprivation in this poem, the protagonist is not mourning or complaining about the loss of his "infancy," or sadly remembering it as in the preceding sequence. He is, in fact, returning through that denial to his "infancy"; but it is better, "improved," just as in "Repose of Rivers" the replication of the "steady sound" of his youth is better comprehended when he is able to hear it again in maturity.

"Passage" begins, as just about all Crane's poems do, with a meticulous drawing of the scene in which crucial images are cast to be gradually metamorphosed as the vision of the protagonist is deepened and dilated:

> Where the cedar leaf divides the sky
> I heard the sea.
> In sapphire arenas of the hills
> I was promised an improved infancy.

Though the protagonist hears the sea, he cannot see it, couched as he is between hills, his sight blocked by cedars so that even the "sapphire" sky is "divided," violated as it were. (Crane's assignment of the sky's blue to the "arenas of the hills" is, of course, characteristic of his "logic of metaphor.") But the sound of the sea is the same kind of "trust" received at the opening of "Possessions"—he is "promised" a better and new life. The images of the "sky" and the "sea" are thematically significant as they will be transformed into the "glittering abyss" and "unpaced beaches" of the last stanza. And the ideal of an "improved infancy" will be accomplished at the poem's end in a symbolic refertilization, as it were, of ovum by sperm: "A serpent swam a vertex to the sun." But it is the "sun," introduced in the next stanza, that is the dominant symbol of the poem.

In this second stanza, the protagonist is "Sulking," moping in discontent, and "sanctioning the sun," presumably submitted to time's passage represented so graphically by the sun's motions. The situation or occasion of the poem is a day-long, meditative walk through the country, which confronts the protagonist with both the limitations of time and of his art, but which finally brings him through a fronting of these realities to a touching of eternity and absolute vision. This process, again, involves denial and starts here with a kind of divestiture, "My memory I left in a ravine." To better "instress" the moment, the protagonist discards his memory almost with contempt, calling it a "Casual louse" that recreates, rearranges, and adorns one's perceptions, "tissues the buckwheat, / Aprons rocks, congregates pears / In moonlit bushels / And wakens alleys with a hidden cough." It is the "inscape" of the instant that matters and from which memory could only distract him.

It is to that moment that the protagonist gives his singular attention in stanza three. The sun, the transcience he merely acknowledged and tolerated in stanza two, he meets now more directly. "Dangerously the summer burned," he says, more fully comprehending time's ravage as he willingly rides its current with the rest of its debris, "(I had joined the entrainments of the wind)." He becomes aware of the light's, the day's, decline, "The shadows of the boulders lengthened my back," and of the devitalizing effects of time, "In the bronze gongs of my cheeks / The rain dried without odor." Water is a key metaphor in the poem implying in its universal acceptation life and renewal, and in its more special signification here a purified understanding. From the initial "promise" of the "sea" to the mysteriously speaking "fountains" at the poem's conclusion, the inception and clarification of the poet's vision is related to the purifying and generative qualities of water. Here the water is burned away without trace, suggesting aridity of mind and spirit.

What the "Bronze gongs of my cheeks" signifies is, as usual with such nebulously charged images, a matter for conjecture. Crane might ask that the image be simply accepted and allowed to penetrate the consciousness and to act upon the unconscious where it might produce emotional and imaginative associations that would not have to be rationalized or articulated. Although there may be no absolute meaning for the image, its import in the poem might be better appreciated by identifying its emergence again in other forms. When the protagonist finds his "stolen book," he smiles an "iron coffin" at the "thief." Both images depict the face, the cheeks, as composed of a base metal, with the deathly stolidity of iron and bronze intensified in the image of the "coffin." The cheeks, part of the anatomical faculty of speech, are depicted as "gongs" in the first image, but their fluid "tolling" seems blasted by the sun. It is not until the transportation to the watery medium through which the serpent swims and where "fountains" recite "icy speeches" that the "tongue" (of the serpent) is wetted to "drum," let us say "toll," its untranslatable message. In the figure of a silenced bronze bell is the premise for the released utterance toward which the poem moves and with which it culminates.

The Word, however, is not spoken by the protagonist; it is heard by him. It remains for "The Wine Menagerie" to loosen his tongue so that hearing again the sound "Tolled once, perhaps, by every tongue in hell," he is freed to speak: "Anguished, the wit that cries out of me." But "Passage," as we shall see, is not a partial or incomplete experience. Though complemented by "The Wine Menagerie" that follows, it is not completed by that poem. As the eyes have been renewed in the sighting of "the inclusive cloud" in "Possessions," so are the ears redeemed in the hearing of "icy speeches" in "Passage" — and so will the tongue be liberated to "Invent new dominoes of love and bile" in "The Wine Menagerie." Each poem is a distinct and independent color on the spectrum of this sequence, but none completes the other; they together make up the spectrum's full scope.

The protagonist's delusory hope against the declination and decimation of time is momentarily lifted in stanza four in his illusion that he is not far from his destination, presumably the sounding sea beyond the wood and hill he has been climbing; for he sees fertile signs in fields and vineyards below: "It is not long, it is not long; / See where the red and black / Vine-stanchioned valleys— . . . ." These words, however, die with the wind "speaking through the ages that you know / And hug, chimney-sooted heart of man!" The protagonist's delusion that time will grant him what he seeks is a replica of the universal mistake of mankind whose heart is so caked and coated, deluded, by the obscuring smoke of the ages that he begins to hug each era as though it would not pass. But the wind sweeps away the lie, the smoke, as it does the "ages" and will not let the protagonist misapprehend time's nature. "So was I turned about and back," the protagonist says, routinely vanquished (as anyone else, it would seem) by time, "much as your smoke / Compiles a too well-known biography." His surrender to time, however, is not defeat; the real defeat would be not to meet time on its own terms—as in "Praise for an Urn" in which the speaker ends in despondency with "no trophies of the sun." There had to be a renunciation of memory so that time could be traveled; now there is a repudiation of the false hope that time will grant fulfillment so that time can be ridden to the climax. The paradox is that in the acceptance of time's limitation, its binding power is broken.

The sun continues as the central symbol of time's passage in stanza five as the shadows lengthen: "The evening was a spear in the ravine / That throve through every oak." We get another hint of time's inexorableness in its inability to, as it were, cut through even the solid oaks. The protagonist has become so immersed in time that he is surprised to realize that twelve hours have elapsed. It is evening and he has been walking since morning: "And had I walked / The dozen particular decimals of time?" (When Crane wishes to bring out the measurability and therefore the limitation of time, he uses language with mathematical overtones: in this poem, "Compiles" and "dozen particular decimals"; in "Paraphrase," "integers of life" and "systematic morn," to mention one other example.) In his wonder and incredulity, we can begin to see the paradoxical effect of the protagonist's absorption into time, which is to make him less mindful of time. He begins to experience time's relativity by joining its resistless flow, by heeding its absolute decree.

There is another related matter, however, that must be settled before time is transmuted into eternity—the effect time has on his art. And so he pauses to look beneath "an opening laurel" (the emblem of honor, victory) where he finds "A thief beneath, my stolen book in hand." In this context, the "thief" can only be time as it may rob his poetry of either enduring fame (suggested by the "laurel") or, to put it another way, as it frustrates the poet's ambition to surpass its finitude through his art. " 'Why are you back here—smiling an iron coffin?' " the thief asks; why have you returned to me with your sterile aspirations? " 'To argue with the laurel,' " the poet says, to protest the limitations of time and persuade fame's condescension to honor my efforts. The poet contends further that his complaint is only proper, for now he has learned that time is the only medium he has to work through; and he accepts that as necessary and right, "Am justified in transcience"—even though this does not ease his desire for the survival of his art and his urgent sense of time's finite and unpredictable allotments, "fleeing / Under the constant wonder of your eyes—."

At that, as though his confession of time's supremacy were the theurgy by which time is paradoxically "contracted" into eternity and its cabala revealed, the benevolent "thief" closes the "book" of the poet's former art to show him what it is he has sought and has now found *through* time: "And from the Ptolemies / Sand troughed us in a glittering abyss." From the astronomical indicators of time's movement, within the very substance of time's instability ("sand" as a conventional symbol of time), the protagonist is siphoned, "troughed," into bright infinity. And there he enters the "improved infancy" in the conception of a new, unbroken rhythm, beyond, but within and through, the "Ptolemies" of "time"—"A serpent swam a vertex to the sun / —On unpaced beaches leaned its tongue and drummed." Then, reminiscent in theme and image of Coleridge's similar testament of vision in "Kubla Khan," the poet hears the language of infinity in an aquatic tongue: "What fountains did I hear? what icy speeches?"

Memory was an impediment to his "instressing" time at the outset of the action; now that he has penetrated time and found there the substance of eternity, memory proves unnecessary and inadequate. Why, in the eternal moment where there is no past or future but only the all-inclusive present, would one need to remember? And reentering time, how could memory recount an event that did not happen in time? The uselessness of finite, natural terms in explaining or comprehending an infinite, supernatural truth is typical of the mystical experience, which the poem at least parallels. Memory has to do with the past, not with the eternal present; and so, "Memory, committed to the page, had broke." The collapse of memory signals the clasping by the protagonist of the "bright logic"—the spying of another of its facets by the delving through time into eternity. Just as at the moment of truth in all of the poems from "Repose of Rivers" on there is a sudden crystallization of vision, a quantum leap to apprehension, so is the pattern of the fusion of the poem's entire experience into one glowing intensity repeated here. Memory and its use has evolved in *White Buildings* from being the only passageway to the Ideal, the preserver of "spiritual gates," to obsolescence in "Passage." There was a prefigurement of this eclipsing of memory by the "inclusive cloud" of eternity in the projections of "Garden Abstract" and "North Labrador" earlier in the book: when Eve is embraced by the Absolute, "She has no memory"; and of the land that "Flings itself silently / Into eternity," the speaker asks the question, "Have you no memories, O Darkly Bright?" Memory is not disdained by Crane. It continues to play a positive and prominent role in his poetry. It is just that memory must melt against the intensity of the truth "Whose heart is fire."

In *The Bridge* memory is virtually celebrated as a subtheme of "Powhatan's Daughter"—as the way, the guide, to "Atlantis": *"Like Memory, / she is time's / truant, shall / take you by / the hand* . . . ," the gloss comments in "Van Winkle" where we are also coaxed to "Remember, remember" that we might later enter "Cathay," the "Everpresence beyond time" at the conclusion of *The Bridge*. Before this, however, we must go through "Migrations that must needs void memory" ("Atlantis"). The voiding of memory begins in *The Bridge* in the "Cutty Sark" section immediately following the recollections of "Powhatan's Daughter" where the old sailor leaves memory to others: "—now remember kid / to put me out at three she sails on time. / I'm not much good at time any more . . . / . . . —that / damned white Arctic killed my time . . . ." From this point on, after the invocation and recollection of Walt Whitman in "Cape Hatteras," *The Bridge* focuses almost exclusively on the present until it finds "one tolling star / That bleeds infinity." The comparable "voiding" of memory begins in *White Buildings* with "Paraphrase" and is climaxed in "Passage" so that a similar consummation with the eternal might be had through the "instressing" of the "world dimensional" in "For the Marriage of Faustus and Helen" toward the gazing into the "great wink of eternity" in "Voyages."

The idea that eternity is entered through time may have had its precedence for Crane in the aforementioned *Tertium Organum* by P.D. Ouspensky, which so enthralled the poet as a young man. Ouspensky speaks much of a "higher consciousness," the expression of which is best accomplished by artists through symbols as it is fundamentally intuitive knowledge (which might explain the allegorically cryptic tropes of "Passage"). Applying a quasi-Platonic epistemology, Ouspensky considers all aspects of three-dimensional reality experience ("phenomena") to be "intersections" of fourth-dimensional realities ("noumena"), so that the way to the fourth dimension of time, which is eternity, is initially through its finite "intersection," its finite dimension, time as we experience it:

> It is necessary to remember that the noumenon and the phenomenon *are not* different things, but merely different aspects of *one and the same thing.* Thus, each phenomenon is *the finite expression,* in the sphere of our knowledge through the organs of sense, of *something* infinite.[26]

Where Crane would differ with Ouspensky, whom he certainly did not swallow whole, is in the philosopher's insistence that the phenomenal intersections of the noumenal realm are insubstantial because partial, and to be rejected: "One must renounce all the beautiful, bright world in which we are living; one must admit that it is ghostly, phantasmal, unreal, deceitful, illusory, mayavic."[27] The author of "Emblems of Conduct" might seem to agree with this, but certainly not the author of "Passage" or "For the Marrige of Faustus and Helen." Crane, I repeat, is not a Neoplatonist or transcendentalist as is Ouspensky in the final analysis. There is no renunciation of the phenomenal in Crane; there is no transcendence to the noumenal—but an incarnation of the noumenal in the phenomenal by an intense, sometimes almost violent, transmutation of the phenomenal. This "buck-

---

[26]Ouspensky, pp. 160–61.
[27]Ouspensky, p. 234.

ling" (to use Hopkins' word), this collapse and fusion as at the end of "Passage," does not catapult the poet out of the "world dimensional" but transfigures that world into a "glittering abyss."

This reconciliation to finite realities as the "spiritual gates" to infinite ones is confirmed in the last poem of this movement, "Recitative," where the protagonist, having heard the sound of eternity in "alternating bells," is content to "walk through time with equal pride." Or again in "Atlantis," as the noumenon is approached, it never loses body: "Sight, sound and flesh Thou leadest from time's realm." Crane does not look beyond for the realm of the ideal but stares steadily into the heart of things, then pronounces, priestlike, the words of transubstantiation before offering, to use Henry Rago's words, "the sign that is called sacrament" to the reader.[28]

In the "Introduction" to this study, "The Wine Menagerie" was cited as an example of Crane's use of the "logic of metaphor," suggesting that the deliberate distortion of perception is integral to that idiom and the necessary medium by which Crane communicates his vision. With that as a premise, I will further examine both the medium and the vision of "The Wine Menagerie" and explain the poem's position in *White Buildings*.

The reader has already been given in this second movement of the collection three consummate experiences of the "bright logic" posited in "Legend" and anticipated, longed for, through the book's first movement. But aside from being shown that there is deprivation, suffering, and sacrifice at the base of that experience—that the contrarieties, limitations, and transitoriness of reality are the very portals to unbroken vision, perfect felicity, and eternal wisdom—we are not shown specifically the epistemology involved in realizing the Ideal. "The Wine Menagerie," as was said earlier, is not an explanation, a manual of the mechanism for grasping "new purities"; it is a testament to, a reproduction of, the process of "inscaping" the "phenomenal"— with an emphasis on the process itself. As a poem focusing on the psychology of transubstantive vision, while participating in the transfigurative

[28]Rago, p. 341.

act dominating this sequence, "The Wine Menagerie" both intensifies and amplifies the movement's thrust.

The first stanza intimates the source or at least the occasion, the catalyst, for deeper understanding:

> Invariably when wine redeems the sight,
> Narrowing the mustard scansions of the eyes,
> A leopard ranging always in the brow
> Asserts a vision in the slumbering gaze.

The protagonist, quite literally in a drunken daze ("slumbering gaze"), attributes the more acutely focused, poignant "scansions" of his seeing to the wine that so "redeems the sight" as to activate the "leopard" of his imagination now vigilant to spring upon whatever objects come its way. This notion that intoxication, narcosis, or some other alteration of the consciousness generates metaphysical insight has a long and broad tradition in both eastern and western, primitive and modern, cultures and is particularly strong in romantic traditions. Crane did not have to be told about the euphoric effects of alcohol or any other intoxicant. In a letter to Gorham Munson, he even speaks rapturously of the hallucinogenic properties of a common anesthetic:

> Did I tell you of that thrilling experience this last winter in the dentist's chair when under the influence of aether and *amnesia* my mind spiraled to a kind of seventh heaven of consciousness and egoistic dance among the seven spheres—something like an objective voice kept saying to me—"You have the higher consciousness—you have the higher consciousness. This is something that very few have. This is what is called genius."? A happiness, ecstatic such as I have known only twice in "inspirations" came over me. I felt the two worlds. And at once. As the bore went into my tooth I was able to follow its every revolution as detached as a spectator at a funeral. O Gorham, I have known moments in eternity. I tell you this as one who is a brother. I want you to know me as I feel myself to be sometimes. I don't want you to feel I am conceited. But since this adventure in the dentist's chair, I feel a new confidence in myself. At least I had none of the ordinary hallucinations common to this operation. Even that means something. You know I live for work,—for poetry. I shall do my best

work later on when I am about 35 or 40. The imagination is the only thing worth a damn.[29]

The above statement was written when Crane was, by his own admission, drunk; but it does demonstrate his valuing of consciousness alteration and comments tellingly on the subject of "The Wine Menagerie." Crane probably found sanction and was perhaps even conditioned for this dental chair experience before it even happened from his reading of *Tertium Organum* where Ouspensky quotes William James on the subject of narcosis as inducing valid mystical states: "Nitrous oxide and ether, especially nitrous oxide, when sufficiently diluted with air, stimulates the mystical consciousness in an extraordinary degree. Depth beyond depth of truth seems revealed to the inhaler."[30] One emendation we could make, however, is that the "seventh heaven," so transcendent seeming here, was to be characteristically located by Crane not through some pseudo teleportation but in the flesh, the "bluet" of Helen's breasts, in "For the Marriage of Faustus and Helen," which Crane had just begun at the time he wrote the letter.

Crane is widely acknowledged to have composed poetry under the combined influence of music and alcohol.[31] He may have had inspirations while intoxicated, but it is hard to believe he did not compose and revise his best poetry in sobriety. His greatest period of creativity spanned little more than a month during his summer stay, in 1926, at the family plantation on the Isle of Pines, during which he wrote most of *The Bridge*. Crane just about always revealed his drinking in his letters by confessing it or writing in an obviously drunken manner. There is no indication in his letters from the Isle of Pines that he consumed anything more than a lot of fruit. The furious and concentrated pace of his work there, clinically I would say, precluded heavy drinking.

I do not think the point here is that Crane used alcohol or any other narcotic to create, but that artistic creation to him was inseparable from a disorientation of normal perception and dis-

---

[29]*Letters*, pp. 91–92.
[30]Ouspensky, p. 270.
[31]See Philip Horton's statement on this, p. 81.

location of the imagination, what Arthur Rimbaud—one of the authors most closely read by Crane—called a "derangement of the senses."

It is noteworthy that many of the writers Crane most valued—including Plato, Blake, Rimbaud, and Nietzsche—spoke of a kind of aberration of consciousness as the means to producing art. Philip Horton describes the passage in Crane's copy of Plato's "Phaedrus" that refers to the poet's "divine madness" as "significantly and heavily underscored."[32] Plato asserts that this possession:

> seizes a tender, virgin soul and stimulates it to rapt passionate expression, especially in lyric poetry. . . . But if any man come to the gates of poetry without the madness of the Muses, persuaded that skill alone will make him a good poet, then shall he and his works of sanity with him be brought to nought by the poetry of madness, and behold, their place is nowhere to be found.[33]

After "The Wine Menagerie," Crane did not again write expressly of alcohol or any other stimulant to the imagination—except that in "Cutty Sark" the speaker says that "rum was Plato in our heads." Joseph Arpad also implies a deemphasis of inebriation as a means for creation when he contends that Crane came to reject Plato's idea of "divine madness" in favor of "rational intuition," the very epistemology recommended by Plato as superior to "possession" for comprehending the higher truths, which Arpad says Crane expressed through the medium of "dream visions."[34]

Nietzsche, in *The Birth of Tragedy*, speaks of a "narcotic draught" as instrumental in the provocation of Dionysian emotions necessary for true art, commenting further that "In these paroxyisms of intoxication the artistic power of all nature reveals itself to the highest qualification of the primordial unity."[35]

---

[32]Horton, p. 125.

[33]*The Collected Dialogues of Plato, Including the Letters,* ed. Edith Hamilton and Huntington Cairns (Princeton, New Jersey: Princeton University Press, 1969), p. 492.

[34]"Hart Crane's Platonic Myth: The Brooklyn Bridge," *American Literature,* 39 (1967), 76.

[35]Nietzsche, pp. 36–37.

It is Rimbaud, however, who, because he is the most radical exponent of consciousness alteration, likely had the greatest influence on the visionary attitude informing "The Wine Menagerie." Rimbaud did use alcohol as well as drugs as stimulants to creativity. In his famous manifesto, the "*Lettre du voyant*," written when he was sixteen, Rimbaud explains his poetic creed:

> The Poet makes himself a voyant through a long immense and reasoned *deranging* of *all his senses.* All the forms of love, of suffering, of madness; he tries to find in himself, he exhausts in himself all the poisons, to keep only their quintessences. Unutterable torture in which he needs all his faith, all his superhuman strength, in which he becomes among all men the great invalid, the great criminal, the great accursed one—and the supreme Savant!—For he arrives at the *unknown*! Since he has cultivated his soul, already rich, more than anyone else! He arrives at the unknown, and although, crazed, he would end up by losing the understanding of his visions, he has seen them! Let him die in his leaping through unheard-of and unnamable things: other horrible workers will come; they will begin on the horizons where the other collapsed![36]

Crane does not leap with quite the abandon of this precocious adolescent. Rimbaud quit writing when he was nineteen, and his poetry does exhibit the impulsiveness and formlessness his own poetics mandates—a carelessness and dogged spontaneity one does not find even in Crane's juvenilia. But the exhortation to deliberately alter the perception, to identify with "All the forms of love, of suffering, of madness," to reach for "unheard-of and unnamable things" seems certainly to have been heeded by Crane in "The Wine Menagerie." And the exhausting in himself of the "poisons, to keep only their quintessences" connects interestingly with the alchemical transmutation of experience I have been describing in Crane's poetry. Rimbaud, however, is indifferent about whether this quintessentializing of experience has malign or benign results. Crane's poems always rarify the goodness, the light, out of their subjects even though the evil, the darkness, may be uncompromisingly "instressed" in the process. A comparative reading of these two poets should not lead to a grouping of Crane

[36]Rimbaud, pp. 7–8.

with Rimbaud and others of the "demonic" ilk if by that term is meant a poet at the mercy of the spirit of creation that "possesses" him—which is the feeling one gets reading the shrieks and random effusions of Rimbaud. Crane is a self-possessed, disciplined, and orderly artist who writes poems about basic human values in an idiom that duplicates the way we come to realize them—by the interaction of sensation, imagination, and reason that Crane calls the "logic of metaphor" and the anatomy of which is exposed in "The Wine Menagerie."

In this regard, Allen Tate sees Crane in "The Wine Menagerie" as "using propitiatory magic, merely material means for spiritual ends: the mere intensity of sensation disguised as spiritual good."[37] Tate's opinion reveals not only a fundamental misapprehension of Crane's poetics but a deeply seated dualism in his own metaphysics by which he cannot or will not admit the basic unity of Crane's incarnational ontology within which matter and spirit are fused or on a continuum—as in Catholic theologian Pierre Tielhard de Chardin's similar conception that matter is perpetually evolving into spirit and so potentially spiritual. Philip Horton answers such objections as Tate's by reference to the mystical consciousness:

> For the desire to expand the consciousness into higher levels of awareness and to achieve the ultimate reconciliation of universal conflicts is one of the chief characteristics and motivating forces of mysticism. In Crane's case this desire for an expansion of consciousness . . . has too often been mistaken for a search for sensation.[38]

The action of the poem takes place in a bar, and in stanza two Crane uses the distorted reflections in the bottles behind the bar to augment the wine's effect upon his perception: "Then glozening decanters that reflect the street / Wear me in crescents on their bellies." Crane took a liberty in altering the progressive form of "gloze" (which would be "glozing") to "glozening," which communicates a double sense of specious explanation and gleaming or shining. These bright reflections are for the moment but

[37]"The Self-Made Angel," *New Republic*, 129 (Aug. 31, 1953), 21.
[38]Horton, p. 129.

shallow, superficial images of what will later in the poem be seen as "new anatomies." But the process of discovery has begun here with the contortion of what and how the protagonist sees. Motion serves to further convolute the crescented reflections so that they seem to run lazily together like lethargic clapping hands, "Slow / Applause flows into liquid cynosures." These "cynosures," like the scintillating "lodestars" to better vision which they are, irresistibly compel the protagonist to a closer study of their import," — I am conscripted to their shadows' glow."

As the protagonist begins to perceive things differently, he applies his senses and imagination more earnestly. He sees the "imitation onyx wainscoting" not with his eyes but with his imagination, so that the fake stone surface appears to him like a "(Painted emulsion of snow, eggs, yarn, coal, manure)" — against which, in a similar fusion of sensation and imagination, he observes the crudely disguised sexual advances of one of the bar's patrons toward a woman, "Regard the forceps of the smile that takes her. / Percussive sweat is spreading to his hair." The sense of violence and pounding introduced in the words "forceps" and "Percussive" do not indicate the subjective action of the imagination on the object as much as a metaphysical comprehension of the truer, deeper nature of the event observed. It takes a "derangement of the senses" to get to that more essential reality. The force of the man's brutish passion is met by a similarly blatant and brutal, pounding response in the woman's rejection (or acceptance, it seems to make little difference) of his hard advances. "Mallets, / Her eyes, unmake an instant of the world. . . ." These ugly aspects of the scene, the disgusting decor, the uncouth clientele, are closely observed, "instressed" by the protagonist because they are inseparable from the "new purities" toward which the poem leads. As in "Possessions," the unlovely, the repugnant, must be almost forcibly scrutinized and by that very act transmuted.

The spirit here is, once again, similar to that of Walt Whitman who declares, "I accept Reality and dare not question it."[39] And, like Whitman, Crane goes beyond acceptance to vision. William Blake anticipates and delineates more precisely what "The Wine

---

[39]Whitman, "Starting from Paumanok," p. 51.

Menagerie" is about: "If the doors of perception were cleansed every thing would appear to man as it is, infinite. / For man has closed himself up, till he sees all things thro' narrow chinks of his cavern" ("The Marriage of Heaven and Hell").[40] R.W.B. Lewis also puts Crane in the above company by calling him "a poet who believed, as deeply as Whitman and Shelley and Blake had believed, that the poet really was the true son of God, and that only the poetic imagination could transfigure ugliness into beauty, hatred into love, death into life."[41]

But what precisely is there in this perversion of love, in this seedy bar, that is "redeemable"? This is the very question asked in the following stanza:

> What is it in this heap the serpent pries —
> Whose skin, facsimile of time, unskeins
> Octagon, sapphire transepts round the eyes;
> — From whom some whispered carillon assures
> speed to the arrow into feathered skies?

The serpent stands for the protagonist himself (or his prying vision), but we can better appreciate Crane's use of serpent imagery if we understand that for him the serpent was almost always a positive symbol. In the preceding poem, "Passage," the serpent is the seed of a new "infancy," the sounder of profound new truths. In *The Bridge*, the serpent appears in various metamorphic forms through the entire poem as a minor leitmotif but figures most prominently in "The Dance" and "Atlantis" as the symbolic complement to the eagle with which it is joined, "The serpent with the eagle in the boughs." Whatever the serpent signifies in *The Bridge* (it at least represents time as the dimension needing to be harmonized with space, the eagle), it is a necessary and valued ontological complement to the eagle. My feeling — and that is all it is since I have no hard evidence to support it — is that the serpent in *The Bridge* represents not only time but a kind of earthly, visceral, primal intuition and reality — the Dionysian vision — as distinct from the more sublime, cerebral, reflective projections of the Apollonian mind, the eagle. The joining of the serpent and the

[40]Blake, p. 150.
[41]Lewis, p. 365.

eagle would in this sense represent the Nietzschean idea of perfectly balanced vision in art in the coexistence of the Dionysian and Apollonian visions.

Clearly the serpent in this fourth stanza of "The Wine Menagerie" stands for time as its skin is called "facsimile of time." But the skin unravels its strange geometry to reveal the snake's eyes—suggestive to me of a piercing vision into primordial things. These octagonal, "sapphire" eye openings are further described as being "transepts," which literally means the arched partitions separating horizontal portions of a cross-shaped church but probably denotes here the slitted forms of the closed eyes before they are "unskeined," opened to pry into the pith of things. This unskeining of the serpent's skin, which like time is measurable (octagonal and partitioned), is, it would seem, symbolic of the unraveling of time itself—often in Crane's poetry a sign of the visionary breakthrough as we have seen more specifically in "Passage."

In "Passage" Crane's transfigured, eternal vision is achieved not by transcendence of time but by an "instressing" and transmutation of "time's realm." It is as though the Apollonian vision—coming at the end of "Passage" in the serpent's "vertex to the sun"—were a sublimation from the temporal, earthbound observations of the preceding stanzas with the Dionysian serpent transported to the Apollonian realm. This is consistent with Nietzsche's thesis that the Apollonian view is really a function, a by-product, of the Dionysian experience: "Out of the original Titanic divine order of terror, the Olympian divine order of joy gradually evolved through the Apollinian impulse toward beauty, just as roses burst from thorny bushes."[42] There is a kind of transformation here resembling Crane's transubstantive way of seeing, but the point is that the serpent's role in both poems is to indicate that vision is borne out of the Dionysian realm and is transformed into the Apollonian without ever transcending or destroying the Dionysian.

And so it is, as the serpent "pries" the "heap," that in his "whispered carillon," his barely audible "tinkling" tongue, is

[42]Nietzsche, pp. 42–43. The translator's spelling of "Apollinian" is a legitimate variant of "Apollonian."

heard the potential for the "chimes" that will be "Tolled" after "new purities are snared" in stanza eight. This incipient power to see and proclaim is confirmed in the last line of stanza four where we are told that in the prodding and quiet hissing of the serpent there is the assurance of "Speed to the arrow into feathered skies." The figure is likely a metamorphosis of the image in "Passage" of the serpent swimming spermlike, arrowlike, a "vertex" (meaning headfirst) to the sun. And it symbolizes exactly the same thing—new conceptions, "New thresholds"—what Samuel Hazo identifies as "the renewal of original thought."[43]

With the premise that in the penetration of even these sordid realities will be found the ring and target of primordial truth, the protagonist continues to "instress" the moment, the scene, in stanza five. "Sharp to the windowpane guile drags a face": perhaps, one might imagine, the embittered wife of the man seeking to seduce the woman in stanza three (wives coming to fetch their husbands has always been a common occurrence at neighborhood bars). "And as the alcove of her jealousy recedes," as her tortured face withdraws from the window, dreamlike, as though through an alcove (although the "logic of metaphor" permits no such linear interpretation), the speaker's attention is drawn to something else: "An urchin who has left the snow / Nudges a cannister across the bar / While August meadows somewhere clasp his brow." The boy is not just a kid running an errand to get beer for his father; to the protagonist's prying eyes, the blondish hair that grows down upon his forehead like "August meadows" speaks of the child's summer reveries of better, freer times. Neither of the persons observed here is happy, and one could hardly call glad the percussive antics of the couple previously described. They must, however, be "essentialized," as the commentary in the next stanza insists, by perceiving them differently.

"Each chamber, transept, coins some squint"; the reflection of each bottle, like partitioned (again, "transepted") pictures, "coins" a new and radically focused slant of insight. And each undeniable individuation is paradoxically better defined as it is seen transfigured in the decanters: "Remorseless line, minting

---

[43]Hazo, p. 44.

their separate wills." There is a "remorseless," an uncompromis-
ing, remaking of each mirrored person and figure signified in the
complementary metaphors of coining and minting. For as the
shoddy customers of the saloon are seen in their motions dis-
tortedly reflected like the gestures in a funhouse mirror, they do
not realize how to their observer each flaw, each "stigma," is
cancelled, healed by that transfiguration: "Poor streaked bodies
wreathing up and out, / Unwitting the stigma that each turn
repeals." And with that discovery, the protagonist exclaims, "Be-
tween black tusks the roses shine!" The "black tusks" would seem
to be the dark brown bottles themselves, the "roses" the trans-
figured reflections in their "bellies," but it is not farfetched to
speculate that this image is a transferral of the above quoted
metaphor Nietzsche used to explain the emergence of the Apol-
lonian vision out of the Dionysian, "Just as roses burst from
thorny bushes." Though the image has a sufficiently clear mean-
ing without tracing its source, this would tend to support the idea
that Crane had in mind here the Nietzschean idea of indulging
the Dionysian toward a realization of the Apollonian vision.

The transubstantiation, facilitated by wine and a "Reflective
conversion of all things," to borrow a phrase from "For the
Marriage of Faustus and Helen," is complete. There is no more
sordidness—it has been "repealed," transmuted; and this break-
through to a radically new vision—to a reality deeper than ap-
pearances but seen in these appearances—is now proclaimed and
celebrated in stanza seven.

Crane once told his mother, "The freedom of my imagination
is the most precious thing that life holds for me, —and the only
reason I can see for living."[44] It is this freedom that is now
affirmed. The protagonist has crossed "New thresholds" into
"new anatomies." It is "Wine talons," both the alcohol he has
drunk and the "glozening decanters" or "tusks" (like "talons"),
which have altered his perception, his consciousness, and given
him the "freedom" to "distill," purify, refine, his "competence" so
that he might enter into the being, however sordid or sad, of
another and know its perfect essence—"to travel in a tear /
Sparkling alone, within another's will." We have a broadening

[44]*Letters*, p. 189.

and deepening of the concept of Crane's transubstantive vision; in the transmutation of objective reality, of another person, the poet somehow, mysteriously, identifies so utterly with his subject as to virtually become it, to move within its "will." One thinks here of Keats's notion of "negative capability," and the idea is related. Crane's desire and ability to "become" someone else is not the parasitical seeking of an identity by one who has none. It is a form of love in which the identification is so complete that its quintessential expression is a "tear"—compassion. This entrance into the perceived phenomena of external reality is not unique to Crane and is in fact characteristic of the mystical consciousness. It represents the liberation Crane as artist, as poet, has sought—to get outside himself and universalize the transfiguration experienced inwardly in the previous three poems.

Ordinarily, Crane's poems end on this epiphanic note, but in stanza eight "The Wine Menagerie" goes on to explore the ramifications of this renovated vision, the conditions of its implementation. The "new anatomies" must be assimilated into the pith of his being, "Until my blood dreams a receptive smile / Wherein new purities are snared." (One thinks again of the felicitous "smiling" of "Possessions," the generative "target smile" of Dionysius, and the "Half-riant" face of Helen.) And these "purities" must be heard deep within himself as the essential ring of truth, "where chimes / Before some flame of gaunt respose a shell / Tolled once, perhaps, by every tongue in hell." The bell is imagined here as a tolling "shell," as the "tongue" of each person in hell. In "Passage," we recall, Crane also compared the cheeks to "gongs," a bell. From "Paraphrase" on, the protagonists have had to pass through a kind of hell (prefigured in the "burning" of "Legend") to arrive at the illuminative vision sought. It is from "hell" that the bell is first tolled, the word of transubstantiation first spoken.

A hint to the meaning of Crane's transformation of a bell into a shell might be found in a comparable image in "O Carib Isle!" (1927): "You have given me the shell, Satan, —carbonic amulet." In the context of this poem, the shell is regarded as a charm against evil, a talisman of occult wisdom, discovered in the paradoxical manner of "The Wine Menagerie" through the "inscaping" of the desolation and violence of a tropical island, "death's brittle crypt." Could not the tolling "shell" here be a similar "amulet" found in the hell of this Menagerie? The "flame of gaunt repose" is redolent to me of a thin, undeveloped vision and peace "before," over and above, which the sure tolling of that "shell" must come. The key word here is, of course, "before"; the sentence only makes sense to me if the puny "flame" of a compromised art and happiness is superseded by the clear "chimes" of a wisdom suffered out of experience.

Until he does dream the "receptive smile" and hear the chime of "new purities," he must upbraid himself: "Anguished, the wit that cries out of me." In stanza nine, we hear what his anguished cry is. The protagonist repudiates his frigid, insubstantial efforts born of mere techniue, not vision, "Alas, —these frozen billows of your skill!" And he admonishes himself to "Invent new dominoes of love and bile," to artistically recast, transubstantiate, the passions of life just as he saw them transmuted in the menagerie of his altered consciousness. For he must know, "Ruddy, the tooth implicit of the world has followed you"; whether Crane means here that there is a price to be paid by the visionary to the world that would punish such unorthodox ways of seeing, or that the violence of life must be reinvented into "new dominoes" because it has "followed you" anyway—or both—I do not know. Either or both readings would fit the context. But the artist/protagonist must not be content with anything less real and substantial than the "new purities" he has for the first time "snared"; he must not "count some dim inheritance of sand" because "How much yet meets the treason of the snow"—his "frozen billows" will be betrayed by their own evanescent substance and melt. Only the solid stuff of "new anatomies" will keep against time. In this sense, "The Wine Menagerie" interprets the "thief's" cryptic answer to the "argument" of the protagonist of "Passage" that his poetry not pass with time. The vision granted at the end of "Passage" is the same substance, "new purities," out of which poetry must be wrought if it is to endure.

And so, in stanza ten Crane articulates the call to freedom implicit in these "New thresholds." In another biblical analogy figurative of liberation from bondage (recall "the inclusive cloud / Whose heart is fire" of "Possessions"), the protagonist thinks of himself as Judith of the Old Testament who, to carry out God's plan to deliver the Israelites from the tyranny of Nebuchadnezzar, gives herself up to the great Babylonian general, Holofernes, so that she might assassinate him. Because he lusts after her and offers her all manner of wealth and comfort, Judith might have been tempted to renege; but she carries out the deed of beheading Holofernes and wins the freedom of Israel. The poet, too, feels tugged toward complacency, is similarly tempted to abandon his mission toward a revolution of consciousness and settle for the safety of mere "skill." He therefore exhorts himself:

> Rise from the dates and crumbs. And walk away,
> Stepping over Holofernes' shins —
> Beyond the wall, whose severed head floats by
> With Baptist John's. Their whispering begins.

What are these more easily won prizes but "dates and crumbs"? As the liberator leaves the scene, the "severed head" of Holofernes is seen "whispering" with "Baptist John's." The introduction of John the Baptist is another puzzling image that yields no easy or absolute meaning. It would probably be a mistake to read too much into the figures by reference to the biblical characters of John the Baptist or Holofernes (unless we consider the ironic contrast of oppressor and oppressed both sharing the same fate, John's prophetic career having been cut off by the "Ruddy . . . tooth" of another of the world's Holofernes). They have one thing in common, decapitation. As such they seem to simply represent a thwarted vision that must be left behind, "Beyond the wall," to mutter whatever pointless poems or slanderous detractions their bodiless brains can conjure. The true poet's vision is not found in floating heads but in the beating "blood."

Judith went back to the welcoming gratitude of her compatriots, but not so the poet/protagonist. As he tells himself, he must, because of his unorthodox vision and like the "mid-kingdom" artist of "Black Tambourine," face alienation: " — And fold your exile on your back again; / Petrushka's valentine pivots on its pin." Petrushka is a character in a Stravinsky ballet by that title (1919) who is slain for his pursuit of his "valentine" or love. Crane knew of and liked the ballet, as a 1925 letter referring to Stravinsky's conducting the piece in Cleveland attests: "Indeed, the *Petrouchka* was the only fine thing on the program."[45] The figure of a mechanical ballerina spinning on its axis can symbolize the poetic ideal for which the poet must be willing to die or be ostracized, or conversely it can stand for the sterile artifacts, the "frozen billows," which the poet has repudiated and which are not worth the investment of his life. I favor the latter interpretation and see the protagonist as packing up to abandon the merely clever, technical contrivances of his poetry which are not radicalized by the new consciousness—pretty parlor ornaments spinning nothing real.

"The Wine Menagerie" does not end on the upbeat note of the previous three poems of the movement. The last four stanzas are like an addendum to a poem which, had it followed Crane's habitual mode, would have ended, as stated above, with the triumphant proclamation of the seventh stanza. "The Wine Menagerie" is the fifth poem in a movement that has brought us beyond memory and artifact, through annihilation, sacrifice, and time, to a sure comprehension of four aspects of the Absolute, but its ending might seem like a relapse back into the futile mood of "Emblems and Conduct." There are, however, two important factors about "The Wine Menagerie" that warrant its position in *White Buildings*. The "sight" *is* redeemed in the poem—it does depict a profound and personal experience had by the protagonist, not a vicarious observation of or longing for the Ideal; and there is a resolve at the poem's conclusion to exercise the freedom of such renewed vision and obey its call though it lead to "exile." This is quite different from the unproductive exile of the artist in "Black Tambourine" whose instrument of art is "stuck on the wall," and there is little redemptive about the alienation of the visionary in "Emblems of Conduct" who has only memory to console him. As a poem portraying another facet of the "bright logic" and recreating the conditions of its perception—while bluntly acknowledging the cost of its pursuit—"The Wine Menagerie" takes the theme of *White Buildings* a step forward.

All of Crane's poetry is a reaching from the duality of human experience toward some form of unity. Oneness, indivisibility, is a

---

[45]*Letters*, p. 200.

primary but, for the most part, implicit attribute of the Ideal sought in *White Buildings*. "For the Marriage of Faustus and Helen" begins with the premise that the mind has become fragmented, "Divided by accepted multitudes," and needs the integrating, healing vision of Helen. In *The Bridge,* this unification of what Crane in his final poem calls "the broken world" is most explicitly identified as the sign of divinity that the Brooklyn Bridge represents—from the poet's apostrophe to it as "Unfractioned idiom" in the "Proem" to his psalmic praise of it in "Atlantis": "Within whose lariat sweep encinctured sing / In single chrysalis the many twain." The classic ontological question of the "one and many" is known to anyone familiar with the history of philosophy: "Recitative" is Crane's formal consideration of and response to life's brokenness that is assumed in all of the poems of *White Buildings*, beginning with the fragmentation implied in the need to "string some constant harmony" in "Legend." "Recitative" is, however, the most express statement in the book of a theme that will become more pronounced in *The Bridge*. As a deeply personal experience in bridging the "nameless gulf"—rather than a detached contemplation of a similar chasm in the "mid-kingdom" of "Black Tambourine" or the surrender to "broken eyes" in "Stark Major"—"Recitative" provides the last rich tone to the "perfect cry" of consummation in the movement it completes. "Recitative" is, therefore, in keeping with the consummate nature of this second sequence. As the poem summarizing the split nature of reality, which is the premise of every poem in the book up to this point, it quite properly is found as the last poem before the two final movements, "For the Marriage of Faustus and Helen" and "Voyages," which gather up all the strands of the collection and fuse them into two inclusive but tonally distinct variations.

In a letter to William Wright, Crane confides that he would like to work "without having to wrestle with either angels or devils to continue with it. I get awfully exhausted sometimes, trying to achieve some kind of consistent vision of things."[46] This remark helps us to understand the motivation and psychology behind "Recitative," the "Janus-faced" nature of Crane's life on which Brom Weber sheds a little more light:

[46]*Letters,* p. 267.

This dualism was far more than an abstract conflict between ideal and reality, between matter and spirit, good and evil, lust and love. It was a dualism that extended through every fiber of his being, sending him in agony from one extremity to another, always in turmoil and never at rest.[47]

> Regard the capture here, O Janus-faced,
> As double as the hands that twist this glass.
> Such eyes at search or rest you cannot see;
> Reciting pain or glee, how can you bear!

In this first stanza, the protagonist describes himself as peering at the "capture" of his visage in a mirror, a "glass." Here, as in "The Wine Menagerie," the device of reflection is used to alter the perception that a deeper truth might be contemplated. Addressing himself as two-faced, like the double-visaged god Janus, he moves, "twists," the mirror to better study, it would seem, the psychic duality suggested by his very physiognomy: the two eyes bespeaking "search or rest" — "pain or glee." There is a sort of unity here, but it is maddeningly manifested in doubles — what philosophers call the "concomitant one and many." And then he cries out his anguish at having to "bear" such contradictions within himself:

> Twin shadowed halves: the breaking second holds
> In each the skin alone, and so it is
> I crust a plate of vibrant mercury
> Borne cleft to you, and brother in the half.

The doubleness so stressed in the first stanza, in the two hands and eyes of the reflection and original of the protagonist's face, is extended in stanza two to the reader so that the duality has ramifications in the distant yet paradoxical correspondence between audience and poet, the two halves of humanity who see each other in each other as in a mirror. If we see the mirror as cracked, "cleft," the language of this stanza and later makes more sense — and the duality is further intensified. The "breaking second" becomes double in its meaning, signifying the split moment of time as well as the other half of the mirror that "holds" half of a severed image: "Twin shadowed halves." The poet addresses the

[47]Weber, p. 233.

reader now (as well as himself) and offers us the mirror, "Borne cleft to you, and brother in the half," as a duplex image of himself/ourselves. In its other sense of fractured time, "the breaking second" underscores and compounds the dividedness of what we see. As I have repeatedly acknowledged, many of Crane's metaphors have no perfectly equivalent or literally describable object that they represent. These images represent the poet's perception and response to an experience and communicate a network of dualities stressed and strengthened as they interact.

But what we see is also superficial, a surface reality in which "the skin alone" is "crusted" on "a plate of vibrant mercury." The vibrancy of the mirror—however realistic—is not truly alive but an imitation of life. There is a subtle sense here that the duality is only apparent, no truer than the specious reality of the mirror's reflection. Perhaps there is a unified truth beneath, within, this duality as real as its double appearance. The poem itself is an exemplar of the very duality it projects because of the rift yet perplexing unity between speaker and auditor. This duality is further compounded when we consider that a recitative in music is a piece half-spoken, half-sung by the performer—as Crane describes the poet below, "on a platform speaking it." Crane explains this dualistic complex in a letter to Allen Tate;

> It *is* complex, exceedingly,—and I worked for weeks, off and on, of course,—trying to simplify the presentation of ideas in it, the conception. Imagine the poet, say, on a platform speaking it. The audience is one half of Humanity, Man (in the sense of Blake) and the poet the other. ALSO, the poet sees himself in the audience as in a mirror. ALSO, the audience sees itself, in part, in the poet. Against this paradoxical DUALITY is posed the UNITY or the conception of it (as you got it) in the last verse. In another sense, the poet is *talking to himself* all the way through the poem, and there are, as too often in my poems, other reflexes and symbolisms in the poem, also, which it would be silly to write here—at least for the present.[48]

Of course, Crane also confirms here the final apprehension of unity toward which the poem moves. But as in all Crane's poems, the Ideal desired is found *through* its seeming opposite: as the

---

[48]*Letters,* p. 176.

ascent to life is begun in the death of "Paraphrase," and the "pure possession" is transmuted from the "stone of lust" in "Possessions," and "perfect spheres" are sacrificed from the "red perfidies of spring" in "Lachrymae Christi," and eternity's "fountains" spring from the "Ptolemies" of time in "Passage," and "black tusks" put forth "roses" in "The Wine Menagerie." Nietzsche, in *The Birth of Tragedy,* senses a "primordial contradiction and primordial pain at the heart of the primal unity," which he says must be known if the unity is to be envisioned.[49] Crane seems to have taken well to heart those words, which comply with the dualistic paradox of "Recitative." Within the very duality of the poem we can already discern a unity that must be "instressed," but not before the agony of duality has been "instressed" through the next four stanzas.

Stanza three invites us to press our observation further, "Inquire this much-exacting fragment smile"—this split picture demands deeper scrutiny. (How different is this "fragment smile" from the "Unmangled . . . smile" of Dionysius.) We must not, however, focus for now on the primitive, wilder self, the jungle that underlies this "much-exacting," civil smile like the id beneath the superego: "Its drumbs and darkest blowing leaves ignore." But neither should we weep yet, recall the "tears" that enable us to interpret the "crucial sign" (only watered with tears do "Betrayed stones slowly speak"; and only in a tear are "new purities . . . snared"): "Defer though, revocation of the tears / That yield attendance to one crucial sign."

The poet asks us to "Defer," to wait, and in stanza four to "Look steadily—how the wind feasts and spins / The brain's disk shivered against lust." In the idiom of the "logic of metaphor," the literal image of the hair being tossed by the wind is transformed through the imagination to stand for the "brain's" dilemma (literally located in the "disk," the cranium, beneath the blowing hair) between lust and shame, which was the subject of "Possessions" and which has here "shivered" his mind. Again, in keeping with the metaphor's literal/figurative logic, a hand-held mirror would tend to tremble and so "shiver" the reflection. There is a substratum of meaning in "Recitative," one of those "other reflexes"

---

[49]Nietzsche, p. 55.

Crane identifies in the above quotation as characteristic of his poetry, which considerably adds to the density of the dualities intertwined in the poem. It is the recognition of humankind's apparently divided nature so elaborately analyzed by Sigmund Freud (whose terminology has already been applied to this poem): the clash between the primal and the civil self. The poet is here "instressing" that civilized half commonly called conscience. In "essentializing" that part of his/our nature, the speaker says, we see the other, darker, bestial, and apelike half drop out of sight as we literally shift the angle of the mirror, "Then watch / While darkness, like an ape's face, falls away, / And gradually white buildings answer day." These "white buildings" stand in the poem as the antithesis to the primitive "darkness" that has now withdrawn, their civilized facades "gradually" brightening the picture. But in the next stanza we learn that they do not provide the "answer" to the poem's anguishing dilemma; for the answer cannot be found in any antithesis, be it ordered light or formless darkness. The answer can only reside in synthesis.

"Let the same nameless gulf beleaguer us," we are instructed in stanza five; let us allow the indefinable dichotomy to annoy, even overwhelm us, for it must be known in its divisiveness if its hidden unity is to be realized. Let us, together, taste fully the frustration of being held aloof, aloft, without communion with each other, our primal selves, or anything else—let the stories and partitions of "white buildings," of civilized restraint, "Alike suspend us from atrocious sums / Built floor by floor on shafts of steel that grant / The plummet heart, like Absalom, no stream." Let us, like Absalom of the Bible, know utterly what it means to hang by the hair, as it were, when all that the "heart" desires is to come down, to "plummet"—to escape the fragmentation, to be unbound and join the "stream" in which, one might infer, all things flow as one. It is not "atrocious sums" we want (again Crane resorting to a mathematical conceit to convey the limitations of experience), but the ultimate number that cannot be multiplied or divided, added or subtracted. The significance of "white buildings," for this poem and the entire book that takes its title from the phrase, is not that they are the answer, but that in their structuring of the unformed, primordial self, which they imply, they are part of, a way to, the answer. The disturbing multiplicity and distinctions of their "floors" and "shafts" are paradoxically the splintered expression of a perfect singularity. In feeling their separateness, their essential unity is grasped. They may be seen as representing the sublimated, delineated, distinguishable Apollonian vision in contradistinction to (yet inseparable from) the libidinous, undefined, undivided Dionysian energy out of which the Apollonian comes—as was elsewhere explained.

P.D. Ouspensky may once again provide a clarifying gloss or perhaps source for Crane's idea of the oneness grasped through multiplicity. In *Tertium Organum* he asserts that the world merely looks to be what it is not, "Thus our language pictures to us before-hand a false universe—*dual*, when in reality it is *one*."[50] And he adds:

> Duality is the condition of *our* knowledge of the phenomenal (three-dimensional) world; this is the *instrument* of our knowledge of phenomena. But when we come to the knowledge of the noumenal world (or the world of many dimensions), this duality begins to hinder us, appears as an obstacle of knowledge. . . . Our language is incapable of expressing *the unity of opposites.*[51]

Yet Crane must have found encouragement in *Tertium Organum* for locating the one in the many: "THE PHENOMENON IS THE IMAGE OF THE NOUMENON. It is *possible* to know the noumenon by the phenomenon."[52] Crane, to repeat, did not assent to Ouspensky's more transcendental idea that phenomena are illusions. The phenomenal realm, the world, was never treated as literally illusory by Crane despite the noumenal realm it shrouded. For Ouspensky and such other transcendentalists as Emerson, the phenomenal is a reflection, a Platonic "shadow," of the noumenal; for Crane the world is a manifestation, an embodiment, of the holy. What Crane got from Ouspensky was either the idea or the confirmation of the idea that there is no split between spirit and matter, that reality is ontologically monistic, and that the Ideal could be found in and through the vicissitudes of earth and flesh.

[50]Ouspensky, p. 170.
[51]Ouspensky, p. 239.
[52]Ouspensky, p. 145.

Having felt deeply the deprivation of the "gulf" and our solitary anguished remove from each other and from all blessed unity, we are now ready to span the "gulf"—to leave our separate "towers" and the "wrenched" treasures walled up within them, those partial goods that are incomplete because they have been stolen from the "Nineveh" where all "gold" is one:

> The highest tower,—let her ribs palisade
> Wrenched gold of Nineveh;—yet leave the tower.
> The bridge swings over salvage, beyond wharves;
> A wind abides the ensign of your will. . . .

In this "bridging" of opposites is our "salvage"—the redemption of our vision—for there "abides," stays constant, the "crucial sign," the "ensign of your will" . . . the signal of the wholeness we have so desired. The image of the bridge, again, clearly prefigures the same unifying quality of the Brooklyn Bridge in "Atlantis": "One arc synoptic of all tides below." It is the "wind" that signals the constancy and singularity beyond flux and multiplicity and shore-bound moorings—"beyond wharves." "Wind" is the same image that contained the "steady sound" of ideality in "Repose of Rivers"—the same symbol of immutability found ironically in the dynamism of its sustained commotion. The poet has not transcended or renounced the mutable realm; he has found in its flux and duality the changeless One:

> In alternating bells have you not heard
> All hours clapped dense into a single stride?
> Forgive me for an echo of these things,
> And let us walk through time with equal pride.

It is in the doubleness of "alternating bells" that the "single stride" of eternity is heard—as in the "Proem" to *The Bridge*, the multitudinous chains of "traffic lights" paradoxically "condense eternity." And finally, the poet apologizes for speaking in an "echo," the inadequate language of duality, which is the only way we can approach the "word" of unity; for as Crane has told us, as Nietzsche and Ouspensky both affirmed, that "word" is unpronounceable. And in the last line, Crane, knowingly or not, breaks company with Ouspensky and all of the Neoplatonic/

transcendental school when he invites us to gladly commit our-
selves to time and its duality, "walk through time with equal
pride," for in our several steps will mysteriously be the "single
stride" to the immutable, indivisible Absolute.

And so "Recitative" concludes this uniquely varied but themati-
cally coherent second movement that reveals six "dimensional"
experiences of the dimensionless Ideal. "Recitative," as a poem
about wholeness in brokenness, seems to draw together, "bridge,"
each distinct motion of the previous five poems so that, "clapped
dense," they may be fused "by strange harmonic laws" in "For the
Marriage of Faustus and Helen." This sequence incrementally
exposes the book's primary theme of transubstantiating/
incarnating the "bright logic" within the quotidian and thus dis-
poses us for the climactic and fully orchestrated celebration of
this truth in "For the Marriage of Faustus and Helen."

Before going on to our consideration of "For the Marriage of
Faustus and Helen," we might pause to consider to what section
of *The Bridge* this movement of *White Buildings* might be counter-
part. It was said earlier that "Paraphrase" does for *White Buildings*
what "Cutty Sark" does for *The Bridge:* both poems deal with the
experience of the negative side of the Absolute—not its inexhaust-
ible fullness but its utter emptiness. The protagonist of "Para-
hrase" is "stunned in that antarctic blaze," and the "man in South
Street" of "Cutty Sark" acknowledges the same annihilation:
"that / damned white Arctic killed my time." Each poem takes us
down from the anticipations of its first movement and readies us
for the hard and rapturous realizations of the second half of
either book's cycle. "Cutty Sark" is located exactly at the center of
The Bridge, just as "Paraphrase," to reiterate, is situated in *White
Buildings*. They are the axes of their volumes, the "dead centers,"
by which the personae of their collections will be converted to a
new vision. We have already seen to what illuminations the per-
sona of *White Buildings* is lifted from "Paraphrase," and through
what kinds of ordeals he passes. The persona of *The Bridge,*
having seen in the old sailor the "frontiers gleaming of his mind,"
will, just as the persona of *White Buildings*, forsake the reveries
and dreams, the pure projections of "Powhatan's Daughter" (af-
ter one last fling in recalling the great ships of old, "clipper

dreams") and enter the crass quotidian to transmute from it the "Bridge of Fire" in "Atlantis." The parallels between *White Buildings* and *The Bridge* are not always perfect and neat. Their movements are not in every detail, obviously, identical but comparable and, to reemphasize, cyclically and thematically the same. In both books, after the purgation, the experience of emptiness, the personae move through various "instressings" of present experiences to recurrent moments of revelation.

Given the strain of eulogy and invocation to Walt Whitman running through "Cape Hatteras" (which really only has counterpart in *White Buildings* in the tribute of "At Melville's Tomb"), this section immediately following "Cutty Sark" is essentially a facing of the potentially oppressive reality of technology within whose power and destruction must be found beauty and truth—but transfigured, newly "conjugated" on "infinity's dim marge." The point again is that both *White Buildings* and *The Bridge* leap immediately to the contrarieties of the phenomenal world to find within them the supreme simplicity of the noumenal after their personae have been readied, shocked still, by the noumenal Void.

From this point on in these two volumes, there is no congruent correspondence as nice as that of their first halves with "Legend," "Black Tambourine," and "Emblems of Conduct" functioning as an introductory suite for *White Buildings* along with "To Brooklyn Bridge" and "Ave Maria" for *The Bridge*; and the section keynoted by "Emblems of Conduct" paralleling "Powhatan's Daughter" as a first preludial movement. Hopefully without forcing an analogy, I would say that "Cape Hatteras," "Three Songs," and "Quaker Hill" do roughly for *The Bridge* what the movement analyzed in this chapter does for *White Buildings*. These three sections search out the holy in the various aspects of multifarious experience, even the crudest—as in "National Winter Garden" where, seeing "Magdalene" in a tawdry stripper so that even she can "Lug us back lifeward," the poet engages in the same transfiguration of the repugnant as in "The Wine Menagerie." We may relate the death/resurrection of "Voyages" to the similar "Lazarus" experience of "The Tunnel"; but there is toward the end of *White Buildings* no direct equivalent to "The Tunnel," "Paraphrase" having already had a similar function. And there is in *The Bridge* no equivalent to "For the Marriage of Faustus and Helen," a single movement encompassing, telescoping, the full range of the entire collection. These are, after all, different books—with the all-important difference being that *The Bridge* was planned as a collection before it was written. But in a broader sense, in their larger cycles, both books move from introductory overture, to a preludial movement, through an obliterating emptiness at their centers, through a grappling with the carnal and time-bound, through incremental apprehensions of the numina, to rapt and grateful hosannas to the Numen.

V

Beyond Despair

Crane's first written reference to *The Bridge* describes it as a poem "which carries on further the tendencies manifest in 'F and H.' "[1] Later, he was again to link *The Bridge* with "For the Marriage of Faustus and Helen" (hereafter shortened to "Faustus and Helen"): "The form will be symphonic, something like 'F and H' with its treatment of varied content. . . ."[2] Crane's comparing of the intentions and structures of these two poems surely confirms what the astute reader has already observed—that "Faustus and Helen," given its obvious distinction as an independent poem, is a prototype of *The Bridge*. In its segmented form and cyclic movement through the welter of the quotidian to the blessed Ideal—in its transubstantiation of "Brazen hypnotics" into the "new and scattered wine"—"Faustus and Helen" anticipates in microcosm the vaster transformation of "panoramic sleights" into "wrapt inception and beatitude" in *The Bridge*.

If "Faustus and Helen" is a paradigm for *The Bridge*, it is also a summary of *White Buildings*; for, as has been my thesis, both books are more than incidentally similar in theme and form. The "bright logic" blazoned in "Legend" as that which the visionary can find only by entry into the "Imploring flame" is found pristine in the "eventual flame" of Helen. The admonition not to languish

[1]*Letters*, p. 118.
[2]*Letters*, p. 125.

112

in "repentance" in "Legend" is matched by a similar renunciation of those who "Laugh out the meager penance of their days" in "Faustus and Helen." "Faustus and Helen" is faithful to the "perfect cry" of "Legend" in the speaker's vow that he "will persist to speak again" and "share with us the breath released."

"Faustus and Helen" relates as well to the other two introductory poems of *White Buildings*. The "mid-kingdom" of "Black Tambourine" exists in "Faustus and Helen" in the protagonist's being "lost yet poised in traffic." His suspension does not, however, result in the stagnation of "The black man, forlorn in the cellar"; but rather, by his dislocation, the protagonist of "Faustus and Helen" is able to discover Helen's "plane": "Then I might find your eyes across an aisle." And the mere "memories of spiritual gates" sullenly contemplated in "Emblems of Conduct" become the "gold-shod prophecies of heaven" that take the protagonist "beyond despair" in "Faustus and Helen."

"Faustus and Helen" responds as pointedly to the thematic statements of the book's three introductory poems as if it were written specifically as an answer to the challenges and questions they pose. And in a sense it was; for "Faustus and Helen" is the first comprehensive statment by Crane of the vision anticipated and approached in virtually all his shorter poems up to that time (early 1923) and manifested and developed in the poems to come after it—including *The Bridge*. It should not be surprising that the poem functions so perfectly in the collection to gather up and fuse the separate strains of the book's preceding poems. Although its placement in the volume does not represent its time of composition in relation to the other poems of the book (no less than seven of the poems preceding it were written after it), it does represent a kind of culmination of Crane's visionary development. Most importantly, "Faustus and Helen" provides an aesthetically pleasing structural and thematic resumé of *White Buildings* comparable to a "recapitulation" movement in a symphony before the advancement into the final movement or "coda." The recapitulation of a symphony usually includes all the elements of the introduction that have been developed piecemeal through the first two or so movements. While commenting on the largely lamentational theme of the book's first movement keynoted by "Emblems of Conduct," "Faustus and Helen" more particularly, as discussed in the previous chapter, incorporates and integrates the six separate colorations of the preceding movement into one intense illumination.

The "speediest destruction" necessary before we can "unbind our throats of fear and pity" in "Faustus and Helen" recalls the "antarctic blaze" of obliteration in "Paraphrase," which produces the first "white paraphrase" toward the canticle of "some constant harmony" pointed to in "Legend." The transformation of the speaker's "bartered blood" into "blown blood and vine" in "Faustus and Helen" accords well with the transmutation of the "fixed stone of lust" into the "bright stones" of "Possessions." In "Faustus and Helen," the speaker remembers how "titters hailed the groans of death" because through that sacrifice is known the "incunabula of the divine grotesque." Similarly, "The ripe borage of death" in the sacrificial rite of spring in "Lachrymae Christi" leads to Dionysius' "Unmangled target smile." And it is through time, "divers dawns" and the "graduate opacities of evening," that the protagonist comes to the "hourless days" of Helen's "plane" in "Faustus and Helen" just as through the "decimals of time" the protagonist of "Passage" enters the "glittering abyss" of eternity. And as the "Brazen hypnotics" of the intoxicated dance—those "Rhythmic ellipses"—yield "new amazements" in "Faustus and Helen," so "wine redeems the sight" to find in "bodies wreathing up and out" the "new anatomies" of "The Wine Menagerie." In "Faustus and Helen," the "stacked partitions of the day" must be turned into something "less fragmentary"; and in "Recitative," the "atrocious sums / Built floor by floor" must be "clapped dense into a single stride." The paradoxes of annihilation/creation, destruction/transmutation, immolation/transubstantiation, time/eternity, perverted sight/transfiguration, dividedness/unity are all "twisted" into "*the love of things / irreconcilable*" in "Faustus and Helen."

This brings us to the syllogism that if "Faustus and Helen" is the summation of *White Buildings* and *White Buildings* is a prefigurement of *The Bridge*, then "Faustus and Helen" is the image of Crane's entire poetic output—including, it could be demonstrated, his projected collection *Key West*. This is not to say that Crane's poetry does not change and evolve after 1923; but the basic scheme, that perfect vision of the holy is incarnated by a suffering transubstantiation of the quotidian, by a transfiguration of normal perception, and through a series of interacting "epiphanies," is fully developed in this poem. "The white wafer cheek of love" aspired to in "Faustus and Helen" is identical to "the visionary company of love" still sought in Crane's final poem "The Broken Tower."

The factor that gives "Faustus and Helen" its special identity as a unique poem that is more than just a comprehensive summary of Crane's poetic vision is its emphasis on synthesizing opposites, seen most markedly up to this point in *White Buildings* in "Recitative" and seen again later in *The Bridge*. The key to this Hegelian dialectic informing "Faustus and Helen" is found in the poem's prologue drawn from Ben Jonson's play *The Alchemist*:

> *And so we may arrive by Talmud skill*
> *And profane Greek to raise the building up*
> *Of Helen's house against the Ismaelite,*
> *King of Thogarma, and his habergeons*
> *Brimstony, blue and fiery; and the force*
> *Of King Abaddon, and the beast of Cittim;*
> *Which Rabbi David Kimchi, Onkelos,*
> *And Aben Ezra do interpret Rome.*

The fact that the speech is spoken farcically by a whore seeking to disguise her identity by mouthing some pedantic bambast either went unnoticed by Crane or simply did not deter him from finding in the words a very appropriate prolegomenon for the marriage of Faustus and Helen. Perhaps the words were intended by Jonson to have thematic significance for his play just as the "nonsense" utterances of Shakespeare's fools and simpletons do; for in her seemingly rambling rhetoric, the prostitute envisions the great synthesis of the sacred tradition of "Talmud skill" and the secular heritage of "profane Greek" in the Renaissance ideal of Christian humanism, "Helen's house," which must stand "aginst the Ismaelite"—against the various forces of barbarism that the great rabbinical exegetes "do interpret Rome."

I do not think Crane had primarily in mind the Renaissance conflict between the secular and eschatological or between the truly humanistic and crassly materialistic views of life. What he found here is a classical type of the reconciliation of opposites to keynote a poem in which a complex of antitheses are synthesized. As Crane himself puts it, the figure of Helen as the "absolute conception of beauty" enabled him to build "a bridge between so-called classic experience and many divergent realities of our seething, confused cosmos of today, which has no formulated mythology yet for religious exploitation."[3] Although Crane acknowledges one aspect of the poem's unifying thrust, he also confesses his need to go outside contemporary culture to find a unifying symbol. Later, of course, he found the perfect sign of reconciliation within the "confused cosmos of today" in *The Bridge*. Babette Deutsche, among other critics, says of Crane, "The religious poet who must live in the climate of an irreligious age is a kind of spiritual Crusoe. He has to forage for himself to get the materials that such men as Dante and Milton took as a matter of course."[4] But the dichotomy of the poem is, to be sure, deeper and wider than the division between the classical and modern worlds.

What do Faustus and Helen symbolize, and what is the significance of their marriage? Crane gestures in the direction we must take to discover the full implications of the two figures: "Helen, the symbol of this abstract 'sense of beauty,' Faustus the symbol of myself, the poetic or imaginative man of all times."[5] To repeat, this statement points the direction; it does not take us the full way to interpretation. An additional hint to the meaning of the character whose name stands for "inordinate" pursuit of beauty and truth and of her whose very image is perfect beauty and truth might be found in *The Birth of Tragedy*, which, it should now be clear, provided a number of conceptual and metaphorical seeds for Crane's poems. Nietzsche says that to live "in wholeness and fullness" it is necessary for the truly "tragic man . . . to desire a new art, the art of metaphysical comfort, to desire tragedy as his own proper Helen, and to exclaim with Faust:

> Should not my longing overleap the distance
> And draw the fairest form into existence?[6]

[3]*Poems*, p. 217.
[4]Deutsch, p. 312.
[5]*Letters*, p. 120.
[6]Nietzsche, p. 113. The verses quoted by Nietzsche are by Goethe.

Elsewhere Nietzsche identifies the Apollonian as a realm of the Olympians in which "wherever they turned, their eyes beheld the smile of Helen, the ideal picture of their own existence, 'floating in sweet sensuality.' "[7] The sense and imagery here resemble rather closely the encounter of Helen in Part II of the poem, "We cannot frown upon her as she smiles, / Dipping here in this cultivated storm / Among slim skaters of the gardened skies." The "tragic man" is for Nietzsche the Dionysian man who finds in his excess, in his revelry, in his tragedy, the "metaphysical comfort" of the Apollonian vision — Helen — which always springs paradoxically from the Dionysian experience. Nietzsche also conceives of this synthesis in conjugal terms when he says that "the continuous development of art is bound up with the Apollinian and Dionysian duality — just as procreation depends on the duality of the sexes."[8] The marriage of Faustus and Helen is fundamentally the conjoining of two incomplete visions. The world of Faustus, until fulfilled by finding Helen in its own "body" (much as Adam finds Eve to be "bone of my bones, and flesh of my flesh"), "Weeps in inventive dust for the hiatus / That winks above it, bluet in your breasts."

The Dionysian/Apollonian paradox is just another expression, borrowed from Nietzsche, of the transubstantive/incarnational vision that is the animus of Crane's art. Additional bases for and correspondences to this vision can be found in most of those who influenced or confirmed Crane in his thinking. Whitman says the same thing only in different terms:

> I will make the poems of materials, for I think they are
>   to be the most spiritual poems,
> And I will make the poems of my body and of mortality,
> For I think I shall then supply myself with the poems of my
>   soul and of immortality.[9]

And he reiterates this poetic statement in the "Preface 1855": "The spirit receives from the body just as much as it gives to the

---

[7]Nietzsche, p. 41.
[8]Nietzsche, p. 33. "Apollinian" is a legitimate variation in the spelling of "Apollonian."
[9]Whitman, "Starting from Paumanok," p. 18.

118

body."[10] We find it also in Rimbaud: "I am restored to the earth, with a duty to seek, and rugged reality to embrace!"; and the very last words of *A Season in Hell* are, "—and it will be permissible for me *to possess truth* in one *soul and one body*."[11] Or as Blake put it, "Man has no Body distinct from his Soul; for that call'd Body is a portion of Soul discern'd by the five Senses, the chief inlets of Soul in this age."[12]

R.W.B. Lewis argues that Crane could have found in Blake or Whitman what he is alleged to have picked up mainly from Ouspensky.[13] Certainly the above quotations would support Lewis's contention, but as Crane admits, "I have also enjoyed reading Ouspensky's *Tertium Organum* lately. Its corroboration of several experiences in consciousness that I have had gave it particular interest."[14] This "interest" cannot be ignored. How "lately" he had read Ouspensky is difficult to say, but this statement was made just after Crane had finished "Faustus and Helen" on which he had worked for almost a year. Unless Brom Weber is right that Crane read *Tertium Organum* sometime during 1921,[15] we must understand Ouspensky as more a gloss than a source for Crane's poetry—or to use Crane's words, as a "corroboration" of his "consciousness." Whichever the case, source or corroboration, Ouspensky's thought provides a valuable commentary on Crane's vision.

Recalling Ouspensky's ontology in which sensible reality, the "phenomenal"—what Crane calls in "Faustus and Helen" "The world dimensional"—is considered a reflection or segment, an "intersection," of "noumenal" reality—which would be nondimensional—we might again benefit by relating Ouspensky's idea of finding the noumenal through the phenomenal to Faustus' finding Helen on a streetcar or in the "cultivated storm" of a roof-garden party. In *Tertium Organum*, Ouspensky teaches:

At the present stage of our development we possess nothing so powerful, as an instrument of knowledge of the world of causes, as

[10]Whitman, p. 726.
[11]Rimbaud, pp. 103 and 105.
[12]Blake, "The Marriage of Heaven and Hell," p. 149.
[13]Lewis, p. 95.
[14]*Letters,* p. 124.
[15]Weber, p. 153.

art. The mystery of life dwells in the fact that the *noumenon,* i.e., the hidden meaning and the hidden function of a thing, is reflected in its *phenomenon.* A phenomenon is merely the reflection of a noumenon in our sphere.[16]

But here too, it is essential that we understand the fundamental difference between Crane's view and Ouspensky's transcendental idea that phenomena are as "phantasmal" as the shadows cast in Plato's cave. Despite his admiration for the Neoplatonic Ouspensky, Crane does not embrace in "Faustus and Helen" the Platonic ethic adopted almost unaltered by Ouspensky as he might have found it in Plato's *Phaedo:*

> Did we not say some time ago that when the soul uses the instrumentality of the body for any inquiry, whether through sight or hearing or any other sense—because using the body implies using the senses—it is drawn away by the body into the realm of the variable, and loses its way and becomes confused and dizzy, as though it were fuddled, through contact of things of a similar nature?[17]

Crane did not write poetry as though "true being" dwells in a nonmaterial realm "without color or shape, that cannot be touched" as Plato repeats his thesis in the *Phaedrus,*[18] which we know Crane read from the notes and underlinings he made in his copy.[19] Unlike Plato and his more orthodox disciples, Crane finds the Ideal, let me again emphasize, in the color, shape, and sensations of Helen's body—which is his own sense life:

> Reflective conversion of all things
> At your deep blush, when ecstasies thread
> The limbs and belly, when rainbows spread
> Impinging on the throat and sides . . .

As John Unterecker concludes in *Voyages: A Life of Hart Crane,* "But it was less dogma than imagery that Crane extracted from Ouspensky."[20] And of Plato himself Crane once said, "Plato

---

[16]Ouspensky, p. 145.
[17]Plato, p. 62.
[18]Plato, p. 494.
[19]See Horton, p. 125.
[20](New York: Farrar, Strauss, and Giroux, 1969), p. 249.

doesn't live today because of the intrinsic 'truth' of his statements: their only living truth today consists in the 'fact' of their harmonious relationship to each other in the context of his organization of them."[21]

Although no critic I have read develops the same argument pursued here, various interpreters of Crane's poetry discern, at least implicitly, the incarnational, non-Platonic ethic in the poems. Crane found "the absolute inextricably wedded to the actual," R.W.B. Lewis observes, "seen and known by means of the actual even as it serves to transform the actual: this was Crane's regular purpose and his brand of totality."[22] Bernice Slote finds "[That] such a spiritual vision might be best accomplished through the whole reality of life, centering on the complete body and its creative force, is suggested by [Crane's] poems."[23] Robert J. Andreach, in *Studies in Structure,* even sees justification for Crane's "essentializing" the horrible in *The Bridge,* for in "not denying the ostensible evil in contemporary society but by piercing through it to its spiritual substratum, the protagonist transmutes the materialistic into the spiritual."[24] A similar view is held by Henry W. Wells in *The American Way of Poetry:* "In his poetical philosophy Crane never doubts that ecstasy and goodness spring from soil torn by misery, as Lazarus ascended from the grave"[25]—an observation particularly applicable to Part III of "Faustus and Helen." And Gordon K. Grigsby in his essay, "Hart Crane's Doubtful Vision," agrees: "The tortured awareness of realistic circumstance is *an integral part of the vision.*"[26]

Crane, in a letter written not long after the completion of "Faustus and Helen," shares his fear of being misunderstood: "But this 'new consciousness' is something that takes a long while to 'put across.' "[27] For every critic who recognized the integrated vision of Crane, there is another who fails to see it—usually

[21]*Letters,* p. 238.

[22]Lewis, p. 374.

[23]"Transmutation in Crane's Imagery in *The Bridge,*" *Modern Language Notes,* 73 (1958), 22.

[24](New York: Fordham University Press, 1964), p. 121.

[25](New York: Russell and Russell, Inc., 1964), p. 202.

[26]*College English,* 24 (1963), 519.

[27]*Letters,* p. 131.

categorizing the poet as either a transcendentalist or empty sensationalist (as we have seen was Tate's assessment). Ironically (or perhaps predictably), many of these misinterpreters were among Crane's friends and contemporaries whom we usually tend to think would know him best. Gorham Munson, to whom Crane wrote more letters than to any other person outside his family, mistakes Crane's enthusiasm for Ouspensky as a profession of the more strictly Platonic aspects of Ouspensky's thesis and simplistically applies a transcendental ontology to Crane's poems: "There is no system but only this: a doubt of the truth of the appearances which the world shows us and intuitions of higher dimensions. . . ."[28] Munson can only explain Crane's inclusion of the sordid aspects of life as lapses from his transcendent ecstasies: "That, I take it, accounts for a tendency in his writing to oscillate between a description of his personal wretchedness of life and the moments of supernal beauty he experiences."[29] Munson does not consider that the "supernal beauty" is wrung out of the very "personal wretchedness" that is its necessary premise. Crane, in responding to Munson's interpretation of his poetry, insists that his poems "would avoid the employment of abstract tags" and "necessarily express its concepts in the more direct terms of physical-psychic experience." He also answers Munson's criticism of his spiritual highs and lows: "What I'm objecting to is contained in my suspicion that you have allowed too many extra-literary impressions of me to enter your essay," and "you arbitrarily propose a goal for me which I have no idea of nor interest in following."[30] The arbitrary "goal," of course, is Platonic transcendence.

In his 1927 review of *White Buildings*, as close and supportive an associate as Waldo Frank, while comprehending the phenomenal revelation of the noumenal in the poems, describes that noumenal presence as strictly analogical, merely reflected by the figures of the poems—as in "Voyages" where he finds a "constructed image of a noumenal world" and concludes that

[28]*Destinations: A Canvass of American Literature Since 1900* (New York: J. H. Sears and Company, Inc., 1928), p. 175.
[29]Munson, p. 176.
[30]*Letters*, p. 239.

"phenomenal qualities and sequences are implicit in its crea-
tion."[31] This might be said of "Emblems of Conduct" but not of
"Faustus and Helen" and "Voyages," which are dynamic penetra-
tions of the phenomenal to the noumenal, not fixed artifacts of
the noumenon. The poems of the second part of *White Buildings*
are more processes of becoming blest than they are "constructs"
of ideality.

Brom Weber is right in seeing Crane's vision of the Ideal as
derived from the "concrete and particular" and seen as "tangible
reality." But in describing Crane's comprehension of "the ar-
chetype of beauty" as a "thoroughly Platonic" ascent to "the
abstract,"[32] he misapprehends the dynamics of Crane's finding,
"instressing," spirituality within rather than beyond the "con-
crete." Crane's description of John Donne as "at once sensual and
spiritual" applies as revealingly to himself and states tersely the
truly incarnational nature of his vision.[33]

The theme, then, of "Faustus and Helen" is the same as that of
the previous movement—a transmutation of the quotidian into
the holy—with a particular emphasis on synthesizing opposites by
the careful "inscaping" of their apparent dividedness. The proc-
ess begins in Part I with an extended observation of the splin-
tered, segmented, overly "defined" nature of experience:

> The mind has shown itself at times
> Too much the baked and labeled dough
> Divided by accepted multitudes.
> Across the stacked partitions of the day—
> Across the memoranda, baseball scores,
> The stenographic smiles and stock quotations
> Smutty wings flash out equivocations.

The "mind" is, like loaved bread, too well packaged and
formed, too thoroughly "Divided" by the "multitudes" of things
that must be considered in ordinary experience. The implication
is, inversely, that we need not analysis and division but a more

---

[31]"The Poetry of Hart Crane," *New Republic,* 50 (March 16, 1927), 117.
[32]Weber, p. 180.
[33]*Letters,* p. 68.

holistic sense of reality. The dividedness is further stressed in words connoting distinguishability, enumeration: "stacked partitions of the day," the precise divisions of the day into seconds, minutes, hours, morning, night, coffee breaks, and lunches; the "memoranda," containing, one by one, their piecemeal messages; and "baseball scores," more numbers to add to "stock quotations" so that even the "smiles" of the stenographers seem to be so many flashing signs — so much double-talk like the blazoned "equivocations" of what appear to be the lingo of blinking neon advertisements whose "winged" words are debased, obscured — rendered "Smutty" — by abuse.

The city is a study in fragmentation, and the numerical conceit continues into the next stanza — except that a subtle shift in perception begins to happen, like the new way of seeing that occurs in "The Wine Menagerie," but without the wine:

> The mind is brushed by sparrow wings;
> Numbers, rebuffed by asphalt, crowd
> The margins of the day, accent the curbs,
> Convoying divers dawns on every corner
> To druggist, barber and tobacconist,
> Until the graduate opacities of evening
> Take them away as suddenly to somewhere
> Virginal perhaps, less fragmentary, cool.

The "Smutty wings" of the previous stanza retain their duality, but they are now "sparrow wings" without the duplicity implied in "equivocations." As the protagonist walks through the streets, he allows his "mind" to be "brushed" by these wings, by all multiplicities. "Numbers" seem to bounce off the pavement and gather at the "margins of the day" ("margins" is particularly suggestive of precise measurement and demarcation), or rest, random and distinct, along the "curbs." Even the word "accent" carries a sense of distinguishability. The awareness of myriad, separate realities is intensified in this inventory of "Numbers," but what these "Numbers" specifically represent is left deliberately vague by Crane. They simply represent numerability. In their "behavior," however, they seem to mimic the action of the "sparrows" alluded to in the first line. Such city birds do tend to shun the busy asphalted streets and sidewalks and "crowd" the edges, the "margins," of the avenues and congregate on "curbs" and ledges. And in their appearance each morning, they seem to be "Convoying," carrying, a new day to all the various merchants compartmentalized in their separate establishments "on every corner." As the punctual indicators of each day's beginning with "divers dawns" (again the unrelenting compounding of time's divisibility in "divers"), they also signal each day's passage by withdrawing at "the graduate opacities of evening." Crane is careful here to point out the "graduate" degrees of darkness with which night comes—the broken successiveness rather than the integrability of each divided moment. Time is not one but many.

In the last two lines, we get the first clear indication that beyond all this shifting diversity—viewed, as indicated above, more tolerantly in this second stanza—there may be "somewhere / Virginal," some realm not violated by the increase and multiplication of species upon species—like the cold, chaste land of "North Labrador" where there is "No birth, no death, no time nor sun"—some place "less fragmentary, cool." Typical of his manner of composition, Crane has established the scene in the first two stanzas, a preparation that is indispensable; for out of the situation at hand always comes the vision. The protagonist is understandably but mistakenly looking to "somewhere" else for the answer to the brokenness of his experience as he pauses to reflect upon his own "twistedness" in desiring a dimensionless world in which all is one:

> There is the world dimensional for
> those untwisted by the love of things
> irreconcilable . . .

But what he is about to learn in the third stanza is that his splintered eyes will be healed by the eyes of Helen found tranquilly "flickering" him "prefigurations" of wholeness through the window of a trolley. The protagonist is half-mindful of escaping the "world dimensional" to find the realm of reconciliation, but after his introduction to Helen, who in Part I presages the "eventual flame" of "hourless days," he will plunge into the "crashing opera bouffe" of Dionysian music and dance to find in that "breathless" escapade the wholeness he has sought. And in that

"Blest excursion," in that "Relentless caper" (to hearken back to "Legend"), he will discover that paradox of immutable singularity in seething plenty where "All relatives" rest "serene and cool." In Part III, the Dionysian songs of revelry will give way to the Dionysian cry of tragedy, an immersion in life's cruelty equally necessary toward the "essentializing" of Helen's "plane"—which turns out to be everywhere here and always now and perfectly still in its dynamism, like the "fury fused" in "To Brooklyn Bridge." Crane's task here is identical to Whitman's in *Leaves of Grass:* "And a song make I of the One form'd out of all."[34]

This mystery is found in Crane's poetry by Bernice Slote as "the union in which opposites are paradoxically identified: Body and spirit, past and present, good and evil," and in which "the encirclement of all experience is necessary to the generation of a spiritual force."[35] It is Crane himself, however, who tells us most explicitly how he discovers Helen and all she stands for: "So I found 'Helen' sitting in a street car; the Dionysian revels of her court and her seduction were transferred to a Metropolitan roof garden with a jazz orchestra; and the *katharsis* of the fall of Troy I saw approximated in the recent World War."[36] And elsewhere he says:

> Part I starts out from the quotidian, rises to evocation, ecstasy and statement. . . . The streetcar device is the most concrete symbol I could find for the transition of the imagination from quotidian details to the universal consideration of beauty,—the body still 'centered in traffic,' the imagination eluding its nets and self consciousness.[37]

Crane is explicit here about universal beauty being found in the here and now with "the body still 'centered in traffic' "—a very un-Platonic statement.

As in the previously quoted passages from "General Aims and Theories" about "spiritual illuminations . . . essentialized from

---

[34]Whitman, "Starting from Paumanok," p. 19.
[35]"Views of the Bridge," *Start With the Sun: Studies in Cosmic Poetry*, with James E. Miller, Jr., and Karl Shapiro (Lincoln, Nebraska: University of Nebraska Press, 1960), p. 139.
[36]"General Aims and Theories," *Poems*, p. 217.
[37]*Letters*, p. 120.

experience directly," Crane similarly defines his poetics in a 1926 letter to Gorham Munson:

> Poetry, in so far as the metaphysics of any absolute knowledge extends, is simply the concrete *evidence* of the *experience* of a recognition (*knowledge* if you like). It can give you a *ratio* of fact and experience, and in this sense it is both perception and thing perceived, according as it approaches a significant articulation or not. This is its reality, its fact, being.[38]

In stating his poetics, Crane, wittingly or not, declared his incarnational ontology, for a poetics must proceed from one's metaphysics however poorly formulated. If you can speak of your metaphysical absolutes as concretely evident and recognized within experience as both "perception and thing perceived," then you are finding the absolute embodied in the relative, divided, limited realm of the quotidian rather than outside it.

Crane described Part I of "Faustus and Helen" as follows: "Meditation, Evocation, Love, Beauty."[39] With Part II précised as "Dance, Humor, Satisfaction" and Part III as "Tragedy, War (the eternal soldier), Resume, Ecstasy, Final Declaration,"[40] we can see that Part I is a preliminary sequence, a postulation or proposition of ideality to be meditated and then acted upon, realized in the next two segments. And so the "Evocation" continues in stanza three except that Helen has now appeared through the fragmentation the protagonist has been experiencing:

> And yet, suppose some evening I forgot
> The fare and transfer, yet got by that way
> Without recall,—lost yet poised in traffic,
> Then I might find your eyes across an aisle,
> Still flickering with those prefigurations—
> Prodigal, yet uncontested now,
> Half-riant before the jerky window frame.

The beginning of realization comes with the protagonist's becoming "lost" physically and mentally. Forgetting, losing mem-

[38]*Letters*, p. 237.
[39]*Letters*, p. 116.
[40]*Letters*, p. 116.

ory, we have seen in such poems as "Passage," is a sign and a means of "instressing" the moment of truth undistracted by the past, for memory must be "broke." The visionary, forgetting his "fare," gets through the stile and onto the car "without recall" — that is, without being called back, but also without the encumbrance of memory. In his suspension, in his perfect balance in and with the very "multitudes" that had so harried him in stanza one, "yet poised in traffic," he is made ready to see Helen's "eyes across an aisle," halfsmiling, "before the jerky window frame" — not in some transcendent realm. And the "prefigurations" of sacred truth those eyes speak (compare their "flickering" with the "lattices of flame" speaking holy "Names" in "Lachrymae Christi") are given freely, prodigally; yet, unlike in ancient times, they now go "uncontested," unwanted, despite their obvious beatitude. It is noteworthy that Helen's eyes "flicker" and are seen through a shaking, "jerky," window. These eyes, if not utterly fragmented as is everything else experienced by the speaker, are, however, "Half-riant" and in a sense winking like the "Smutty wings" of the first stanza. But Helen's constancy is and will remain dynamic, and her eyes are as yet but promises, "prefigurations" of the single, changeless gift. It is the speaker's vision that is imperfect, incomplete — incipient — not Helen; and it is with a glimpse that his apprehension of Helen begins, for even in stanza five Helen's image still "winks" — and only from "above."

In stanza four, the protagonist is confident that he will hold as well as see Helen; and he knows that it will be within the urban vulgarity in which he finds himself: "There is some way, I think, to touch / Those hands of yours that count the nights / Stippled with pink and green advertisements." The "equivocations" of glaring signs in stanza one have become here the very element through which Helen is to be known. With that understanding, the protagonist is moved to prayer — of petition first and then praise of Helen: "And now, before its arteries turn dark / I would have you meet this bartered blood." He asks Helen, before he dies, to "meet" him just as he is, "bartered," virtually sold out to the "world dimensional." The pose here is the classic one of the supplicant before his God, unworthy but repentant, seeking to be redeemed. Then, like the Psalmist of Scripture, he makes bold to claim his salvation because of his devotion, his faithfulness to the blessed way: "Imminent in his dream, none better knows / The white wafer cheek of love, or offers words / Lightly as moonlight on the eaves of snow." He, Poet/Faustus, already "knows" Helen's delicate goodness, which has appeared to him so "Imminent," so nearly grasped, "in his dream." And no one else has found "words" that touch so finely upon her "love" that they do not violate her "white wafer cheek" any more than "moonlight" does fragile ridges of snow on "eaves." If anyone has claim to Helen, surely Faustus/Artist does; for he has, to use the previously quoted words of Goethe, drawn "the fairest form into existence."

The prayer of petition and faith in stanza four shifts to a recitation of Helen's attributes in stanza five:

> Reflective conversion of all things
> At your deep blush, when ecstasies thread
> The limbs and belly, when rainbows spread
> Impinging on the throat and sides . . .
> Inevitable, the body of the world
> Weeps in inventive dust for the hiatus
> That winks above it, bluet in your breasts.

"Reflective conversion" is the pivotal term for the entire poem, for within Helen's "deep blush," all of reality is transformed, reflected back, "essentialized," like the transfigured images in the decanters of "The Wine Menagerie." This transubstantiation occurs not transcendently but carnally, almost erotically, in the flush of ecstasy that spreads over the body of Helen like "rainbows." The rainbow is a natural symbol of unity because its spectrum, though each of its colors is distinct, is a single continuum. We shall see that Crane again uses the rainbow figure more prominently but with similar suggestiveness in "Voyages" as well as in the "Atlantis" section of *The Bridge*. Helen's transmuting passion and beauty are desired by "the world," her rightful lover that "Weeps" for the "hiatus," the missing factor that will make it whole but as yet "winks above it" still at a remove. Though "inventive," until consummated with the "bluet," the virginal, floral innocence of Helen's "breasts," the "body of the world" remains "dust — not yet converted in that blessed "blush."

In stanza six, the protagonist admits that because the world no

longer "contests" for Helen's saving beauty, it might very well slip
to its demise:

> The earth may glide diaphanous to death;
> But if I lift my arms it is to bend
> To you who turned away once, Helen, knowing
> The press of troubled hands, too alternate
> With steel and soil to hold you endlessly.
> I meet you, therefore, in that eventual flame
> You found in final chains, no captive then—
> Beyond their million brittle, bloodshot eyes;
> White, through white cities passed on to assume
> That world which comes to each of us alone.

The word "diaphanous," which means sheer or transparent, con-
notes the insubstantialness, perhaps the emptiness, of an "earth"
unfulfilled by Helen. Unlike the soiled and hardened "troubled
hands" of the world (hands appropriately "alternate," inconstant,
like all else), which cannot hope to "hold" Helen, Faustus' sensi-
tive hands will reach for her. In a sense, Helen is "above" the
"dust" and "soil," which need her transforming touch; but, in his
typically paradoxical manner, Crane makes us see that Helen is
implicit in the very earth that aches for her: "But if I lift my arms it
is to bend. . . ." Helen is not sublime if by that is meant of a
celestial sphere; reaching up to her we must reach down—just as
the vision of Apollo derives from the dance and death of
Dionysius. So Faustus now makes his covenant with Helen to
enter her "eventual flame" of transmutation—but not in some
far-flung, aerial, uncontainable realm.

Helen, her power to transform, is to be met in her "final
chains." (Of course, there is a runing analogy throughout the
poem to the actual story of Helen's rape and captivity as told by
Homer, which Crane acknowledged in a letter to Waldo Frank.[41])
We must not hope to transcend the maddening limitations and
partialness of experience described in the first two stanzas, for
that is where Helen abides; but she is, again paradoxically, "no
captive." Nor are we. While we avoid with Helen the "press" of

---

[41]*Letters*, p. 120.

vulgar clutches, the senseless ogles of the "million brittle, blood-
shot eyes" of those who lust for her rather than love her, "we can
still love the world," as Crane says it in "Chaplinesque." We must
not confuse Helen's beauty and innocence with unearthliness.
Though she be "White" and pass through "white cities," she is in
the world, but not for those who violate her sanctity. As Robert J.
Andreach puts it, "For Crane, man loses his spiritual poten-
tialities when he denies life because it is ugly and materialistic, not
realizing it is ugly and materialistic because he has denied its
spiritual possibilities."[42] And as we find Helen "in that eventual
flame," we find our world transfigured into "That world which
comes to each of us alone." No one can experience that "mystical"
(Crane's own word in a letter to Munson[43]) truth for us. With that
knowledge, Faustus lifts his prayer in the last stanza from petition
and meditation into pure praise:

> Accept a lone eye riveted to your plane,
> Bent axle of devotion along companion ways
> That beat, continuous, to hourless days—
> One inconspicuous, glowing orb of praise.

Faustus appears by his "lone eye" to be the alien or outcast
introduced in "Black Tambourine" and "Emblems of Conduct."
But like the protagonist of "The Wine Menagerie," his "exile" is
not unredeemed, for he has located Helen's "plane." The com-
paring of his vision to a "Bent axle of devotion along companion
ways" is Crane's way of figuratively representing the continuum,
the true indistinguishability of the phenomenal/sensorial and the
noumenal/spiritual planes—his own and Helen's. The two wheels
mounted on the same axle are of one mechanism though we
speak of them as distinct and independent; they are "Bent" al-
ways in the same direction and by nature travel "along companion
ways." Though separate, they are one. So does Faustus' earthly
vision through measurable time and space extend on an unbro-
ken continuum into Helen's dimensionless, eternal realm so that
the two "ways / . . . beat, continuous, to hourless days." Establish-
ing the true unity between himself and Helen, Faustus asks her to

---

[42]Andreach, p. 108.
[43]*Letters*, p. 129.

"Accept" his solitary gaze, though "inconspicuous," as "One . . . glowing orb of praise." The singularity of his eye, its oneness, linked with its spherical quality as an "orb" communicates a sense of undivided unity—like the circle encompassing their planes as one. It is as though the unbroken sphere represents the oneness of the phenomenal and noumenal, with the phenomenal as a section of the unending noumenal circle. If we can bring our eyes to follow the path of a phenomenal curve, it will unfailingly take us into the infinite curve of the noumenal that is continuous with it.

In a letter to Waldo Frank, Crane explains his intentions in the second section of "Faustus and Helen": "Part II is, of course, the DANCE and sensual culmination."[44] Part I has given the "Evocation" of Helen, her "Love" and "Beauty"; the "Meditation" must now spring into "Dance" toward "Satisfaction"—to quote again Crane's summarizing terms. We have been conditioned in Part I not to be shocked if we find the apotheosis of all that is true within the "sensual." Apropos of this, if we were to hear Part II as a musical piece (which it is not far from being), it would open abruptly with the blatant blare of brazen horns:

> Brazen hypnotics glitter here;
> Glee shifts from foot to foot,
> Magnetic to their tremolo.
> This crashing opera bouffe,
> Blest excursion! this ricochet
> From roof to roof—
> Know, Olympians, we are breathless
> While nigger cupids scour the stars!

Indeed, the "glitter" of brass instruments and everything else at the roof-garden party—replete with its jazz ensemble—does have a "hypnotic" effect. One is irresistably magnetized by the music's "tremolo" to a gleeful dance of abandon. And the "crashing" high steps of the party's participants seem like absurd gambols in an operatic farce. But this is a "Blest excursion"; for its hyperbolic, "breathless" bounding "From roof to roof" will take the postulant

[44]*Letters*, p. 121.

to the home of the gods. The "stars" of these "Olympians" are not beyond the racket of the party as evidenced by the "nigger cupids" (black waiters?) who, by the "logic of metaphor," polish those "stars" as so many platters and trays . . . or perhaps as the negro musicians "cleanse" the very heavens with their raspy jazz.

Here too, Crane must have been reinforced by those writers most influential upon him in his belief that felicity and knowledge are approached through Dionysian indulgence. In "The Marriage of Heaven and Hell," Blake asserts, "The road of excess leads to the place of wisdom."[45] And in *The Illuminations,* after describing a bizarre "hypnotic theater" — more sinisterly depicted than Crane's "opera bouffe" — Rimbaud tells us, "I alone possess the key of this wild pageant,"[46] which is exactly what Crane would say of his "Brazen hypnotics." Ouspensky would also encourage the intensity of this part of the poem, for "the more powerful, the brighter the inner emotions are, so much the more quickly will the moment of consciousness of the unreality of life come."[47] Crane would amend that to "consciousness of the deeper reality of life," for the reality of this "Blest excursion" does not recede as Helen emerges.

Nietzsche, in *The Birth of Tragedy,* has the most to say about the Dionysian dance into which Faustus leaps to find the Apollonian vision of Helen: "In this magic transformation the Dionysian reveler sees himself as a satyr, *and as a satyr, in turn, he sees the god,* which means that in his metamorphosis he beholds another vision outside himself, as the Apollinian complement of his own state."[48] Crane's poem seems to me a perfect illustration of Nietzsche's principle of how the Apollonian grows out of the Dionysian — whether or not Crane deliberately applied it. And he was to use the Dionysian revel again as a means of drawing out the holiness, the wholeness, implicit in the heaving earth and pulsing body in "The Dance":

> We danced, O Brave, we danced beyond their farms,
> In cobalt desert closures made our vows . . .

[45]Blake, p. 150.
[46]Rimbaud, p. 119.
[47]Ouspensky, p. 155.
[48]Nietzsche, p. 64.

Now is the strong prayer folded in thine arms,
The serpent with the eagle in the boughs.

In a letter to Alfred Steiglitz, quoting from an essay he was writing on the photographer's work, Crane explains that the "essences of things . . . are suspended on the invisible dimension whose vibrancy has been denied the human eye at all times save in the intuition of ecstasy."[49]

The ecstasy continues in stanza two:

A thousand light shrugs balance us
Through snarling hails of melody.
White shadows slip across the floor
Splayed like cards from a loose hand;
Rhythmic ellipses lead into canters
Until somewhere a rooster banters.

It is significant that in all the apparent confusion and disorder there is "balance." The shoves on the crowded floor offset each other, and one stands with aplomb beneath the raucous "hails of melody" and amidst the surrealistically "White shadows," the dancers or the notes of music, which are strewn like so many "cards" across the roof—from an appropriately "loose hand." The divided "multitudes" that so disturbed the protagonist in Part I are now gladly received in all this frenzy, for though "Splayed," they are seen as somehow single.

From the "hypnotics" opening the section, the alteration of perception, including the tactile and auditory senses, has been assumed. Aided by the frenetic movement of his body—which does in fact have a rapturous effect and is used in some religious traditions to induce spiritual transport—Faustus is sensing the "plane" of Helen. As the "Rhythmic ellipses" of his dance intensify into less restrained, wilder "canters," the bantering cry of a "rooster" (probably the equivalent of a high-pitched bar from one of the "cornets" Crane refers to in the next stanza) signals the climax of the "instressing" of the scene. The "Numbers" so random and "fragmentary" in Part I have begun to harmonize within these "Rhythmic" circles. The tempo of the music has reached its

[49]*Letters*, p. 132.

breaking point and, as in most of Crane's poems, the "minor epiphany" now collapses to the "major." The deeper reality begins to unfold in stanza three.

"Greet naively—yet intrepidly / New soothings, new amazements / That cornets introduce at every turn," Faustus says. Indeed, through his "relentless caper," he has approached the "metaphysical comfort" of Nietzsche much as the protagonist of "The Wine Menagerie" snares "new purities." But if we are to possess these flashes of illumination we meet "at every turn," we must take them "naively," openly, and "intrepidly," without fear or inhibition. We must "be as little children" one might say. And we must be willing to "fall downstairs / With perfect grace and equanimity"; for in abandoning ourselves to this seeming mayhem, we do gain "grace and equanimity"—a paradox prefigured in Part I when Faustus allows himself to be "lost yet poised in traffic."

Then in our tranquil equilibrium, we are able to "plaintively scud past shores / Where, by strange harmonic laws / All relatives, serene and cool, / Sit rocked in patent armchairs." These "shores" correspond to the timeless "unpaced beaches" of "Passage"; it is the place of "hourless days" where all "relatives" are absolute. Through this frenetic and fiery escapade, come "serene and cool" intimations of the "constant harmony" anticipated in "Legend." One can imagine Crane affirmed in seeing this correspondence between time and eternity by such statements as William Blake's "Eternity is in love with the productions of time."[50]

But the absolute is not static; its energy, experienced through incrementally intensified "Rhythmic ellipses," is not eliminated but accelerated to a kinetic frequency that can only be called absolute—so that there is rest, stillness, in its utter dynamism. This, I would suggest, is the significance of all life's variables, "All relatives," rocking peacefully, not motionless, and so perfectly balanced as to be in repose and in unison one with the other—like the taut balance in the dynamics of Heraclitus' strung bow. Their "armchairs" are uniform, all alike—"patent"—suggesting the sameness within their differences. The problem of consciousness being "Divided by accepted multitudes" is solved by truly "accept-

---

[50]Blake, "The Marriage of Heaven and Hell," p. 150.

ing" and "instressing" that dividedness and finding the "multitudes" made one and the consciousness made whole "by strange harmonic laws."

The organized riot of Helen's realm sustains its perfect equilibrium in stanza four:

> O, I have known metallic paradises
> Where cuckoos clucked to finches
> Above the deft catastrophes of drums.
> While titters hailed the groans of death
> Beneath gyrating awnings I have seen
> The incunabula of the divine grotesque.
> This music has a reassuring way.

These visions are, like the "gold mosaic" of Yeats's "holy city of Byzantium," "metallic paradises"—enduring and incorruptible; and in these holy places, the monotonous call of "cuckoos" makes a pleasing contrapuntal melody to the spritely warbles of "finches." So utterly charmed is Helen's realm that these cuckoos, notorious for using the nests of other birds, do not seem to want to exploit the gentle finches, or the finches do not mind hatching cuckoo eggs. Peace and harmony are so absolute that the "deft catastrophies of drums," evoking in their blunt percussions thoughts of death and war, blend with the blithe rhythms of bird talk. The "groans of death" set off nicely the unlikely counterpoint of the "titters" that greet them. For death is as strongly implied here as in "The Dance" of *The Bridge*: "Know, Maqnokeeta, greeting; know death's best; / —Fall, Sachem, strictly as the tamarack!" All is one within "This music," which "has a reassuring way."

Crane must have been as mindful as Nietzsche "that music stands in symbolic relation to the primordial pain in the heart of primal unity. . . ."[51] The various horns in a jazz band could, for Crane's purpose, aptly approximate the whistles of cuckoos and finches to the accompaniment of "deft" drums. The "metallic" quality of the scene might be explainable—recognizing that no such literal explanation is necessary—by the brass instruments; and we might go so far as to assign the contrasting sounds of the

---

[51]Nietzsche, p. 55.

birds to whatever wind instruments we think fit. In its tendency to yoke together widely variant tones and tempos and to achieve harmony by the interplay of seemingly independent, broadly drawn circles of sound, the mode and style of jazz music itself suits well the theme of unity and balance through multiplicity and antithesis. Crane deliberately sought to give a jazz quality to his poetry, as he states in a letter written just at the time he was composing "Faustus and Helen": "Let us invent an idiom for the proper transposition of jazz into words! Something clean, sparkling, elusive!"[52]

The circle imagery of Part I in the "Bent axle" and "orb of praise" is picked up again here in the "gyrating awnings." In its ceaseless "ellipses," the "tremolo" beneath the canopies on the roof seems to have the entire place turning carousellike—again projecting a sense of all distinctions spun into the undivided sphere and perfect glide of merry-go-round. Within that gyre, Faustus sees "The incunabula of the divine grotesque"—the most original, pristine picture of God; but "grotesque" suggests that the image of God is bizarre, misshapen. I think Crane is simply saying the same thing he said in "The Wine Menagerie" and elsewhere: not that such "new anatomies" are found finally to be distorted but that these "new amazements" are seen *through* a distortion, a "twisting" of the consciousness. In wrenching the perception, the face of God appears paradoxically *through* all "things irreconcilable" but at first with the look of Dionysius, contorted in agony and ecstasy.

In the last stanza, however, God's "grotesque" is metamorphosed as Helen "smiles" once again:

> The siren of the springs of guilty song—
> Let us take her on the incandescent wax
> Striated with nuances, nervosities
> That we are heir to: she is still so young,
> We cannot frown upon her as she smiles,
> Dipping here in this cultivated storm
> Among slim skaters of the gardened skies.

Helen is the "siren" who lures by her irresistible chant all who search; hers are "the springs of guilty song." But unlike Homer's sirens, if she calls us to destruction, we find therein our lives; and if she lies to us, we learn the truth. Her song is "guilty" in an ironic sense, for Crane is saying that God is found not by repression of the senses—not by denial of the flesh—but by a celebration of the body. In the context of a law-oriented Christianity that has become largely convinced that the flesh is evil and therefore to be mortified as a form of punishment (rather than moderated for its own sake and for love of God), such a "song" of "limbs and belly" would be "guilty." But Christ himself refutes the false ascesticism of the Pharisees who complain about his feasting rather than fasting: "The Son of man is come eating and drinking; and ye say, 'Behold a gluttonous man, and a winebibber, a friend of publicans and sinners!' But wisdom is justified of all her children" (Luke 7:34–35). If in this poem Crane is coaxing us to an orgiastic, hedonistic, unbridled indulgence of the senses, we could hardly call it Christian even by analogy; but if Crane is calling us to appreciate the body, the earth, as a sacred tabernacle of the holy and to exercise rather than numb the senses and emotions as the means by which we touch divinity, then this poem accords well with the incarnational tradition of Christianity initiated by Christ himself when he took bread and wine, ointments and tears, kisses and scourges—the sputum of his mouth—all as sacraments of beatitude.

Helen is here imagined as a jazz songstress (accompanying the party's orchestra) whose singing collects and articulates all the "new amazements" Faustus has encountered. The next several lines have been variously interpreted and do pose a puzzle. Considering that Helen's song is an oracle worthy of preservation, it might properly be imagined as a jazz tune to be recorded. In this sense, the "incandescent wax" would be the record (made in 1923 from a form of paraffin) figuratively glowing hot with the song it holds. A record disc could quite accurately be described as "Striated with nuances," minutely furrowed or grooved with the impressions of those "nuances" and "nervosities" of voice that make up Helen's hymn "That we are heir to."

How can we "frown upon her as she smiles"—revelling in the

joy of her own rhythm and "Dipping" through the "storm"? This is no random fury but a "cultivated" orchestration of energies and "Numbers" into the wind's one "steady sound" (to take a phrase from "Repose of Rivers")—a storm of which Crane might exclaim, as he does in his poem, "The Hurricane": "Lo, Lord, Thou ridest!" These "gardened skies" are like Eden filled with graceful dancing children, "slim skaters." But this is not the prelapsarian garden of innocence. It is paradise regained through the redemptive tragedy of Part III.

In the "groans of death" of Part II, we were given a foretaste of the "slain numbers" of Part III where the full taste of death is now given. As Crane himself points out:

> This last part begins with *catharsis,* the acceptance of tragedy through destruction (the Fall of Troy, etc., also in it). It is Dionysian in its attitude, the creator and the eternal destroyer dance arm in arm, etc., all ending in a restatement of the imagination of Part I.[53]

The need for "destruction" as the inseparable other side of the generative Dionysian dance is clearly expressed here; and so that other face of Dionysius glimpsed in the "divine grotesque" of Part II is fully visible in the person of the "eternal gunman" of Part III. But Dionysius, whether creating or destroying, inevitably brings us to "the arc of Helen's brow" where the opposites of "blessing and dismay" are bridged. This classically tragic attitude in the poem is confirmed by Crane in a letter to Gorham Munson:

> After this perfection of death—nothing is possible in motion but a resurrection of some kind. . . . All I know through very much suffering and dullness (somehow I seem to twinge more all the time) is that it interests me to still affirm certain things. That will be the persisting theme of the last part of "F and H" as it has been all along.[54]

In the quest for the Holy, nothing is shunned as too carnal or terrible to hold it—not trolleys or jazz parties, not "A goose,

---

[53]*Letters,* p. 121.
[54]*Letters,* p. 115.

tobacco, and cologne," not "speediest destruction" itself. For the "spiritual gates" through which we must pass to the divine are of the body that dances and dies and lives again.

The speaker of Part I of "Faustus and Helen" is singular, "I"—Faustus/Artist. Faustus remains the protagonist of Part II, but the pronoun is mostly pluralized, "we"—a way of drawing the reader more intimately into the poem's process. In Part III there seems a shift to another persona because the poem is addressed to the "religious gunman" who is apparently Faustus. But there is really no change of person; the poem has simply moved to internal dialogue, the speaker now talking to the Faustus within himself—and, as we know from Part II, the Faustus within us. The point of view is comparable to the inner conversation of "I" and "Psyche" in Poe's "Ulalume."

The first stanza begins with the address of Faustus, the fighter pilot, the "religious gunman" who performs the sacred rite of slaughter and who "faithfully," himself, "will fall too soon":

> Capped arbiter of beauty in this street
> That narrows darkly into motor dawn,—
> You, here beside me, delicate ambassador
> Of intricate slain numbers that arise
> In whispers, naked of steel;
> religious gunman!
> Who faithfully, yourself, will fall too soon,
> And in other ways than as the wind settles
> On the sixteen thrifty bridges of the city:
> Let us unbind our throats of fear and pity.

The scene is World War I, as an earlier quotation from Crane has told us. In his leather cap, the pilot seems commissioned as the "arbiter of beauty," given absolute authority to slay or spare lovely or unlovely alike. And that other self, the reveller of Part II, rides beside the "delicate ambassador / Of intricate slain numbers"— he who though he immolates, priestlike, also speaks for the victims. There is another appearance of the "Numbers" that so "divided" the "mind" of the speaker in Part I, only they are here "slain." In Part II, the numerosity of things was "inscaped" and the perfect, indivisible Number was found. The other way to get to the Number within all numbers is to kill each number, for they will then paradoxically "arise"—but transfigured, stripped of the clamant hardness that made them so "intricate" and distinct. They will return "In whispers, naked of steel." This paradox of generative, healing, revelatory death is found, again, in Nietzsche's concept of the tragic Dionysian who has a "premonition of a highest pleasure attained through destruction and negation, so he feels as if the innermost abyss of things spoke to him perceptibly."[55]

In Chapter IV, I briefly discussed Crane's attitude toward the machine that he saw to be as inevitable to modern poetry as castles to medieval. Crane particularly used the flying machine as the epitome of modern technology. In "Cape Hatteras" Crane would again idealize the pilot—though victim to his own "high bravery" and those "Vast engines outward veering with seraphic grace"— as the one who in his flight is most apt "To course that span of consciousness." L.S. Dembo discovers the peculiar but illuminating fact of Crane's brief allegiance to an aesthetic movement called "Verticalism," which partially explains the poet's use of airplanes and their operators as metaphors of vision in "Faustus and Helen" and "Cape Hatteras" (the poem Dembo concentrates on in his article).[56] The main principle of "Verticalism," founded by Eugene Jolas and promulgated through the French magazine *Transition* (where Crane's name is signed to a verticalist manifesto along with that of Harry Crosby and others), is that cosmic consciousness comes most readily through motion, especially ascent or flight, and that it is best expressed, after the necessary facing and exorcising of demonic fear, in a "hymnic vocabulary"—such as in the last two stanzas of "Faustus and Helen," I would add.

As pilot and copilot descend to strafe "this street / That narrows darkly into motor drawn"—still partly obscured by the shadows that fill its caverns at daybreak and, according to the "logic of metaphor," filled with the roar of the airplane's motor, which comes ironically in place of dawn's light—they are aware that the "priest" must, true to his calling as immolator, himself be immolated. For death itself must die—and not gently as the "wind settles / On the sixteen thrifty bridges of the city." Vincent Quinn

[55]Nietzsche, p. 126.
[56]"Hart Crane's 'Verticalist' Poem," *American Literature,* 40 (1968), 77–81.

agrees that "The pilot is placed in a priestly, even deific role at the same time he is recognized as destroyer."[57] Death will die calamitously in the crash and explosion of his craft over the city, for this is the violent way of transmutation. The "sixteen thrifty bridges"—while they represent the multiplicity that is being made one by obliteration—stand as congruent foreshadows of the "thrifty," the direct and unlabored spanning of opposites toward which the entire poem reaches. And then, once again obedient to the original call of "Legend" to give the "perfect cry," Dancer/Destroyer proclaims: "Let us unbind our throats of fear and pity"—let us not turn our faces from the cup but drink full of its agony and pathos, for therein is our triumph.

The "inscape" of that destructive horror is fiercely "essentialized" through the next three stanzas where the crucible is heated to incandescence that the elixir might be distilled.

> We even,
> Who drove speediest destruction
> In corymbulous formations of mechanics,—
> Who hurried the hill breezes, spouting malice
> Plangent over meadows, and looked down
> On rifts of torn and empty houses
> Like old women with teeth unjubilant
> That waited faintly, briefly and in vain:
>
> We know, eternal gunman, our flesh remembers
> The tensile boughs, the nimble blue plateaus,
> The mounted, yielding cities of the air!
>
> That saddled sky that shook down vertical
> Repeated play of fire—no hypogeum
> Of wave or rock was good against one hour.

The "speediest destruction," the "spouting malice," even though savage in its loud annihilation of already "torn and empty houses," as helpless, sad, and vulnerable as grimacing "old women," is uncompromisingly "instressed" as the ironically "thrifty" gateway to peace. This paradox is most notably apparent in the

---

[57]Vincent Quinn, p. 55.

terms "corymbulous formations of mechanics" and "Plangent over meadows." The cylinders of a World War I aircraft motor are visible and arranged in a circular pattern about the crankshaft they drive—something like the sharing of one stalk by a cluster of flowers, which is what "corymbulous" literally refers to. Or the metaphor might be intended to convey the clustered flying formation of a squadron of fighter planes. Either way, the image does more than just provide a physical picture of an airplane engine or a flight formation; in its curious blending of deathly "malice" and delicate beauty, it functions to communicate the new life and vision implicit in this "religious" devastation. And "Plangent," which denotes the repeated racket of a machinegun, in its secondary meaning connotes a plaintive reverberation, a mourning over "meadows"; so that the calamity is as sorrowful as it is malicious, as lovely as it is abhorrent.

The honor-bound and anointed mission of the "eternal gunman" is additionally stressed by his cavalier running of the craft over "nimble blue plateaus" of the "saddled sky"—the clouds giving themselves to be "mounted" like celestial "cities of the air." (We must not seek in the "logic of metaphor" literal explanation for the sky being "nimble" and "saddled" rather than the airplane.) This is, however, no insubstantial, airy dream, for "our flesh remembers" real, firm wings ("tensile boughs") and real bullets "shook down" again and again in such a "play of fire" that "no hypogeum"—no cellar or shelter even tunneled beneath "wave or rock"—could withstand for long the onslaught.

Crane is not relishing or promoting war, death, and destruction (as Nietzsche approaches doing in his "highest pleasure attained through destruction"); but since tragedy is a fact of life, its horror can be transfigured by recognizing and accepting the redemptive sacrifice, the rebirth, inherent in annihilation—as in "The Tunnel":

> And yet, like Lazarus, to feel the slope,
> The sod and billow breaking,—lifting ground,
> —A sound of waters bending astride the sky
> Unceasing with some Word that will not die. . . !

There is in *The Birth of Tragedy* another corroboration of Crane's attitude toward the demolition of phenomena that

Nietzsche calls the tragedian's "vast Dionysian impulse" that "devours his entire world of phenomena, in order to let us sense beyond it, and through its destruction, the highest artistic primal joy, in the bosom of the primordially One."[58] In stanza five, however, the speaker seems not as impelled to destruction as Nietzsche's tragedian: "We did not ask for that, but have survived, / And will persist to speak again. . . ." By pronouncing the Word of "fear and pity," we will continue to transubstantiate and redeem all catastrophes that can be recalled, "All stubble streets that have not curved to memory." For all reality must be transmuted in the "Reflective conversion" of Helen's "deep blush" —here called the "ominous lifted arm / That lowers down the arc of Helen's brow / To saturate with blessing and dismay."

"Onimous" is the perfect word because it contains almost antithetical meanings; more currently it means "threatening," but originally it meant (and can still mean) having the import of an "omen"—for either good or evil. It does not matter whether Helen lifts her arm, makes the sign, over the fertility dance or the dance of death. Either can be transformed; both must be made one within the circle, the "arc," of her blessed countenance. Whether we are smitten with "blessing" as in Part II or "dismay" as in Part III, we must allow ourselves to be "saturated" with either so that we might grasp the singular oracle across "Helen's brow." Crane is saying something very similar to what Whitman declares in "Song of Myself":

> I am the poet of the Body and I am the poet of the Soul,
> The pleasures of heaven are with me and the pains of hell
>   are with me,
> The first I graft and increase upon myself, the latter
>   I translate into a new tongue.[59]

This comprehension of the unity within the duality of "blessing and dismay" also has precedent for Crane in Nietzsche: "All that exists is just and unjust and equally justified in both."[60] And Scripture puts the paradox this way: "But where sin abounded, grace did much more abound" (Romans 5:20).

[58]Nietzsche, p. 132.
[59]Whitman, p. 48.
[60]Nietzsche, p. 72.

This "restatement" of the imagination of Part I," to use Crane's description, continues into stanza six:

> A goose, tobacco and cologne—
> Three-winged and gold-shod prophecies of heaven,
> The lavish heart shall always have to leaven
> And spread with bells and voices, and atone
> The abating shadows of our conscript dust.

In Part I we learned that "all things" are transformed in Helen's "eventual flame." Nothing, not the most ordinary and mundane aspects of our lives, is exempt from that "conversion." The protagonist at the beginning of "Faustus and Helen" was unsettled by the "labeled" distinctions "on every corner" between "druggist, barber, and tobacconist." Now the once disturbingly "stacked," distinct stuff of his experience, "A goose, tobacco and cologne," are "three-winged and gold-shod prophecies of heaven." Their previous density, their "opacities," have been penetrated to truth; their multiplicity and dividedness fused into one triple-pinioned emissary of heaven's one Word; their previous ordinariness is now perceived as sublimely "gold-shod"—like the divine messenger, but abiding with us rather than with the gods. It is interesting to note the heavy sense quality of these objects, which appeals to the olfactory or gustatory faculties—avoiding the more "intellectual" senses of sight and hearing. Crane is stressing the materiality of those things in which he grasps spirituality.

But the prophecies are not automatic, for they must be fermented, so to speak, within that "labeled dough" of experience much as yeast gives life and form to flour and water: "The lavish heart shall always have to leaven / And spread with bells and voices, and atone / The abating shadows of our conscript dust." It takes a generous, a magnanimous spirit, a "lavish heart," to "raise" the seemingly flat material of our days—to "leaven" and lace it with music and prophecy—with the "bells and voices" that proclaim its latent blessedness. Lest the vital, fleshy substance of what we meet be always "abating," reducing to "shadows" and, like the "earth" in Part I, left to "glide diaphanous to death" or to resolve to "dust," we must "atone" it. We must not see our flesh as "conscript," fated to "dust." We must redeem and transfigure it by loving it and releasing the hidden holiness it is, which is not very unlike the way Christ said we would see the sanctity of life: "The kingdom of heaven is like unto leaven, which a woman took, and hid in three measures of meal, till the whole was leavened" (Matthew 13:33). Here as in "Faustus and Helen," an immersion, a burial within the "meal" of things, is necessary for the heavenly transformation and incarnation to occur.

Most of the writers referred to as influencing or solidifying Crane in his sensitivities professed a similar attitude toward the quotidian and ordinary as portents of the divine. William Blake has Isaiah speak this prophecy: " 'I saw no God, nor heard any, in a finite organical perception; but my senses discover'd the infinite in every thing. . . .' "[61] And Ouspensky describes how it will be once one acquires the "higher consciousness": "It is impossible now to imagine the nature of this newness which we shall sense in familiar things, and once felt it will be difficult to understand";[62] or "Desiring to understand the *noumenal world* we must search for *the hidden meaning* in everything."[63]

R.W.B. Lewis also finds in Crane's poem that "enroute to ecstasy, we must take the most commonplace elements that the world has to offer as prophecies of heaven."[64] In "Modern Poetry" Crane tells us that:

> poetic prophecy has nothing to do with factual prediction or with futurity. It is a peculiar type of perception, capable of apprehending some absolute and timeless concept of the imagination with astounding clarity and conviction.[65]

It is important to note Crane's language here; these absolutes are not conceived of but *perceived* clearly as "concepts of the imagination" in smells and tastes—in "the body of the world."

And just as Helen was coveted in antiquity by Anchises, so has her ideality, her "gold hair," been the object of the fervent desire of that other great age, the Renaissance, in the person of Erasmus. Helen's "plane" is timeless, classic:

[61]Blake, p. 153.
[62]Ouspensky, p. 142.
[63]Ouspensky, p. 143.
[64]Lewis, p. 116.
[65]*Poems,* p. 263.

Anchises' navel, dripping of the sea,—
The hands Erasmus dipped in gleaming tides,
Gathered the voltage of blown blood and vine;
Delve upward for the new and scattered wine,
O brother-thief of time, that we recall.
Laugh out the meager penance of their days
Who dare not share with us the breath released,
The substance drilled and spent beyond repair
For golden, or the shadow of gold hair.

In the figure of Anchises, the Trojan father of Aeneas, the
founder of Rome, we have the bridging of the two grand, ancient
cultures of Greece and Rome. As the lover of Venus, to whom
Aeneas was born, and as one of the contestants for Helen in the
Trojan War, he represents one who aspires to divinity and pur-
sues beauty. Erasmus was the great Renaissance humanist of the
sixteenth century who sought to rid the church of its repressive
superstitions and abuses and to wed the medieval Christian out-
look with the more human-centered values of classical antiquity.
Both figures together exhibit the desire for synthesis: of God and
man, of past and present. Both seek and meet the divine not
eschatalogically but immanently, with their bodies: Anchises in
Venus and in Helen, Erasmus in his application of the Christian
faith to the visible, the "secular." They are together the *"Talmud
skill / And profane Greek to raise the building up / Of Helen's house
against the Ismaelite."* With the "Faustus" persona of the poem, the
restless seeker and creator/destroyer of the modern age, they
span the entire history of civilization. And the three are united by
overstepping normal boundaries in their pursuit of beauty and
truth: Anchises dared to cross the threshold between gods and
humans to embrace an Olympian; Erasmus was censured as ir-
religious for criticizing what he thought were ungodly, inhumane
church practices; Faustus (both the contemporary protagonist of
the poem and he of medieval Wittenberg) tapped "the springs of
guilty song" for higher knowledge and the hand of Helen.

Like Faustus, then, Anchises and Erasmus find the holy not in
transcendence but in the "world." They have "dipped" into divin-
ity as into the sea and emerge "dripping" of the sensible "sub-
stance" of the blessed. They have, like the reveler/gunman,
"Gathered the voltage of blown blood and vine" and have utterly

transmuted the "gleaming tides" into the "wine" that is "blood" of divinity (rather than the "bartered blood" of Part I). This apprehension of the heavenly "voltage" with which all of life is charged or "blown" can only be sensed (not "understood") by plunging—"navel" and "hands"—into its "sea." For in our immersion, we experience the paradox of the Ideal incarnate; and just as Faustus says that "if I lift my arms it is to bend" to Helen, his brethren reach down for what is above them, "Delve upward for the new and scattered wine." The transfigurative process of this holy vision is stated in explicitly eucharistic, transubstantive terms. Priestlike, Anchises and Erasmus change water into wine into blood—finding their life-giving drink in the elements of the earth. The imagery here is, of course, biblical—the more obvious source being Christ's giving wine to be drunk as his, God's, Blood whereby the communicant "dwelleth in me, and I in him" (John 6:56). A likely secondary source is Christ's comparison of a new way of seeing to "new wine" that must be placed in new skins as it would just burst the old containers capable of holding only old wine—old attitudes (Matthew 9:17). Faustus has communed with divinity, and the old and narrow categories of consciousness have been burst and cannot hold the "new and scattered wine" of his transfigured vision. The eucharistic imagery here conveys both the transubstantive and the sacred nature of the vision. As Samuel Hazo sees it, "It is worthwhile to note here how Crane has transmuted several conventional Christian images to suggest the redemptive and sustaining effect of beauty upon man. The allusion to the 'new and scattered wine' has an obvious Eucharistic significance."[66]

And so, the speaker of the poem reflects upon these two predecessors in the visionary way as he addresses his other self, the "eternal gunman," his "brother-thief of time." The protagonist has stolen from time its relativity and the "stacked partitions" of its divisions by redemptive destruction just as in Part II he found the absolute in relativity by generative dancing. But he must do more than "recall"; he must not be as those who inhibit themselves and who do not "Delve" or "unbind their throats," or who "Laugh out the meager penance of their days." "Penance" con-

---

[66]Hazo, p. 54.

notes, here as elsewhere in Crane, a repression of body and therefore of spirit. In keeping with the dictum of "Legend," Anchises and Erasmus—Faustus—do not "match regrets." But they "dare" to "atone," to fathom the "tides" and clutch the "dust" of their days and give us the good news of what they transmute from them; they "share with us the breath released"—even if cried out in anguish.

As one who "spends out himself again" ("Legend") with Anchises and Erasmus, Faustus knows that the "substance" of the quotidian must be "instressed," "drilled," shot through (with bullets and vision) and, as the "stones" of "Possessions," utterly "rased"—"spent beyond repair"—that a new substance, the "new wine," the transubstance of "golden, or the shadow of gold hair" can be had.

With that consummate realization of the vision posited in Part I, the poem returns to and reaffirms the praises proffered in Part I:

> Distinctly praise the years, whose volatile
> Blamed bleeding hands extend and thresh the height
> The imagination spans beyond despair,
> Outpacing bargain, vocable and prayer.

Faustus knows the essential unity and prophetic nature of things now that they have been transfigured and seen as they really are in Helen's "deep blush," through dance and devastation. He can now "Distinctly praise the years," for in time's "multitudes" is discovered the eternal One. And so can all the brotherhood of Faustus be as distinct in their praise, "whose volatile / Blamed bleeding hands extend and thresh the height"—always ready to reach for blessedness, ever outcast and suffering in their aspiration. For their "imagination," their transfigurative vision, casts the "arc" that "spans" "beyond despair," connecting all things in its curve—like the "bridge" that "swings over salvage" in "Recitative" and the "curveship" of Brooklyn Bridge that can "lend a myth to God." This is the perfect circle of vision, the antiphonal song, the "constant harmony" that outreaches any "bargain," approximation, or compromise of beatitude—"outpacing" any "vocable" or sayable word, for it is the "single, new *word,* never before spoken and impossible to actually enunciate."[67] Such apprehension goes "beyond despair" but not before it has gone through the dark night of near despair. As in the "Palm and pain" of "Lachrymae Christi," the "Blamed bleeding hands" of betrayal and crucifixion are the signs of redemption, touching in their thrashing agony the very "height" of heaven. And as in the "illumination" of St. John of the Cross, even "prayer" is eliminated in the sense of a communication between God and man. For God and man and all creation are one in the communion, the marriage of Faustus and Helen.

[67]*Poems,* p. 221.

VI

The Incarnate Word

In 1923, about a year before he began to write "Voyages," Crane revealed to a friend his fundamental attitude toward suffering:

> I have had enough of it, anyway, to realize that it is all very beautiful in the end if you will pierce through to the center of it and see it in relation to the real emotions and values of Life. . . . The true idea of God is the only thing that can give happiness,—and that is the identification of yourself with *all of life*.[1]

In his belief that suffering can yield something "beautiful" if you "pierce through" to the "real," Crane comments quite pointedly on the theme of "Voyages," which is the finding of the "fervid covenant" through the anguish of wrecked love. But if this is a comment on "Voyages," it is also a statement of the vision that informs all of *White Buildings* and, by extension, all of Crane's poetry. "Voyages" is unlike anything else Crane wrote in its deeply sorrowful and exquisitely sustained theme of broken love and tragic regeneration; but in its discovery of "happiness," "The true idea of God," by an "identification . . . with *all of life*"—what is called in the poem "the incarnate word / . . . in mingling / Mutual blood"—it is integral to the incarnational vision of the holy that

---

[1]*Letters*, p. 140.

has been described in this study. "Voyages" partakes fully of the general mode of Crane's poetry to transubstantiate from the pain and the inconstancy of life an undying faith and felicity—"the unbetrayable reply."

As the closing movement of the "symphony" of *White Buildings*, responding to the call of "Legend" and conforming to its ethic of sacrificial "cleaving" and "burning" for the "bright logic," "Voyages" maintains the integrity and completes the theme of the book. "Voyages" further unifies the collection by returning, as I indicated earlier, to the graver, more elegiac mood and more gradual tempo of the collection's first movement (keynoted by the lamentational "Emblems of Conduct"). I repeat, however, that "Voyages" is true to the call of "Legend" to "string some constant harmony." This closing suite does not reiterate the largely resigned, more purely meditative outlook of the first movement. That preludial sequence of *White Buildings*, as we have seen, does not "step / The legend . . . into noon"—does not "pierce through" to the "bright logic"—but rather mourns its loss or inaccessibility, or constructs artifacts of its perfection to be but contemplated, not possessed. "Voyages," on the other hand, clasps the "bright logic" in the "imaged Word" and hears its "constant harmony" in "Creation's blithe and petaled word." Although this final movement does not recapitulate and gather the book's distinct variations upon the theme stated in its overture, as does "For the Marriage of Faustus and Helen," it does serve to clinch the theme by partaking of the consummate vision of the book's second and third movements while sounding the melancholy note of the first sequence. This gives a truly satisfying aesthetic as well as thematic unity and balance to the artistic whole that is *White Buildings*.

Yet, in its unrelieved preoccupation with the sea and love and death as replicas of each other, "Voyages" *is* different, standing out more uniquely in the collection than any of the other movements. The first two movements of the book are comprised of complementary but originally independent poems and so exhibit a wider range and variety within their common subthemes. "For the Marriage of Faustus and Helen," though, like "Voyages," composed as a multipart but single poem before its inclusion in *White Buildings*, serves as a summary or "recapitulation" of the entire cycle and so contains within it elements found in just about all the individual poems. But viewed as analogous to the "coda" or concluding movement of a symphony, the "eccentricity" of "Voyages" as a sequence much more narrowly focused than the others makes good "musical" sense. A "coda" is not, in a classically structured sonata or symphony, intended to be perfectly homogeneous with the work's preceding movements. While contributing, of course, to the composition's main (and perhaps secondary) theme, it is usually designed to introduce a new, previously unstated emotion or strain. With the thematic restatement or résumé having been given in the immediately preceding movement, the piece can conclude with a vital and pleasurable sense of new direction. "Voyages" functions in *White Buildings* just as the "coda" in a symphony, responding to and closing the theme posited in its introduction but leaving the reader with a sense of continuation and of the theme's many possible manifestations.

"Voyages" stands out as unique in *White Buildings*, and it does not parallel exactly any single movement in *The Bridge*. Though the introduction and the three other movements of *White Buildings* do parallel a comparable overture and kindred movements in *The Bridge*, "Voyages" does not so closely resemble "Atlantis," either in content or function, as a last movement in its collection. Of course, there are similarities between these two concluding sequences. "Voyages" does give to *White Buildings* the rapturous ending "Atlantis" gives to *The Bridge*. And there is a most important functional and thematic similarity between "Voyages" and "Atlantis" in that both do point in the direction of complete beatitude, of divinity, and so fulfill the prayers and promises of their introductions. The last two stanzas of "Voyages VI" and the last stanza of "Atlantis" communicate visions so close that they require similar language and imagery for their expression:

> Still fervid covenant, Belle Isle,
> — Unfolded floating dais before
> Which rainbows twine continual hair —
> Belle Isle, white echo of the oar!
>
> The imaged Word, it is, that holds
> Hushed willows anchored in its glow.

It is the unbetrayable reply
Whose accent no farewell can know.

"Voyages VI"

So to thine Everpresence, beyond time,
Like spears ensanguined of one tolling star
That bleeds infinity—the orphic strings,
Sidereal phalanxes, leap and converge:
—One Song, one Bridge of Fire! Is it Cathay,
Now pity steeps the grass and rainbows ring
The serpent with the eagle in the leaves. . . ?
Whispers antiphonal in azure swing.

"Atlantis"

There are other correspondences in metaphor and meaning between "Voyages" and "Atlantis," but "Voyages" does not reflect anything like the high liturgy ritualistically intoned in "Atlantis," and "Atlantis" never slows down enough to speak that other, softer voice of God. It is the difference between the "still small voice" of Yahweh heard by Elijah and the "voice as of the sound of many waters" speaking of the last days to St. John in the Apocalypse. *White Buildings* is thematically and structurally analogous to *The Bridge*, but it is a different book with its own special identity—an identity given it mainly by the subdued and pensive voice of "Voyages."

Up to this point, reference has been made only to the six parts of "Voyages," but this last movement of *White Buildings* also includes "At Melville's Tomb." This poem, though of course conceived independently, was written at about the same time as "Voyages" and projects a common symbolism, finding in the contemplation of death and the sea a vision of the Absolute. The "silent answers" of "At Melville's Tomb" are heard in the "unbetrayable reply" of "Voyages." "At Melville's Tomb," in its persona whose "Frosted eyes . . . lifted altars" and in its paradoxical sense of "death's bounty" and depiction of a sea whose cruelty is "charmed and malice reconciled," provides a most appropriate introduction to a cycle of poems with almost identical subjects. The persona of "Voyages" similarly seeks "The seal's wide spin-

drift gaze toward paradise" and finds that "death, if shed, /
Presumes no carnage" and that the sea, though a "sceptred
terror," "lifts, also, reliquary hands."

"Voyages" itself, like the other movements of *White Buildings*,
contains its own thematic progression as a cycle within a cycle. "At
Melville's Tomb" keynotes and initiates that cycle not only
thematically, as demonstrated above, but tonally as well. I men-
tioned that "Voyages" exhibits an elegiac mood; "At Melville's
Tomb" is literally a "Monody" to the "fabulous shadow" from
whom the poem takes its title. In its quiet, eulogistic manner, "At
Melville's Tomb" conditions the reader for the almost purely
elegiac tenor and restrained pathos of the six poems that follow it.
At the same time, it provides a transition and buffer between "For
the Marriage of Faustus and Helen" and "Voyages" comparable
to a "bridge" passage in a symphony. "At Melville's Tomb" picks
up the mystical and prayerful attitude of the last stanza of "For
the Marriage of Faustus and Helen" and carries forward its
feeling of reconciliation and repose — which will be realized again
in "Voyages" but in another way. Such a "bridge" provides both a
structural and visionary continuity most gratifying to the aes-
thetic sense and powerfully unifying to *White Buildings*.

Herbert A. Leibowitz, in his book *Hart Crane: An Introduction to
the Poetry*, statistically confirms what even the casual reader of
Crane's poems has sensed — that the sea and things related to the
sea provide the richest source of imagery in Crane's poetry.[2] *The
Bridge* is, to be sure, dominated by sea imagery from its opening
"Proem" to "Atlantis"; and, including the six parts of "Voyages,"
no less than a third of the poems of *White Buildings* contain
central, crucial images of the sea. This last movement is, of
course, given wholly to an "inscaping" of the sea and all that it
signifies of death and love and vision.

Thus, this introductory poem tells of the voyage we shall take
through the sea:

> Often beneath the wave, wide from this ledge
> The dice of drowned men's bones he saw bequeath
> An embassy. Their numbers as he watched,
> Beat on the dusty shore and were obscured.

[2](New York: Columbia University Press, 1968), pp. 151 ff.

The protagonist, Herman Melville, whose *Moby Dick* Crane had
admired enough to read at least four times and the imagery of
which is recognizable in this poem and elsewhere,[3] is depicted
first as one who knew the totality, the finality, of death as he saw
from his vantage point (both geographically and metaphysically
"wide") the unmistakable evidence of death's power: "The dice of
drowned men's bones" as they are pounded and sifted to powder
"beneath the wave" and "on the dusty shore." But these bones are
not without meaning, for they "bequeath / An embassy"; they
carry messages from another land, the mystic meaning of which
we shall learn in the succeeding stanzas. (This explication of "At
Melville's Tomb" is consistent with Crane's own partial explana-
tion of the poem in that important general statement of his
poetics to Harriet Monroe.[4]) The dead men's bones are like
"dice"—literally reduced to little cubes by the beating action of
the water and sand. Dice are known in slang parlance as "bones,"
but the analogy runs deeper than the physical resemblance of
fragmented, polished bones to dice. The bones are also called
"numbers," which seems to play on the idea of the numerical
markings on gaming dice. In previous contexts (particularly in
my discussion of "Recitative"), it was pointed out that Crane often
uses mathematical or quantitative language to indicate both the
fragmentation and limitation of time and "the world dimen-
sional." These images of "dice" and "numbers," while com-
municating the finitude of life, also suggest the unpredictability
of death, like a game of chance.

In stanza two, the "instressing" of death by water continues in
the ghostly image of soundless "wrecks" passing. These ruined
ships as well as their mariners' "bones" also speak portentous
messages:

> And wrecks passed without sound of bells,
> The calyx of death's bounty giving back
> A scattered chapter, livid hieroglyph,
> The portent wound in corridors of shells.

In the "calyx," the vortex, of their sinking, death returns a cor-
nucopian "bounty" of wisdom in the "scattered" debris that arises

[3]*Letters*, p. 404.
[4]*Poems*, pp. 238–39.

as a "livid hieroglyph"—as a pale and cryptic but decipherable language. But the "chapter" can only be translated through "The portent wound in corridors of shells," for "about as much definite knowledge might come from all this as anyone might gain from the roar of his own veins, which is easily heard (haven't you ever done it?) by holding a shell close to one's ear," as Crane comments on this last image.[5] Although real and palpable, the word that the sea, that death, speaks is—as always with Crane's most profound truths—unpronounceable, given as the "silent answers" of the next stanza:

> Then in the circuit calm of one vast coil,
> Its lashings charmed and malice reconciled,
> Frosted eyes there were that lifted altars;
> And silent answers crept across the stars.

As the vision that derives paradoxically from "death's bounty" is approached, there is an appearance of circle imagery, which, we have seen in other poems, signifies ideality, perfection, and the unification of opposites—here of "numbers" that are "scattered." The "portent" of stanza two is "wound," and it is "in the circuit calm of one vast coil" of the sea that the vision is had. For if the sea is "cruel," as we will learn in "Voyages I," she is also kind once her "lashings" have been "charmed" and her "malice reconciled" within her own "coil." It is then that the "Frosted eyes," crystallized, as it were, in their unstinting search, lift "altars" of supplication and "reverence" to the "deity" they seek through death.[6] And the prayer is answered, but in silence, in the unsearchable truths spelled out "across the stars."

The "tides," the horizonless realm of these "answers," are "farther" than any navigational instrument can "construe" in its computations:

> Compass, quadrant and sextant contrive
> No farther tides . . . High in the azure steeps
> Monody shall not wake the mariner.
> This fabulous shadow only the sea keeps.

---

[5] *Poems,* p. 239.
[6] These terms, "reverence" and "deity," are used by Crane in his explanation of the line in his letter to Harriet Monroe, *Poems,* p. 239.

For through the fragmentation of death's "numbers" comes the understanding of eternity's unbroken arc. And so the song is single, a "Monody" — an ode to be sung by one voice — signifying the oneness, the integrity of the vision gained by the "mariner" who rests now in that unchartable place, "High in the azure steeps." His understanding is beyond the mere approximations of this eulogy, and so he will not hear it or be awakened by it in his stillness. The protagonist's sleep here is not unconscious, but, on the contrary, more like a state of consciousness so absolute and final as to resemble sleep. Melville has been transfigured by death to find the vision of eternity toward which he gazed in life. And "This fabulous shadow only the sea keeps," for only "this great wink of eternity" ("Voyages II") can hold such a spirit, contain such a vision.

The idea of time or death as "spiritual gates" to absolute vision has been seen a number of times in *White Buildings* up to this point (most notably in Part III of "Faustus and Helen") and will be seen again throughout *The Bridge*. And this ode to Melville is the third time in *White Buildings* that Crane uses the persona of a "patron saint," a fellow seer or questor from history or fable as an embodiment of vision. To his invocations of Charlie Chaplin, Faustus, and Herman Melville in *White Buildings*, Crane will add reverences and prayers to Columbus, Rip Van Winkle, Walt Whitman, Emily Dickinson, Edgar Allan Poe, and others in *The Bridge*. "At Melville's Tomb" represents Crane's proclivity to associate himself almost for guidance with those who have known "silent answers" — much as the classical poet calls upon the muse or some other deity or "angel" for inspiration.

With this keynote of vision coming through "death's," the sea's, "bounty," we move on to "Voyages," where death and the sea join with love as a trinity of transfigurative truth.

It was mentioned above that "Voyages" has a structure of its own and is, like "Faustus and Helen," a cycle within a cycle. "Voyages I" posts a premise: "The bottom of the sea is cruel." This admission of the sea's savagery is also a challenge to vision, a hard reality to be translated into hope — as are all the apparently cruel facts of life transfigured in Crane's poetry. "Voyages II," "III" and "IV" — constituting together a second sequence — peer steadily into the sea's "sceptred terror" to begin to transmute from it its inverse truth: to hear the sea "Laughing the wrapt inflections of our love" ("II"), and to discover that "The sea lifts also reliquary hands" ("III"), or to see written upon it the "signature of the incarnate word" ("IV"). Finding the sea to be the image of life, love, and felicity as well as of death, indifference, and inconstancy, "Voyages V," as a third movement within a movement, returns to the "merciless" side of the sea and tells of the loss, the "piracy," of love by time and mutability, by the sea's "drifting foam." Then "Voyages VI," comparable to the last reconciling stanzas of "For the Marriage of Faustus and Helen" and similar to the synthesizing thrust of "Atlantis," posits finally a single, healed vision from the torturing ambivalence of the sea. It finds in the "splintered garland" of broken hope the "fervid covenant" signaled in the arch of "rainbows" and preserved in the everlasting "imaged Word."

"Voyages I" opens with the image of children, "Bright striped urchins," playing "Above the fresh ruffles of the surf," throwing sand or contending for shells or crumbling dried seaweed or "Gaily digging and scattering." The carelessness and frivolity of their games, however, is answered by a far more austere voice than their mindless "treble interjections" might have asked for. For the sea speaks in response a violent tongue: "The sun beats lightning on the waves / The waves fold thunder on the sand. . . ." "And could they hear me," the speaker says of the children, "I would tell them:"

> O brilliant kids, frisk with your dog,
> Fondle your shells and sticks, bleached
> By time and the elements; but there is a line
> You must not cross nor ever trust beyond it
> Spry cordage of your bodies to caresses
> Too lichen-faithful from too wide a breast.
> The bottom of the sea is cruel.

The persona of the poem would warn these "brilliant kids," unheeding in their play of the sea's strong message, to see in the susceptibility of "shells and sticks, bleached / By time and the elements," the same frailty and vulnerability in their now "Spry . . . bodies." They must not be fooled by the sea's ambivalence or "trust" those "caresses / . . . from too wide a breast." They must be wary of a sea that is "faithful" only to her own who know her such as "lichen," a hearty rock vegetation thriving on the "caresses" of the sea.

And yet, despite his prudent admonition, the persona of "Voyages" himself crosses the "line"; and in the next three parts of the poem he does "trust beyond" the limits he cautioned the innocent children against. But if he finds that "The bottom of the sea is cruel," he also finds "upon the steep floor flung from dawn to dawn / The silken skilled transmemberment of song" ("III"). Though he would spare the "kids" the agony, the speaker knows that unless baptized into its cruelty, he will not know the sea's, life's, "secret oar and petals of all love" ("IV"). "Voyages II" is where the line is crossed and the revelation begun.

The symbolic aspects of the poem aside, the description of the sea in "Voyages" evokes as genuinely and affectingly the physical nature and behavior of the sea as any poetry I have ever read—as in this first stanza of "Voyages II":

> —And yet this great wink of eternity,
> Of rimless floods, unfettered leewardings,
> Samite sheeted and processioned where
> Her undinal vast belly moonward bends,
> Laughing the wrapt inflections of our love.

The speaker receives from the sea in its seeming endlessness, in its "rimless" expanse and "unfettered" motions, a glimpse, a "wink of eternity." And he sees sovereignty in its "samite sheeted" surface, like the motley-rich tapestries of medieval royalty interwoven with silver and gold, and in its stately, "processioned," gait. This metaphor serves remarkably well the double purpose of picturing the blotched texture of the ocean's surface and conveying its grandeur. And by crossing the boundary and entering the sea, the protagonist uncovers the sea's sexuality as well as its sovereignty; for, like the immortal goddess Undine, yearning for a mortal lover, her "vast" tides are imagined as a "belly" bent erotically "moonward" and in its undulation "Laughing the wrapt inflections of our love." If the sea destroys, she also breeds and emulates, sanctions, the sensuality of the speaker and his lover.

But her tyranny is not forgotten as the conceit of the sea's regal majesty of stanza one is advanced into the "sceptred terror" of stanza two:

> Take this Sea, whose diapason knells
> On scrolls of silver snowy sentences,
> The sceptred terror of whose sessions rends
> As her demeanors motion well or ill,
> All but the pieties of lovers' hands.

The word "Sea" is here capitalized as though she were now "entitled," and indeed she does rule. The full, rich range of her many-valved voice, like a "diapason," tolls "snowy sentences" across her foamy surface ("scrolls of silver"), which like writs hold the record, the edict, of her royal proclamations, of her queenly "sessions." This "sceptred terror" in her sovereignty, in her absolute authority, decrees "As her demeanors motion well or ill." And she will break or sever anything—"All but the pieties of lovers' hands." This she will not do, the protagonist naively believes, for he has now seen her as the very image of his love.

The sea continues to reveal herself, to "Complete the dark confessions her veins spell," in stanza three. She continues to speak her own peculiar, lovely language in the "bells off San Salvador" that "Salute the crocus lustres of the stars" and "In these poinsettia meadows of her tides." "San Salvador" literally translates "Holy Savior." This island was the first land seen by Christopher Columbus in his discovery of the New World. In the context of this poem it appears as a pledge of the "covenant" with which "Voyages" ends and as a promise of that hope fulfilled that will be similarly signaled in "Belle Isle." The sense of sovereign power and majesty has now given way to an aura of grace and delicate beauty dominated by flower imagery ("crocus" and "poinsettia"). Even her islands move as in "Adagios"—as in a graceful, slowed, and measured dance. The hard "knells" of stanza two have been metamorphosed into softer "bells."

The point of view, the actual angle of observation of the protagonist, is from a moving ship, which would explain the "dancing" of islands and the general sense of shifting scenery. The ship is traveling northward beginning here in the Caribbean and ending off the coast of Newfoundland, from "San Salvador" to "Belle Isle." It is appropriate that the "voyage" be from a tropic to a near arctic region as it parallels the course and scope of the protagonist's love—as we shall see again in "Voyages IV." And the persona of "Voyages II" is speaking his observations to someone who in stanza three is addressed directly for the first time as "O my Prodigal," and who will be the addressee through the next three parts of the poem up to "Voyages VI." Just as the sea in her lavish power and beauty, the lover to whom the poem is spoken is prodigal, all-giving—"all granting," to use a term from "Legend." What the speaker has not yet realized is that his lover's generosity can also be as errant as the "prodigal son" of the parable or as whimsical as the sea in bequeathing love as his "demeanors motion well or ill."

Unless one knows something of Crane's life, one could not guess that the writing of "Voyages" was occasioned by an intense homosexual affair Crane had with a sailor in 1924. There is virtually nothing in the poem to suggest homosexuality, and it is best to read the poem without deliberate reference to its biographical origin as it is not a poem about homosexuality. Despite his actual homosexual exploits, Crane did not cultivate homosexuality as a desirable or even acceptable lifestyle. He seemed, on the contrary, deeply disturbed by his homosexual tendencies. Not long before his death, after Crane had experienced what was probably his first heterosexual love relationship with Peggy Baird, he was heard to say, "I'm very happy because I have discovered that I am not a homosexual."[7] But if I use "he" to identify the lover of the protagonist in "Voyages," it is to be consistent with the gender of the actual person to whom the poem is addressed.

"Voyages" is a poem about anyone's desire to love and be loved and, failing to realize that love, finding in and through the resultant sorrow an "unsearchable repose" in the apprehension of something more permanent, more faithful, than human love. What can that unexplainable peace, that "imaged Word," be but God or "The true idea of God," which comes as you "*accept everything*" and which gives "such happiness, glorious sorrow, or whatever you want to call it"—to enlarge upon a previously quoted statement by Crane.[8] "Voyages," as regenerative, re-

[7]Unterecker, *Voyages*, p. 739.
[8]*Letters*, p. 140.

demptive tragedy and in its resignation to the "will of God," partakes of the spirit of classical and Christian tragedy.

In stanza four, the protagonist does not yet know that his "Prodigal" will all too well live up to his ambivalent name; but sensing that such felicity, such love, cannot endure, he calls his partner to "hasten" to share them "while they are true":

> Mark how her turning shoulders wind the hours,
> And hasten while her penniless rich palms
> Pass superscription of bent foam and wave,—
> Hasten, while they are true,—sleep, death, desire,
> Close round one instant in one floating flower.

For the sea, in her ceaseless, shifting swells—her "turning shoulders"—is also the likeness of time, seeming to "wind the hours" in her currents. The speaker twice exhorts his lover to "hasten" while the hollows between the risings of the sea like cupped hands, "palms," (or while the tropical palm trees, like empty hands), though "penniless," offer them something richer than material wealth. "Hasten," he pleads, to take what these proffering hands "superscribe," signal, across "bent foam and wave." The gift will not long be offered, for "sleep, death, desire, / Close round" to form a delicate balance of abeyance only for "one instant." It will not be long before the precarious "floating flower" of the moment, of their love, will be lost to sleep or death or mere desire. The call is *carpe diem,* but not in the conventional sense. In seizing the day and perishing in its brevity, the speaker also paradoxically grasps eternity.

We have seen several times in *White Buildings* (and in *The Bridge,* for that matter) that when the poet is fronted with the limitation of time, he does not seek to transcend it but rather accepts its transitoriness and embraces whatever portion of gladness or goodness or wonder it grants—then transmutes from the partialness and resultant anguish something absolute. And so the plea, the prayer, in the last stanza of "Voyages II": "Bind us in time, O Seasons clear, and awe." He asks also those other servants of time, the stars, the "minstrel galleons of Carib fire," not to guide them to land until they have found in time, in the sea and all it signifies—in their love and even in death—the ultimate vision: "Bequeath us to no earthly shore until / Is answered in the vortex

of our grave / The seal's wide spindrift gaze toward paradise."
The image of the "seal" seeing "paradise" through the sea
spray—through the very elements of the temporal and im-
permanent—is the first reiteration in "Voyages" of the theme-
setting vision in "At Melville's Tomb": "Frosted eyes there were
that lifted altars / And silent answers crept across the stars."
There is a similarity in imagery here that is self-evident. The
"vortex of our grave" also relates back to an almost identical
image in the theme-setting poem, "The calyx of death's bounty";
both metaphors portray death and destruction as cornucopian
vortices yielding portentous fruits.

"Voyages II" flings out again the hope, first shown in "At
Melville's Tomb," that the incompleteness and relativity of the
human condition will be transmuted into absolutes as we "bind"
ourselves to them—in the sea, in love.

It is that correspondence between the sea and life—in their flux
and unpredictability, yet constancy and consistency—that is
stressed at the beginning of "Voyages III":

> Infinite consanguinity it bears—
> This tendered theme of you that light
> Retrieves from sea plains where the sky
> Resigns a breast that every wave enthrones;
> While ribboned water lanes I wind
> Are laved and scattered with no stroke
> Wide from your side, whereto this hour
> The sea lifts, also, reliquary hands.

The "Infinite consanguinity"—the fathomless blood kindredship
that is more than an analogy—is between the sea and the lover or
between the sea and the protagonist's love: "This tendered theme
of you" (with a likely pun on the word "tender"). It is with and by
the "light" above these "sea plains" that the speaker "Retrieves"
his offered theme of love; for in their behavior, these skies and
waters imitate that love—like the protagonist's body received in
the act of love, embraced against his lover's body: "the sky /
Resigns a breast that every wave enthrones." The language in
these lines carries a sense of intimacy and gentleness softly con-
trasting with the slightly declamatory last stanza of "Voyages II."

If the sea is the image of the lover as well as of their love, the protagonist receives from the sea a foreshadowing of the eventual departure of his lover and cessation of their love. He can see in the various currents and motions of the sea's "ribboned water lanes"—which are activated, "laved and scattered," to move "Wide from your side"—a sign of the inexorable passage of things that need "no stroke," no reason or cause for their slipping away. Like the sea, things change.

But there is also "Infinite consanguinity" of theme in this: though the sea shifts and speaks so unalterably of love's decline, like the protagonist who seeks at least for "this hour" to hold the precious and blessed vestige, the holy relic of their love, "The sea lifts also reliquary hands." The sea will for now offer them in its "penniless rich palms" their brief hour of love.

The first part of the second stanza of "Voyages III" is another masterful description of the sea's endless motions:

> And so, admitted through black swollen gates
> That must arrest all distance otherwise,—
> Past whirling pillars and lithe pediments,
> Light wrestling there incessantly with light,
> Star kissing star through wave on wave unto
> Your body rocking!

As with all of "Voyages," however, the physical details here have symbolic value. The "black swollen gates" through which the protagonist is admitted represent the large, dark water swells between which the ship passes and which "arrest all distance otherwise"—blocking the view on the horizon except within their portal. But they are also "spiritual gates" through which the protagonist must pass to beatitude. For only between these "gates" is the "distance" visible, the "spindrift gaze" possible. The "gates" are, however, ominous seeming, "black swollen." Entering them, the protagonist will find that they are indeed "swollen" with ire and anguish. And in peering through them to have the unimpeded "vision" that they do in fact grant, he will first see only the darkness of his own tragedy before he perceives that final light of "Belle Isle."

The "whirling pillars and lithe pediments"—tropes that perfectly convey the action of the crests and risings of the ocean—are also architectural shapes we ordinarily associate with temples. Though one could not insist that this is Crane's intention here, linked with the images of "gates," which always in Crane's poetry signify spiritual entry ways, these "pillars" and "pediments" might serve to add to the ambience of sacred rite toward which the entire movement progresses. In the next three lines, the interaction of the sea with its reflected light resembles the erotic actions of lovers in their "wrestling" and "kissing" and "rocking," and yet this is a remarkably exact observation of a restless sea surface shining in shivers with the brilliance of the sun.

As this second stanza splits abruptly at the center of a line, the mood changes with similar suddenness. In the intense energy of that love described above and found through ominous "gates," there is an implicit and dire metamorphosis.

> and where death, if shed,
> Presumes no carnage, but this single change,—
> Upon the steep floor flung from dawn to dawn
> The silken skilled transmemberment of song.

If death does mark the true climax of that seething, carnal love, it brings not "carnage" (a word well chosen because of its affinity with "carnal") but transfiguration, not dismemberment but "transmemberment" (Crane's coinage). The sea is the medium of this "single change," for on its "steep floor" bodies "flung from dawn to dawn" are made new by its "song," "silken skilled" in its gentle ability to transform death and sorrow into something beautiful. This is not the same "cruel" sea bottom of "Voyages I." The "song" or vision of the poet, the love he experiences, and the sea are all so intricately interwoven as to overlap in their functions. The sea is his song, his love is the sea, his song is his love. Nor should we seek to extricate them, for this is the nature of the "logic of metaphor"—of the single ontological truth of which they all partake. All three transfigure and are transfigured—the love or death, the sea, the vision—into something new, something undying. Crane's metaphors, Henry Rago observes, "move in ritual transformations, in which love and death and the sea are constantly metamorphosed into one another."[9]

[9]Rago, p. 341.

The poem then ends with the affirmation, the supplication, of the last one-line stanza, "Permit me voyage, love, into your hands . . . ," which is the destination to which the "gates" ten lines back led. Is "love" here the partner to whom the poem is spoken or the sea? Or is it death or the vision beyond death? It makes little difference, for any of these "hands" are "prodigal"—ever fickle but "all granting."

With that second glimpse in "Voyages III" of the transubstantive power of love, of death—of the sea as it is properly "instressed"—"Voyages IV" answers for a third and final time the challenge of "Voyages I," that "The bottom of the sea is cruel," before moving into the actual transubstantiation of love that dies in "Voyages V" to be redeemed in "Voyages VI." In addition to being studies of the nature of mortal life, of love, through the images of the sea, "Voyages II," "III," and "IV" are premonitions of the tragedy and transubstantiation yet to happen (comparable to the lamentations over and the artifacts of the incarnate Ideal seen in the first movement of *White Buildings* before its realization in the second movement):

> Whose counted smile of hours and days, suppose
> I know as spectrum of the sea and pledge
> Vastly now parting gulf on gulf of wings
> Whose circles bridge, I know, (from palms to the
>   severe)
> Chilled albatross's white immutability)
> No stream of greater love advancing now
> Than, singing, this mortality alone
> Through clay aflow immortally to you.

This first stanza continues the identification of the sea with the lover and his "counted smile" (another mathematical term) limited and, in a sense, rationed out by the "hours and days" of their lives that resemble the temporal "spectrum of the sea" so amply described in the previous parts of "Voyages." This realization, struck again for the third time, evokes not stoicism but a "pledge"—to love in time and in "mortality." This commitment to that "sweet mortality" that "stirs latent power," as it is said eight years later in "The Broken Tower," is always with Crane the way to immortality. For as the sea, whose "spectrum" stretches from gulf to gulf—whose "circles," currents and tides, "bridge," like those "wings" of the seabird, the fecund, tropical zone of "palms" and the arctic pole of the "severe / Chilled albatross's white immutability,"—so does mortal love stretch from its torrid mutability into the changeless reaches of the Absolute. For the sea, like the flight of the albatross, offers no "bridge," "no stream of greater love," than this the protagonist's song of love that flows, though earthly, undyingly: "Through clay aflow immortally to you." The concept of mortal clay being transmuted into the stuff of immortality is as fundamental and strong an image of Crane's incarnational vision as one finds in his poetry.

Other than the sea, there are in this first stanza a number of terms and images that in the context of Crane's total works carry the import of visionary "passwords": "circles" and "bridges" and the "white immutability" of arctic regions. I have already discussed in detail the function of each of these figure types in previous chapters and would just remind the reader that bridges and circles always bring a unification of fragmentation or opposites (here the mortal and immortal, carnal and spiritual); and "A land of leaning ice," as it is called in "North Labrador," always suggests an imperviousness to corruption and change, which, though its lifeless inverse, points in its absolute stillness to the living Absolute. We have, too, in the arching of "gulf on gulf" by the bird a type for the symbolic "inviolate curve" of the seagull's flight that will be used in "To Brooklyn Bridge" as complement to the bridge's own mystic "curveship."

What the protagonist seeks here through fleshly love is not the passion of hot fecundity or the permanence of frozen sterility but their synthesis: the truth that does not die though it has body, "the incarnate word" of stanza four; or the love that burns though it be never consumed, the "fervid covenant" of "Voyages VI."

Then that "pledge" to "clay" is made good in the remainder of the poem as the protagonist knows he can find the "incarnate word" only "in mingling / Mutual blood." The syntax of this poem is, even for Crane, unusually involved and, linked with the typically dense imagery and multiconnotative language, makes difficult and unsure even the approximate paraphrase at best possible with all genuine poetry. We must first understand that

stanza two is the condition preceding the question asked in stanza
three, the two forming one complete sentence:

> All fragrance irrefragibly, and claim
> Madly meeting logically in this hour
> And region that is ours to wreathe again,
> Portending eyes and lips and making told
> The chancel port and portion of our June—

What stanza two posits as a premise to stanza three might be put
as follows: If all this "fragrance" of the sea (of the material world
generally) is "irrefragibly" (undeniably) in its sensible nature a
sign or portent of our flesh—of the "eyes and lips" that are
"Madly meeting logically" as flesh will at this time and in this place
that "is ours to wreathe again," ours to encircle, to have and mark
as our own if only again for an hour . . . if the sea signifies our
mortal love and tells of this holy "port" of meeting like the
"chancel," the sacred place about the altar of our love's "sacrifice"
. . . if the sea comments infallibly in its own carnal "fragrance" on
the limited "portion" of time and pleasure we have in this brief
"June" of our lives, then:

> Shall they not stem and close in our own steps
> Bright staves of flowers and quills to-day as I
> Must first be lost in fatal tides to tell?

If the sea sanctions our love, shall not our "eyes and lips," the
protagonist concludes, "stem," drive into, the tide of love's sea
"to-day" and "close," cast and fold behind us "in our own steps,"
as in the wake of a ship, the "bright" evidence of our love like
"staves of flowers" tossed from the ship's stern? Or let us in our
flight across the latitudes of love, the speaker urges, like the bird
whose migration parallels the range of the sea, the range of our
love, leave "quills," lovely remnant feathers of our love as we fly
across gulfs and span the "spectrum" of love.

They must enter the sea's sensuality, the protagonist is saying,
even if that consummation brings death, in order to find "The
secret oar and petals of all love"—"Must first be lost in fatal tides
to tell."

In signature of the incarnate word
The harbor shoulders to resign in mingling
Mutual blood, transpiring as foreknown
And widening noon within your breast for gathering
All bright insinuations that my years have caught
For islands where must lead inviolably
Blue latitudes and levels of your eyes,—

In this expectant, still exclaim receive
The secret oar and petals of all love.

Like stanzas two and three, the last two stanzas constitute to-
gether one sentence. Stanza four, like stanza two, is a complex of
conditions premising the statement of the poem's last line. The
rationale for receiving "The secret oar and petals of all love" is
given in stanza four where the speaker tells the lover why, how, he
is to understand his "expectant, still exclaim," his hopeful, word-
less proclamation of love's "secret." It is "In signature," in the
name of the "incarnate word" of love and flesh that they have
found replicated in the sea, that the meaning of love is to be
known. "The harbor shoulders" the "incarnate word"; it holds
the ship that carries the lovers who incarnate the word and that
has now come to "port" as we were obliquely told in stanza two.
The "incarnate word" can only be rewritten if the lovers "resign"
(pun?), yield themselves to "mingling / Mutual blood" in the
physical communion of love, which, to the understanding of the
protagonist at this point, is its only name. The protagonist has not
yet fully comprehended that his carnal love, like the "lust" of
"Possessions," will break; but as in "Possessions," it will be the
medium to a better and no less incarnate love. And so he avers
that lovers must make their separate blood one if the mystery of
love is to be discovered.

The protagonist, whose proposition is more elaborately
reasoned than that made in "To His Coy Mistress," argues
further. This love is already "transpiring" as it was "foreknown,"
and it will be "widening noon within your breast," he explains to
his lover: will fill him with felicitous light. This enlightenment in
turn will suit the lover for "gathering / All bright insinuations that
my years have caught," will enable the lover to comprehend who

his beloved is with all the subtle, precious wisdom he has accumu-
lated through the years. But these glimpses of truth, these "bright
insinuations," it must be known, have always been as "islands"
leading "inviolably" to his beloved, the implicit destination of the
voyage of the protagonist's life. For any hints the speaker had
ever had of happiness or love were as "islands" upon the horizon
to the ultimate expanse in the "Blue latitudes and levels of your
eyes."

In that spirit, then, knowing that their love must be consum-
mated as the "signature" of all love, the speaker offers to share
with his lover "The secret oar and petals of all love" — one of the
"silent answers" Melville knew. The image of the "oar" might, as
R.W.B. Lewis believes, be phallic.[10] But whether it is or not, it also
appears as a sign, unexplainable in itself, but held forth as a
cabalistic key to inexplicable truth — like the cryptic symbols of
unsearchable knowledge we find in tombs and temples. Perhaps
Crane used the figure of an "oar" to suggest that love has the
power to propel or impel the lover to the consummate vision.
"Petals" is a similarly cryptic but pregnant sign of love's beauty
and rareness, which also adds to the minor floral motif of "Voy-
ages." We need not find anything more specific or literal in its
symbology than we do in the "oar."

"Voyages IV," likely the most difficult poem of *White Buildings*
and certainly of this movement, completes the second sequence
of the movement by repeating the themes of "II" and "III": that
the sea, in its motions and expanse, is the paradigm of love and
that by immersion in the sea of love we come to the apprehension
of what the "secret oar" stands for. It differs from "II" and "III"
in that there is no mention of the cruelty, the death, the sea holds.
It is as though that inevitability were forgotten in the urgency to
"Madly" meet one more time before being "overtaken" by time in
"Voyages V."

The scene of "Voyages V" is off a northern shore at the mouth
of a harbor, the literal end of the journey over water if not the end
of the spiritual voyage of the poem. "Voyages V" marks the
realization by the protagonist that the sea has only too faithfully

---

[10]Lewis, p. 168.

foretold the mortality of his love in its windings, and that his prayer that "paradise" be envisioned if even in "the vortex of our grave" will now be more cruelly answered than he had been able until now to comprehend, though he had foreseen it. "Voyages V" marks the death of the carnal love he had idolized and rationalized as the perfect expression of the same ontological wisdom spoken by the sea. It is not that the love is now to be repudiated because it has ended since it is only through its passion, thwarted joy, and the almost unbearable sadness it brings that the "Belle Isle" he thought he had found in his sexual affair is found beyond it. This love affair is not the answer, but it is the material out of which the answer is transmuted, itself not so much destroyed or transcended as transubstantiated in the process.

Stanza one establishes the scene and time:

> Meticulous, past midnight in clear rime,
> Infrangible and lonely, smooth as though cast
> Together in one merciless white blade —
> The bay estuaries fleck the hard sky limits.

The "estuaries," where the harbor waters meet the sea, are as "Meticulous," as "Infrangible" and smooth in their flowing together, as the inviolable edge of "one merciless white blade." The word "Infrangible" suggests a healing of dividedness, but the image of a knife ironically contradicts this. For there is a last dramatic intensification of opposites as the poem approaches the resolution of its conflict. And in this hour "past midnight" but not yet dawn, these knifelike waters seem to cut or mark, to "fleck," the horizon, which is as "hard" as they are "lonely." This is the time of "clear rime" — by the logic of the pathetic fallacy employed here and throughout "Voyages," the time of cold and hard and "merciless" clarity of understanding. But it is not the "time of sundering" experienced in the "lover's death" of "Stark Major" in the first movement of *White Buildings* where the protagonist ends seeing only "doors and stone with broken eyes." This broken love will yield quite another vision.

The inexorable advance of time against love is the subject of the next two stanzas. " — As if too brittle or too clear to touch!" the protagonist says of their night of love, which has been shattered, sullied by the finger of time. And there is a sense of severance in the image of their sleep as "cables . . . so swiftly filed," hanging now as "shred ends," cut off from the love now as distant as a dream or as "remembered stars." "One frozen trackless smile" he sees the moon to be, so different from the warmly indulgent smile of Helen and the all-bequeathing "target smile" of Dionysius seen previously in *White Buildings*. And redolent of the same experience of love's betrayal by time in *Romeo and Juliet*, the speaker pleads, "What words / Can strangle this deaf moonlight?" Then, by splitting the next sentence between stanzas two and three, Crane communicates with great poignancy the protagonist's final surrender to the brokenness of his love:

> For we
>
> Are overtaken.

The understatement of this pained admission is accentuated by its contrast with the tensed anguish of the statements that bracket it—the impulse to strangle the impervious moon and the lament, "Now no cry, no sword / Can fasten or deflect this tidal wedge, / Slow tyranny of moonlight, moonlight loved / And changed. . . ." This is not the moon that had made love to the sea's "wrapped inflections" of "Voyages II." It is in its "slow tyranny" rather like the "sceptred terror" of the sea, which the protagonist had thought would not rend "the pieties of lovers' hands." No word or "sword" can now beat back this "tidal wedge," itself a cutting edge like the "merciless white blade" of stanza one, from doing its work of severing "lovers' hands."

The response of the protagonist's lover to the situation, also split between stanzas, is anything but poignant—or is poignant by ironic contrast. He seems as "deaf" and insentitive as the moon in his comprehension of the tragedy:

> "There's
>
> Nothing this in the world . . ."

Though the desire and love of the protagonist for his partner appears undiminished, the shallowness of both his partner and his partner's love for the protagonist is unmistakable. Though he too knows they "Are overtaken," the lover seems more interested in observing the growing splendor of a predawn sky than he is affected by its encroachment upon their love. There is even a trace of emotional hardness in the protagonist's partner standing at the porthole, as the speaker says it, "knowing I cannot touch your hand and look / Too, into that godless cleft of sky / Where nothing turns but dead sands flashing." The speaker's partner does not see the impending severance written in the "cleft of the sky," which to him is not at all "godless" and "dead" as it is to the grieving protagonist. The first line of the next stanza confirms our doubt that this paramour was ever as desperately committed to the protagonist as the protagonist to him: " — And never to quite understand!" The comment seems to be about the mystery of nature he is observing in the sky, but the protagonist hears it in the bitterly ironic but almost comic, double sense unintended, of course, by his partner.

Not only does the lover not "quite understand" what the protagonist is feeling, but the protagonist had not understood either — even though he saw it predicted in the cruelty of the sea — that it would be this hard and apparently pointless: "No, / In all the argosy of your bright hair I dreamed / Nothing so flagless as this piracy." The nautical conceit maintained throughout "Voyages" is here evident in the terms "argosy," "flagless," and "piracy"; but the word "flagless" is particularly rich in suggestiveness. Pirate ships, as renegade vessels belonging to no nation or fleet, would be "flagless," but this "piracy" is "flagless" in the sense that it bears no insignia of meaning — no explanation of its purpose. If the protagonist forgot in "Voyages IV" that "The bottom of the sea is cruel" as he rushed to seize that "hour" of love, he has here in his utter sorrow forgotten what he knew in "Voyages III," that "death, if shed / Presumes no carnage." And just as the death of which he had had prescience before it came was more "godless" than he had anticipated, the rebirth he has yet to experience will be more marvelous. He does not remember or know yet that this harbor of death's demise is also the "harbor of the phoenix breast" ("VI") where his love will rise newer and brighter from the ashes.

Nor is he ready for the transformation though he now has full awareness of his love's end. In the last stanza, pathetically, he prefers to take the last few moments they have to love:

> But now
> Draw in your head, alone and too tall here.
> Your eyes already in the slant of drifting foam;
> Your breath sealed by the ghosts I do not know:
> Draw in your head and sleep the long way home.

The unaffected lover is content to be "alone" and "too tall," too removed, from the speaker. For, unbound by the present and undisturbed by transience, he "already" looks to the future in "the slant of drifting foam." And "already" he has had enough of conversation, of revealing himself, his "breath sealed by the ghosts I do not know." His "breast" has not been at all "widened" to receive all those "bright insinuations" of the protagonist's life, which in "Voyages IV" the protagonist thought would be the issue of their love's communion. Still the speaker calls him to his side in the last line.

"No one has ever begun to really appreciate life, or lived, until he has recognized the background of life as essentially Tragedy."[11] These words, paraphrasing Samuel Butler, author of *The Way of All Flesh*, are spoken by Crane as though his own. But one could not from this comment deduce the nobility and magnanimity of Crane's attitude toward personal tragedy. In "Voyages V," despite the agonizing recognition that the destruction of his love is as much a result of his partner's insensitivity and insecurity as it is of time's erosion, there is no trace of bitterness in the speaker's voice.

Crane's life and letters give us fuller insight into the poet's response to betrayal and pain. In his tortured anger over the many crippling hurts he had received from his parents and their unending feud, of which he himself once said he was the "bloody battleground,"[12] Crane often did compulsively give vent to his insufferable anguish in vicious counterattacks of his father first, then later of his mother, and then, increasingly toward the end of

[11]*Letters*, p. 99.
[12]*Letters*, p. 18.

his life, retaliating against just about anyone. But in the center of his being, as in the eye of a hurricane, he always cherished the value of forgiveness and never extolled vengeance as a desirable thing. He repeatedly expressed this attitude, significantly enough, most directly to his mother:

> I have a revived confidence in humanity lately, and things are going to come very beautifully for me—and not after so very long, I think. The great thing is to Live and NOT Hate (3/23/24).[13]

> Remember, that suffering does, if borne without rancour, it does build something that only grows lovelier with time—and it is a kind of kingdom among those *initiated,* a kingdom that has the widest kind of communion (3/29/26).[14]

> Anger is a costly luxury to you—and resentment and constant self-pity, I have to fight these demons myself. I know they are demons—they never do me anything but harm. Why look at yourself as a martyr all the time! It simply drives people away from you. The only real martyrs the world ever worships are those devoted exclusively to the worship of God, poverty and suffering—you have, as yet, never been in exactly that position. Not that I want you to be a martyr. I see no reason for it—and am out of sympathy with anyone who thinks he is—for the *real* ones don't think about themselves that way—they are too happy in their faith to ever want to be otherwise (12/22/26).[15]

This is the "faith" the poet is granted in "Voyages VI," a faith both born of and bearing the unconditional love given through suffering at the end of "Voyages V."

"Only dare to be tragic men; for you are to be redeemed," Nietzsche says.[16] But we cannot look to Nietzsche's explanation of tragic regeneration as the source for or equivalent to Crane's explanation. For Nietzsche, the "metaphysical comfort" of Apollonian vision derives almost automatically from the Dionysian fall, "Necessary effects of a glance into the inside and terrors of nature; as it were, luminous spots to cure the eyes damaged by

---

[13]*Letters,* p. 180.
[14]*Letters,* p. 243.
[15]*Letters,* pp. 280–81.
[16]Nietzsche, p. 124.

gruesome night."[17] There is no talk in *The Birth of Tragedy* of love or forgiveness as the answer to calamity and sorrow. Here Crane parts company with the passionate philosopher who, we have seen, so profoundly affected in other ways his sensitivities and even his metaphors.

Nor will the metaphysics of Ouspensky in finding noumenal, transcendent love as analogous to but above and beyond phenomenal, human love provide an origin for or analogue to the meaning of "Voyages." Crane would not have said with Ouspensky, "Love in relation to our life is a deity, sometimes benevolent," which "mercilessly revenges itself upon those little mortals who would subordinate *God* to themselves and make Him serve them."[18] Though Crane would agree that God or Love should never be subordinated, the closer Crane came to God or "Love" in his poetry, the more mercy he always found, from the trust that "Vibrant reprieve and pardon thou dost show" in the "Proem" to the propitiating prayer of "Atlantis" in *The Bridge*: "Unspeakable Thou Bridge to Thee, O Love. / Thy pardon for this history, whitest Flower, O Answerer of all. . . ." We are not likely to find any strong analogy for Crane's response to tragedy in any of the major sources of or influences upon his poetry discussed in this study (excluding Gerard Manley Hopkins, who is not treated here as a major *influence*).

The protagonist of "Voyages" has passed through a carnal love, dashed by time and indifference as the sea said it would be, but he has not passed beyond human love or the "incarnate word" that he mistook that carnal love to be in "Voyages IV." As I have certainly often enough said, that carnal love, or the need for communion that impelled it, is transmuted. In a letter to Waldo Frank written at the time when Crane was in the midst of the affair out of which "Voyages" came, one can discern both the idea and the figures of the poem already forming: "I think the sea has thrown itself upon me and been answered, at least in part, and I believe I am a little changed — not essentially, but changed and transubstantiated as anyone is who has asked a question and been

[17]Nietzsche, p. 17.
[18]Ouspensky, p. 151.

answered."[19] This is, as far as I know, the only time Crane uses the word I have been using so frequently, "transubstantiated." Since this statement was made before the final severance of his relationship with the sailor, the transubstantiation is understandably still "in part," "a little." But this prose statement, like the poetic statements of "Voyages II," "III," and "IV," does not anticipate the "essential" change that occurs in "Voyages VI," where the "question" is "answered" consummately through tragedy in the "unbetrayable reply."

The physical circumstances in "Voyages VI" are still the same as in "Voyages V," but a metamorphosis is about to happen:

> Where icy and bright dungeons lift
> Of swimmers their lost morning eyes,
> And ocean rivers, churning, shift
> Green borders under stronger skies,

The description in this first stanza is little different from that of the first stanza of the previous section. This is the subarctic region of "Belle Isle"—an island (as well as a strait) between Newfoundland and Labrador, Canada, at the entrance to the St. Lawrence harbor on the Atlantic coast. The "voyage," we recall, originated somewhere near San Salvador, which is part of the Bahamian chain, and it has covered the "spectrum" from "poinsettia meadows" to these "Green borders under stranger skies." The protagonist as yet still feels only the "carnage" of his tragedy, and does not yet hear "The silken skilled transmemberment of song" foretold in "Voyages III." So this is the place of "icy and bright dungeons" whose frozen formations suggest bondage rather than the "azure steeps" of freedom known by Melville's "fabulous shadow." And those whose "eyes" are "lifted" by the frigid forms gleaming in the "morning" light (with a probable pun on "mourning") are "lost" like "swimmers," like the speaker himself, in "ocean rivers, churning." The sea is seen again as it was in "Voyages II" as the replica of time's constant "shift." But there is hope and meaning beneath these "stranger skies," which is revealed

---

[19]*Letters,* p. 182.

first obliquely, as an aspiration rather than an affirmation, through the next few stanzas.

> Steadily as a shell secretes
> Its beating leagues of monotone,
> Or as many waters trough the sun's
> Red kelson past the cape's wet stone;
>
> O rivers mingling toward the sky
> And harbor of the phoenix' breast—
> My eyes pressed black against the prow,
> —Thy derelict and blinded guest

The protagonist's first reaction to his sorrow is to stare with "eyes pressed black against the prow," as the wrecked and uncomprehending "guest" of this alien port. Though he seems not to fully understand that, as the "harbor of the phoenix' breast," this bay of his ruination is also the haven of his rebirth, there is beneath his blank gaze a transformation in process. For he sees as "steadily" as the seashell secretes its pulsing sound. (In my treatment of "The Wine Menagerie" the case was made for shells signifying in Crane's poetry omens of higher wisdom and consciousness. And even in this movement, this metaphor is anticipated in "At Melville's Tomb" with "The portent wound in corridors of shells.") With the constant "beating leagues" of the shell's voice, the speaker's vision shares also its "monotone" or quality of singleness. Linked with the steadiness of the speaker's glare, this singularity of focus, though as yet seeing nothing, seems to provide the basis for the answer to the unsteady and divided experience he has just had. We have seen this oneness of vision wrought out of the brokenness, duality, and impermanence of life throughout *White Buildings*, especially in "Recitative" and "Faustus and Helen"; and it is a major aspect of *The Bridge* in its central symbol's synthesizing power as "Unfractioned idiom" ("Proem") and "One arc synoptic of all tides below" ("Atlantis"). These blinded eyes are being healed to wholeness—to the single vision of the "mariner" told in the "Monody" of "At Melville's Tomb."

These eyes are also as constant as the "waters" that channel ("trough") the sun as it moves in its burning arc ("Red kelson") across the "cape's wet stone" (presumably Cape Bauld just southeast of Belle Isle). The adverb "steadily" describes both the secreting of the shell and the troughing of the sun. Along with the arch image (again, the unmistakable sign of unity in Crane's poetry) in the comparison of the sun's motion to the "kelson" or keellike structure reinforcing the hull of a ship, we have another figure of the integration of the persona's consciousness, which is beginning to apprehend an immutable truth at the core of his tragedy.

In stanza three, the protagonist begins his supplicatory prayer, which so often in Crane's poetry precedes the visionary transfiguration. He prays to the "rivers" or estuary currents, which in their "mingling toward the sky" signify synthesis while they recall the "mingling / Mutual blood" the protagonist mistook for the final synthesis of the "incarnate word" in "Voyages IV." He prays to them for what they point to in their flow: the "harbor of the phoenix' breast," the renewal of his spirit from the embers of his burned-out love.

What he asks of these "rivers" is contained in stanza four:

> Waiting, afire, what name, unspoke,
> I cannot claim: let thy waves rear
> More savage than the death of kings,
> Some splintered garland for the seer.

The fire imagery, merely kindling in the metaphor of the "sun's / Red kelson" and in the "phoenix' breast," bursts into full flame in the picture of the protagonist "Waiting afire" for the "name" he cannot speak or "claim"—again, the unpronounceable word. Though changeless and undivided, the vision gained will not be static or frigid, as is this frozen coast. We have repeatedly observed and considered that in such poems as "North Labrador" and "Paraphrase" arctic absoluteness, though a sign and indicator of the permanence desired, in its sterility and stasis is *not* the Ideal sought. Love does stretch to the "Chilled albatross's white immutability"; but unless its frigid whiteness turn hot and its immutability be dynamic, it is not the "voltage of blown blood and vine" we find in "For the Marriage of Faustus and Helen"—ever charged with, ever generating life though itself unchanging and undiminished, like the Brooklyn Bridge whose vibrant dynamics have, as the poet apostrophizes it, "Some motion ever unspent in thy stride" ("Proem"). The blessed truth the speaker finds must be burning in its cold immutability, as the "fervid covenant" of "Belle Isle."

Like the protagonist of "Possessions" who seeks to have "the white wind rase / All but bright stones wherein our smiling plays," the speaker of this poem asks the "waves" to "rear" in a manner as "savage," as dire, as nature convulsing (according to lore) at the "death of kings"—for this death is as momentous. And the sympathetic convulsion of the seas must produce something—"Some splintered garland for the seer"—some prize or compensation, even if itself as shattered as the speaker's heart. But, exceeding the expectation of the supplicant, the garland he receives will not be "splintered" but whole, unbroken in its floral circle as the "petalled word" of stanza six. In nautical language, a "garland" is a woven ring of rope used as a gasket. In view of the consistent floral and nautical imagery of this movement, including its introductory poem, I think Crane intended both kinds of garlands, of rope and flowers, to be represented by the term that suggests once again the circular oneness of vision found in and through contrary and fractured experience.

The last four stanzas unfold the vision only sensed as innuendos and petitioned for in the first four. Once again, in stanza five, the protagonist "instresses" the scene, "Belle Isle." "Beyond siroccos harvesting / The solstice thunders": he is beyond the hot winds of the West Indies from which he has come and which at the time of the winter "solstice" (the apparent time of the journey's start in the Caribbean) "harvest" of "thunders" the violent, heavy rains of that region rather than the "bright dungeons" precipitated here. But the synthesis of tropic and arctic opposition, of dying passion and the passionless absolute, is now to be known in "Belle Isle"—"crept away, / Like a cliff swinging or a sail / Flung into April's inmost day." "Belle Isle" is not the turbulent place of "solstice thunders"—whether of December or June—but the serene balance of "April's inmost day." This "beautiful island" floats by like a "sail" to carry the protagonist the last part of his voyage. Like San Salvador in the south, Belle Isle is well known by mariners as the first land visible to a vessel crossing the

Atlantic at that northern latitude. We learn more particularly in
stanza six what she represents:

> Creation's blithe and petalled word
> To the lounged goddess when she rose
> Conceding dialogue with eyes
> That smile unsearchable repose —

"Belle Isle," as the essence of the "word" sought, is first creative;
like the words of Genesis, she brings into being. And this genera-
tive, "petalled word" (the true fulfillment of the "petals of all love"
looked for first in the carnal love of "Voyages IV") is spoken to a
"lounged goddess."

The "goddess" referred to here is probably Aphrodite or
Venus who was born of the sea foam gathering about the genitals
of Cronos, castrated by his son Uranus who then threw his
father's severed parts into the sea. The origin of Aphrodite is a
fitting complement to a poem in which ideal love derives from
merely genital love. As the patroness of erotic love as well as an
immortal goddess, Aphrodite is herself a kind of synthesis of
carnal and supernal beauty, and in mythology she is always imag-
ined as tranquilly and alluringly smiling. Though undying, she
too had to hear "Creation's blithe and petalled word" before she
"rose." And now this apotheosis of love is ever "Conceding
dialogue" with those who seek the "incarnate word" in her
"eyes / That smile unsearchable repose." But before there was
Aphrodite, "lounged" in all her earthly/heavenly beauty upon the
shell that bore her, there was the "Word," "Belle Isle," which gave
her body. The "trackless smile" of the moon over dark, cold
waters has been metamorphosed into this "smile" full of the
"peace that passes understanding."

Crane, as usual, has located perfection incarnated — not in the
body of his faithless lover but in the body of Aphrodite, another
of the "women" Crane uses to embody divine goodness from
"Helen" to "Powhatan's Daughter." And "Belle Isle" is no lifeless
abstraction of beauty or permanence but "blithe" rather than
motionless in its absoluteness. "Belle Isle" represents the holy
truth the protagonist has internalized and made his own so that
he himself is the incarnation of its blessedness. In his sacrificial

death, he has been, liked the "lounged goddess," created, born
again to a better, a purer, a more enduring goodness than that in
which he had hoped. But he has not transcended the "body of the
world" anymore than he did in "For the Marriage of Faustus and
Helen." His "body," his person, has been divinized, transubstan-
tiated by the "imaged Word" he now possesses. L.H. Dembo saw
the same process in *The Bridge* as a movement "beyond tragedy to
a knowledge of divinity."[20] And R.W.B. Lewis interprets "Voy-
ages VI" as "a process of poetic transubstantiation" in which
"once, again, Crane is redeeming, as it were perfecting, the actual
world by the resources of poetry."[21]

The last two stanzas celebrate in litany the faithfulness and
constancy of what the protagonist has found through the faith-
lessness and inconstancy of dashed desire.

> Still fervid covenant, Belle Isle,
> —Unfolded floating dais before
> Which rainbows twine continual hair—
> Belle Isle, white echo of the oar!
>
> The imaged Word, it is, that holds
> Hushed willows anchored in its glow.
> It is the unbetrayable reply
> Whose accent no farewell can know.

The concept of "covenant" as a "fervid," ever ardent bond be-
tween this fallen son and "Creation's . . . word," is complemented
by the image of the "rainbows," which "twine continual hair" of
beauty and testament across the Strait of Belle Isle. Aside from
being another arch or bridge image signifying unification and
reconciliation, the rainbow might also be understood, in its situa-
tion at the entrance to the great St. Lawrence waterway, as
perhaps another form of "spiritual gates." And the rainbow is one
of the most prominent symbols in Scripture of God's covenant
with his people given to Noah after the deluge. It is Yahweh's
promise that never again would such calamity, such death by
water, be visited upon the sons of men: "I do set my bow in the

[20]Dembo, *Hart Crane's Sanskrit Charge*. p. 18.
[21]Lewis, p. 177.

cloud, and it shall be for a token of a covenant between me and earth" (Genesis 9:13). Richard H. Rupp finds here the same meaning in the rainbow, calling it "the Christian archetype of redemption."[22] Neither will the protagonist be so destroyed again, for he has found in "Belle Isle" the palpable word of the "secret oar" heard now as the "white echo of the oar."

The figure of the "word," as both the incarnation and the medium of blessedness used implicitly and explicitly throughout "Voyages" (and throughout Crane's poetry), is most manifest through these later stanzas of "Voyages VI," leading to the proclamation of "Belle Isle" as "The imaged Word" in the last stanza. And this vital emblem offers in the context of this poem something akin to what the Eternal Word offers believers in the Christian tradition. For like the Word made Flesh—to which this figure of the "imaged Word" surely alludes, as did the "incarnate word" of "Voyages IV"—"Belle Isle" abides with humankind as "the way, the truth, and the life" (John 14:6). This "Word" is as a rock in its solidarity but utterly alive in its dynamism, in "its glow," which "holds / Hushed willows anchored"; and it speaks to the betrayed no "farewell" but the "unbetrayable reply" of absolute fidelity.

As an "Unfolded floating dais," "Belle Isle" might be seen as the altar of sacrifice—one of the "lifted altars" of "At Melville's Tomb"—a table of divine communion. And so, "This cleaving and this burning" of "Voyages"—of all of *White Buildings*—ends on this "Hushed" note of "repose," answering in flawless pitch and cadence the call of "Legend" for "a perfect cry" of "constant harmony." This is "The imaged Word," the "bright logic," "won" through immolation to the "Imploring flame." It is the "Bleeding eidolon" transmuted from flesh and found tangible, incarnate, in "Belle Isle."

"Voyages," true to its function as "coda" to *White Buildings*, is unique also in that it does not alternate strongly from part to part in either its tempo or mood, as we have seen *White Buildings* generally does through "For the Marriage of Faustus and Helen." "Voyages VI" keeps the same melancholy, "monodic" tone set in

---

[22] "Hart Crane: Vitality as *Credo* in 'Atlantis,' " *The Midwest Quarterly*, 3 (1962), 269.

"At Melville's Tomb" and sustained until the last two stanzas, which, though the breakthrough is made, is less an alleluia or hosanna (as is "Atlantis") than it is a deeply felt and quietly spoken, almost sighed, prayer of gratitude. It is both a curious and satisfying conclusion to this book given to an often fervent search for, and sometimes high-pitched proclamation of, "The imaged Word."

VII

Conclusion

White Buildings is a book of religious verse, even though not every poem in the collection is explicitly concerned with God or man's relationship to a personal God. What I have striven to show in this interpretation is that all of the collection's poems possess a psalmic quality as contemplations, praises, or celebrations of — prayers to or lamentations over the loss of — a worshipful ideal, often reflecting the character of a personal divinity. I have further sought to exhibit that Crane's faith as a poet is not in a purely transcendent or abstract ideality, but in a beauty, unity, trust and love — a permanence — incarnated paradoxically within the impermanent; and that through sacrificial immolation and a radical transformation of the perception of the poet, this Ideal is transubstantiated from the often unlovely, fragmented, and suffering life of humankind. Although no critic I have read corroborates fully or precisely this thesis, R.W.B. Lewis comes closest: "The effect of that art is, in the poetic sense, to redeem the fallen world; not, finally to transcend and abandon it, but . . . to find the means of praising it; in one of the oldest and greatest of theological formulae, not to destroy but to perfect it."[1]

The focus of this study has been the religious theme of *White Buildings*, but it has been a crucial aspect of my thesis to point out

[1]Lewis, p. 102.

that *The Bridge* and all of Crane's poetry is informed by the same basically holy vision. It has also been integral to my purpose to demonstrate a thematic unity and structural design in *White Buildings* analogous to the integrity and cyclic structure of *The Bridge*.

I did not ever find Crane's poems easy to explain and occasionally found phrases and passages impossible to explicate with certainty; but I hope this study has added to the growing testimony that Crane is not an obscurant—deliberate or otherwise—and that he is concerned in his poetry with conveying valid and basic truths; or to use Crane's own words in a letter to his father, that his poetry is "simply a communication between man and man, a bond of understanding and human enlightenment—which is what a real work of art *is*."[2]

Crane searched ardently through the disintegration and corruption of ordinary experience for a healing and saving power, which spoke to him most eloquently as Love, intimate and merciful. The "bright logic" within the "Imploring flame" of "Legend" is actualized in various forms throughout *White Buildings* but most poignantly as love—as it is transmuted from lust as the "pure possession" in "Possessions," or touched in Helen's "white wafer cheek of love" in "For the Marriage of Faustus and Helen," or held as the "petals of all love" in "Voyages." And in *The Bridge* this vision, so palpable in the body of Pocahontas, is hailed at its beginning as the "Prayer of pariah and the lover's cry" and at its end is simply adored as "O Love." A passage from Dante's *Divine Comedy* copied by Crane into a notebook would serve well as a schema to Crane's poetry as it reaches for God—for the mending, unifying, beatifying "smile" of Love:

> O grace abounding, wherein I presumed to fix my look on the eternal light so long that I consumed my sight thereon! Within its depths I saw ingathered, bound by love in one volume, the scattered leaves of all the universe; substance and accidents and their relations, as though together fused, after such fashion that what I tell is of one simple flame. The universal form of this complex I

[2]*Letters*, p. 170.

think that I beheld, because more largely, as I say this, I feel that I rejoice.[3]

Allen Tate agrees that "The impulse in *The Bridge* is religious," but adds that "the soundness of an impulse is no warrant that it will create a sound art form."[4] I have undertaken in this study to illustrate the "soundness," the integrity, of both the "impulse" and the "form" of *White Buildings* and, by analogy and extension, of *The Bridge*.

In discussing Crane's poetry in certain aspects of his vision and diction as kindred to biblical or Christian ideas, images, and expressions, I did not intend to make a case for Crane's incipient or latent Christianity. These similarities were noted because they are there and worthy of note as insights into Crane's, into humankind's, pursuit of truth and beauty and the meaning of existence — which is the point of our study of literature. Crane, in fact, cannot be facilely grouped with more orthodoxly religious poets, despite his sharing of their "faith" in and fervor toward divinity. As M.D. Uroff so aptly puts it, "Unlike traditional poets, Crane did not have the assuring belief in God's presence, the sense of reciprocity between the human and the divine."[5] But it would be a mistake to conclude that Crane never experienced God. Like John Donne, though Crane did not share his professed certainty of faith in a revealed God, he groped for God and did, in "epiphanies," find him in "that flesh which was worn / By God," to use Donne's words. Crane's poems are the record of that search and of the moments of personal revelation he was granted.

Samuel Hazo reads *The Bridge* as "a poem of pilgrimage,"[6] which is a valid characterization of *White Buildings* as well: a never-ending pilgrimage to a Holy City that is never entered but with consummate visions of the holy, real glimpses of God, found through pain and in a myriad of earthly things along the way. In a

---

[3]Horton, pp. 269–70.
[4]"Hart Crane," *The Merrill Studies in "The Bridge"* ed. David R. Clark (Columbus, Ohio: Charles E. Merrill Publishing Co., 1970), p. 32.
[5]Uroff, p. 13.
[6]Hazo, p. 118.

letter to a friend, Crane says something about living that applies
with equal truth to his poetry:

> I feel very much at peace with experience, so-called, which at
> present I feel inclined to believe, is the effort to describe God. Only
> the effort,—limitless and yet forever incomplete.[7]

[7]Unterecker, *Voyages,* p. 362. This letter to Jean Toomer is not included in the
collected *Letters.*

Selected Bibliography

Andreach, Robert J. *Studies in Structure*. New York: Fordham University Press, 1964.

Arpad, Joseph J. "Hart Crane's Platonic Myth: The Brooklyn Bridge." *American Literature*, 39 (1967), 75–86.

Bartra, Augustí. "New York: Two Poetic Impressions." *Américas*, 18 (1966), 14–22.

Beach, Joseph Warren. "Hart Crane and *Moby Dick*." *Western Review*, 20 (1956), 183–96.

Bewley, Marius. "Hart Crane's Last Poem." *Accent*, 19 (1959), 75–85.

Blackmur, R. P. *The Double Agent: Essays in Craft and Elucidation*. Gloucester, Massachusetts: Peter Smith, 1962.

Blake, William. *Blake: Complete Writings with Variant Readings*, ed. Geoffrey Keynes. London: Oxford University Press, 1972.

Brown, Susan Jenkins. *Robber Rocks: Letters and Memories of Hart Crane, 1923–1932*. Middletown, Connecticut: Wesleyan University Press, 1969.

Cargill, Oscar. *Intellectual America: Ideas on the March*. New York: Cooper Square Publishers, Inc., 1968.

Coffman, Stanley K., Jr. "Symbolism in *The Bridge*." *PMLA*, 66 (1951), 65–77.

Colum, Padraic. *Myths of the World*. New York: Grosset and Dunlap, 1972.

189

Cowley, Malcolm. "A Preface to Hart Crane." *New Republic,* 62 (April 23, 1930), 276–77.

Crane, Hart. *The Complete Poems and Selected Letters and Prose of Hart Crane,* ed. Brom Weber. New York: Liveright Publishing Corp., 1966.

_____. *The Letters of Hart Crane, 1916–1932,* ed. Brom Weber. Berkeley: University of California Press, 1965.

_____. Notebook P.S. 0642, The Hart Crane Collection. New York: Rare Book and Manuscript Library, Columbia University.

Dembo, L. S. *Conceptions of Reality in Modern American Poetry.* Berkeley and Los Angeles: University of California Press, 1966.

_____. *Hart Crane's Sanscrit Charge: A Study of "The Bridge."* Ithaca, New York: Cornell University Press, 1960.

_____. "Hart Crane's 'Verticalist' Poem." *American Literature,* 40 (1968), 77–81.

Deutsch, Babette. *Poetry in Our Time.* New York: Henry Holt and Co., 1952.

Eliot, T. S. *Selected Essays.* New York: Harcourt, Brace and World, Inc., 1960.

Fowlie, Wallace. *Love in Literature: Studies in Symbolic Expression.* Bloomington, Indiana: Indiana University Press, 1965.

Frank, Waldo. *Our America.* New York: Boni and Liveright, Inc., 1919.

_____. "The Poetry of Hart Crane." *New Republic,* 50 (March 16, 1927), 116–17.

Gregory, Horace. "Far Beyond Our Consciousness." *The Merrill Studies in "The Bridge,"* ed. David R. Clark. Columbus, Ohio: Charles E. Merrill Publishing Co., 1970.

_____ and Marya Zaturenska. *A History of American Poetry: 1900–1940.* New York: Harcourt, Brace and Co., 1946.

Grigsby, Gordon K. "Hart Crane's Doubtful Vision." *College English,* 24 (1963), 518–23.

Gross, Harvey. *Sound and Form in Modern Poetry.* Ann Arbor: University of Michigan Press, 1965.

Hazo, Samuel. *Hart Crane: An Introduction and Interpretation.* New York: Barnes and Noble, Inc., 1963.

Herman, Barbara. "The Language of Hart Crane." *Sewanee Review*, 58 (1950), 52–67.

Hoffman, Frederick J. *The Twenties: American Writing in the Postwar Decade.* New York: The Viking Press, 1955.

Hopkins, Gerard Manley. *Poems and Prose of Gerard Manley Hopkins*, ed. W.H. Gardner. Baltimore: Penguin Books, 1953.

Horton, Philip. *Hart Crane: The Life of an American Poet.* New York: W.W. Norton and Co., Inc., 1937.

Ignatius of Loyola, St. *The Spiritual Exercises of St. Ignatius: A New Translation Based on Studies in the Language of the Autograph,* trans. Louis J. Puhl, S. J. Westminster, Maryland: The Newman Press, 1959.

Jennings, Elizabeth. *Every Changing Shape.* Philadelphia: Dufour Editions, 1962.

Joyce, James, *Critical Writings of James Joyce,* ed. Ellsworth Mason and Richard Ellman. New York: Viking Press, 1966.

Kramer, Maurice. "Hart Crane's 'Reflexes.' " *Twentieth Century Literature,* 13 (1967), 131–38.

Landry, Hilton. "Of Prayer and Praise: The Poetry of Hart Crane." *The Twenties: Poetry and Prose,* ed. Richard E. Langford and William E. Taylor. Deland, Florida: Everett/Edwards, Inc., 1966.

Leibowitz, Herbert A. *Hart Crane: An Introduction to the Poetry.* New York: Columbia University Press, 1968.

Lewis, R.W.B. *The Poetry of Hart Crane: A Critical Study.* Princeton, New Jersey: Princeton University Press, 1967.

Lohf, Kenneth A. "The Library of Hart Crane." *Proof,* 3 (1973), 283–34.

Lyon, Melvin E. "Crane's 'The Mango Tree.' " *Explicator,* 25 (1967), Item 48.

Metzger, Deena Posy. "Hart Crane's Bridge: The Myth Active." *Arizona Quarterly,* 20 (1964), 36–46.

Miller, James E. "The Poetics of the Cosmic Poem." *Start with the Sun: Studies in Cosmic Poetry,* with Karl Shapiro and Bernice Slote. Lincoln, Nebraska: University of Nebraska Press, 1960.

Morgan, H. Wayne. *Writers in Transition: Seven Americans.* New York: Hill and Wang, 1963.

Munson, Gorham. *Destinations: A Canvass of American Literature Since 1900.* New York: J. H. Sears, 1928.

Nietzsche, Friedrich Wilhelm. *Basic Writings of Nietzsche,* trans., ed. Walter Kaufmann. New York: The Modern Library, 1968.

O'Connor, William Van. *Sense and Sensibility in Modern Poetry.* New York: Barnes and Noble, Inc., 1964.

Ouspensky, P.D. *Tertium Organum: A Key to the Enigmas of the World.* New York: Random House, 1970.

Parkinson, Thomas. "Hart Crane and Ivor Winters: A Meeting of Minds." *Southern Review,* 11 (1975), 491–512.

Paul, Sherman. *Hart's Bridge.* Chicago: University of Illinois Press, 1972.

Pearce, Roy Harvey. *The Continuity of American Poetry.* Princeton, New Jersey: Princeton University Press, 1961.

Perry, Robert L. *The Shared Vision of Waldo Frank and Hart Crane.* Lincoln, Nebraska: University of Nebraska Press, 1966.

Plato. *The Collected Dialogues of Plato, Including the Letters,* ed. Edith Hamilton and Huntington Cairns. Princeton, New Jersey: Princeton University Press, 1961.

Quinn, Sister M. Bernetta. *The Metamorphic Tradition in Modern Poetry.* New Brunswick, New Jersey: Rutgers University Press, 1955.

Quinn, Vincent. *Hart Crane.* New York: Twayne Publishers, Inc., Twayne's United States Authors Series, #35, 1963.

Rago, Henry. "The Vocation of Poetry." *Poetry,* 110 (1967), 328–48.

Richman, Sidney. "Hart Crane's 'Voyages II': An Experiment in Redemption." *Wisconsin Studies in Contemporary Literature,* 3 (1962), 65–78.

Riddel, Joseph. "Hart Crane's Poetics of Failure." *Journal of English Literary History,* 33 (1966), 473–96.

Rimbaud, Arthur. *A Season in Hell* and *The Illuminations,* trans. Rhodes Peschel. New York: Oxford University Press, 1973.

Rupp, Richard H. "Hart Crane: Vitality as *Credo* in 'Atlantis.'" *The Midwest Quarterly,* 3 (1962), 265–75.

Schwartz, Joseph. *Hart Crane: An Annotated Bibliography.* New York: David Lewis, 1970.

Shapiro, Karl. "Study of 'Cape Hatteras' by Hart Crane." *The Merrill Studies in "The Bridge,"* ed. David R. Clark. Columbus, Ohio: Charles E. Merrill Publishing Co., 1970.

Slote, Bernice. "Views of *The Bridge.*" *Start with the Sun: Studies in Cosmic Poetry,* with Karl Shapiro and James E. Miller. Lincoln, Nebraska: University of Nebraska Press, 1960.

———. "Transmutation in Crane's Imagery in *The Bridge.*" *MLN,* 73 (1958), 15–23.

Spears, Monroe K. *Hart Crane.* Minneapolis: University of Minnesota Press, 1965.

Tate, Allen. "Hart Crane." *The Merrill Studies in "The Bridge,"* ed. David R. Clark. Columbus, Ohio: Charles E. Merrill Publishing Co., 1970.

———. *Reactionary Essays on Poetry and Ideas.* Freeport, New York: Books for Libraries Press, 1968.

———. "The Self-made Angel." *New Republic,* 129 (August 31, 1953), 17, 21.

Taylor, Frajam. "Keats and Crane: An Airy Citadel." *Accent,* 8 (1947), 34–40.

Trachtenberg, Allan. "The Shadow of a Myth." *The Merrill Studies in "The Bridge,"* ed. David R. Clark. Columbis, Ohio: Charles E. Merrill Publishing Co., 1970.

Unterecker, John. "The Architecture of *The Bridge.*" *The Merrill Studies in "The Bridge,"* ed. David R. Clark. Columbus, Ohio: Charles E. Merrill Publishing Co., 1970.

———. *Voyager: A Life of Hart Crane.* New York: Farrar, Straus and Giroux, 1969.

Uroff, M. D. *Hart Crane: The Patterns of His Poetry.* Chicago: University of Illinois Press, 1974.

Waggoner, Hyatt H. *American Poets: From the Puritans to the Present.* Boston: Houghton Mifflin Co., 1968.

Weber, Brom. *Hart Crane: A Biographical and Critical Study.* New York: Bodley Press, 1948.

———. "Hart Crane." *Sixteen Modern American Authors: A Survey of Research and Criticism,* ed. Jackson R. Bryer. New York: W.W. Norton and Co., Inc., 1973.

Wells, Henry W. *The American Way of Poetry.* New York: Russell and Russell, Inc., 1964.

Whitman, Walt. *Leaves of Grass: Authoritative Texts, Prefaces, Whitman on His Art, Criticism,* ed. Harold W. Blodgett and Sculley Bradley. New York: W.W. Norton and Co., Inc., 1973.

Widmer, Kingsley. "Crane's 'Key West.' " *Explicator,* 18 (1959), Item 17.

Wilder, Amos N. *The Spiritual Aspects of the New Poetry.* Freeport, New York: Books for Libraries Press, 1968.

Willingham, John R. " 'Three Songs' of Hart Crane's *The Bridge: A Reconsideration." American Literature,* 27 (1955), 62–68.

Winters, Yvor. *In Defense of Reason.* Denver, Colorado: Alan Swallow, 1947.

———. "The Progress of Hart Crane." *The Merrill Studies in "The Bridge,"* ed. David R. Clark. Columbus, Ohio: Charles E. Merrill Publishing Co., 1970.

Yannella, Philip R. "Toward Apotheosis: Hart Crane's Visionary Lyrics." *Criticism,* 10 (1968), 313–33.